The
New-Skipper's
BOWDITCH

By the same author

Adobe Walls . . . *a Western?*

The
New-Skipper's
BOWDITCH

Piloting from Here to There
—and Home Again—
With Maximum Pleasure
and Minimum Trauma

JAMES LOUTTIT

W·W·Norton & Company   New York·London

The text of this book is composed in Times Roman, with
display type set in Baskerville. Composition and manufacturing by
The Maple-Vail Book Manufacturing Group.
Book Design by Bernie Klein.

First Edition

Library of Congress Cataloging in Publication Data

Louttit, James.
   The new skipper's Bowditch.

   1. Navigation.   2. Pilots and pilotage.   I. Title.
VK555.L59 1984   623.89   83–8235
ISBN 0–393–03292–2

W. W. Norton & Company, Inc., 500 Fifth Avenue, New York, N. Y. 10110
W. W. Norton & Company Ltd., 37 Great Russell Street, London WC1B 3NU

1 2 3 4 5 6 7 8 9 0

*Dedicated with affection to a
poodle named Hammett, the only
one aboard with enough sense to
be scared; and to all you Old
Salts and New Skippers, whoever
and wherever you may be.*

Contents

Part II. WAVES, WIND, AND WEATHER

Part III. THE PILOT'S LOCKER

Introduction

It all started with one hairy fellow on a log. Nobody knows exactly where or when. He wasn't a navigator, he wasn't a pilot, and he wasn't even a seaman; he was simply a barefoot, bare-bottomed adventurer who wanted to cross a river or a pond that was too wide to swim and too deep to wade. He wanted, like most of us, to get from here to there with the least amount of trauma. It wasn't until he paddled back from "there" to "here" that he invented piloting.

Nothing much has changed—we're still trying to get from here to there, and home again, with the maximum amount of pleasure and the minimum amount of trauma.

The New-Skipper's Bowditch will not tell you how to splice a line, trim a jib, tie a bowline, or clean your boot top. It won't tell you how to back a fat Bertram into a skinny slip. It won't even tell you how to use a sextant or compute a star sight. Don't confuse this *Bowditch* with that other *Bowditch,* old Nat Bowditch's *American Practical Navigator.* That *Bowditch* is a marvelous book, deserving of every honor. You will probably get to it later. This *Bowditch* is exclusively for you— the new skipper.

If the author has done his job, *The New-Skipper's Bowditch* will help you pilot your little ship from here to there and home again—with maximum pleasure and minimum trauma.

And isn't that what it's *really* all about?

Acknowledgments

The Crew of *Ellös* and *Lady Brett*—
 the "M," "K," and "D" in three yacht logs
Howard Foster, who took us sailing
Hammett, who thought we were mad
Harper, who jumped ship at the first opportunity
Dana, demon typist
Jim and Orilla
The United States Coast Guard, especially one lieutenant (j.g.)
Uncle Jack, who showed the author there was a world beyond the horizon
Nathaniel Bowditch, for obvious reasons
Joshua Slocum & Company
Araner, Wedderburn, and *St. Paul*
The good folks at NOS who draft those beautiful charts
March 19, 1941
Old Salt and that hairy fellow on his log
And all those others who go down to the sea in small ships—
 and care enough to learn.

I

Rocks and Shoals

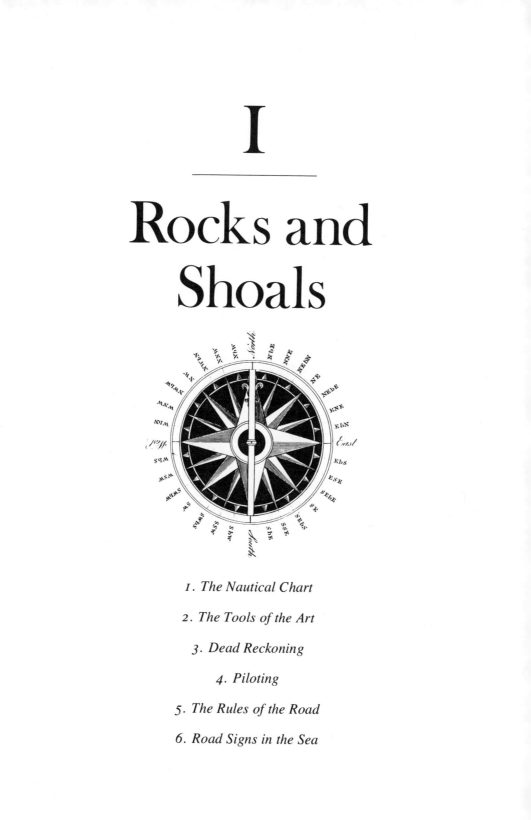

1
The Nautical Chart

Let's start with the nautical chart, for without it you are figuratively and literally lost. Nautical charts are the beginning, middle, and end of any successful cruise or passage. If the marine compass is the single most important instrument aboard your boat (and it is), the marine chart ranks a close second.

Christopher Columbus, a marvelous seaman, found and explored the New World without charts, but don't forget that he later lost his *Santa Maria* on a reef off the northern coast of Hispaniola. He had an excuse. You don't. If Columbus had been able to purchase the charts that are available to you, he would probably have sailed home to Spain in *Santa Maria* instead of in *Nina*'s cramped sea cabin.

Don't confuse nautical charts with maps. And above all, don't call them ''maps.'' Maps tell you where to go; charts tell you where *not* to go. Maps are for landsmen, lubbers, and backpackers—all those folks who turn them upside down to determine if they should turn left or right at the next fork in the road.

Don't skimp on charts. If you must save money, save it someplace else. Your chart inventory should be limited only by the geographic boundaries of your cruising area, not by stowage space or your pocketbook. You can't have too many; the chart you don't have is almost certain to be the one chart you will need—desperately.

Nautical charts are a bargain. If you compare the modest price of a full set of charts with the investment in your boat, you'll see that you can't buy cheaper ''insurance.'' You are certain to meet skippers who sail or cruise without charts. They are either fools or dilettantes. Even if the price per chart goes up, as it surely will, sell the dinghy if you must, but keep your chart inventory *complete* and *up-to-date*.

Bowditch ON CHARTS

The nautical chart is a graphic representation on a flat surface of a navigable portion of the surface of the earth. It shows the depth of water by soundings, soundings *and* depth contours, the shoreline ("hard edge") of adjacent land, topographic landmarks, aids to navigation, dangers, and other information of interest to pilots and skippers. It is a work-sheet of which courses may be plotted and positions ascertained. It assists the navigator in avoiding dangers—that is, piloting your boat from here to there and back again, with minimum trauma and maximum pleasure.

Most nautical charts are constructed on the Mercator projection—i.e., the cartographers have flattened (and distorted) our round globe

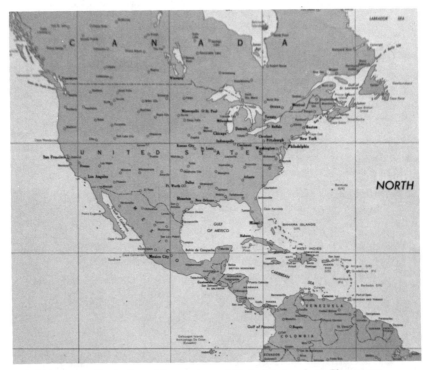

World Mercator Projection of the continental United States, from Chart 3090.

onto a flat piece of paper. Don't worry about the distortion—it's minimal from chart to chart and in limited cruising areas. Charts for special purposes, such as great-circle sailing, are usually on the "gnomonic projection," with no distortion and the round ball of the earth shown as slices or wedges of a great watery apple.

The *scale* of a chart is the ratio of a given distance on the chart to the actual distance it represents on earth. It may be expressed in various ways. The most common are:

1. A simple ratio or fraction: 1:80,000 or 1/80,000 means that one unit (such as an inch) on the chart represents 80,000 of the same unit on the surface of the earth.
2. A statement of distance on the earth, shown in one unit (usually an inch) on the chart. For example, "30 miles to the inch" means that 1 inch on the chart represents 30 miles of the earth's surface.
3. A line or bar may be shown at a convenient place on the chart and subdivided into nautical miles, yards, or feet.

All charts vary somewhat in scale from point to point, and in some projections the scale is not the same in all directions from a single point. A single subdivided line or bar for use over an entire chart is shown only when the chart is of such scale that the scale varies a negligible amount over the chart, usually one of about 1:75,000 or larger. Since 1 minute of latitude is nearly equal to 1 nautical mile, the latitude scale also serves as a graphical scale. On most charts the east and west borders are subdivided for easy measurement.

A chart covering a relatively large area is called a *small-scale* chart, and one covering a relatively small area is called a *large-scale* chart. Confusing? Not really, if you think about it—and if you keep in mind that you really want a very large picture of a very small area, especially if that area is littered with rocks, shallows, and shoals. Since the terms are relative, there is no sharp division between large scale and small scale. A chart of scale 1:100,000 is "large scale" when compared with a chart of 1:1,000,000, but "small scale" when compared with a one of 1:25,000.

Charts are published in many different scales, ranging from about 1:2500 to 1:14,000,000 (and even smaller for some world charts). Small-scale charts covering large areas are used for planning and for offshore navigation. Large-scale charts are used in pilot waters. The following chart classifications are used by the National Ocean Survey:

Sailing Charts are the small-scale charts used for planning, for fixing position at sea, and for plotting dead reckoning while on a long voyage. The scale is generally smaller than 1:600,000. The shoreline and topography are generalized and only offshore soundings, principal navigational lights, outer buoys, and landmarks visible at considerable distances are shown.

General Charts are intended for coastwise navigation outside outlying reefs and shoals. The scales range from about 1:150,000 to 1:600,000.

Coast Charts are intended for inshore coastwise piloting where your course may lie inside outlying reefs and shoals, for entering or leaving bays and harbors, and for navigating large inland waterways. The scales range from about 1:50,000 to 1:150,000.

Harbor Charts are intended for navigation and anchoring in harbors and small waterways. The scale is generally larger than 1:50,000.

Hidden dangers lurk on any chart, even the most up-to-date. Even a detailed survey may have failed to locate every rock, sands shift with the tides, boats sink and lie like booby traps just below the surface, and lobstermen and fishermen may have placed their pots and traps along the best courses from here to there. Changes in the contour of the bottom are rapid in areas where there are strong currents or heavy surf, particularly when the bottom is soft mud or sand. The entrances to bar harbors must be regarded with suspicion, and dredged channels, especially if they are surrounded by sand or mud, or if cross currents exist, should be approached with caution. Grounding in a narrow channel at the entrance to a busy harbor is guaranteed to spoil the best of days. Shifting bottoms are sometimes shown on the chart, but the absence of such a note should not be regarded as evidence that rapid change does not occur. When in doubt, lay off for a while and watch how the "locals" go in and out. Note particularly the size and probable draft of local vessels.

Changes in aids to navigation are more easily determined, and charts are generally correct in this regard to the date of printing. However, there is always the possibility that a change occurred since the chart was printed. Issues of *Notice to Mariners* printed after that date will ensure the accuracy of your charts. Part of the responsibility for the continuing accuracy of charts lies with you, the user. If charts are to remain totally reliable, they must be corrected as indicated by the *Notice to Mariners*. Also, your reports of errors and changes and your suggestions are useful to the publishing agencies in correcting and improving all charts. Local *Notice to Mariners* may be obtained free from the commander of your local Coast Guard district.

Charts published by the Defense Mapping Agency Hydrographic Center and the National Ocean Survey are dated as follows:

First Edition: The original date of issue of a new chart is shown at the top center margin:

5th Ed., Sept. 1950

New Edition: A new edition is made when the numerous corrections make previous printings obsolete. The date of the first edition is retained at the top margin. At the lower left-hand corner it is replaced by the number and date of the new edition. The latter date is the same as that of the latest *Notice to Mariners* to which the chart has been corrected:

5th Ed., July 11, 1970

Revised Print: A revised print published by NOS may contain corrections which have been published in *Notice to Mariners* but does not supersede a current edition. The date of the revision is shown to the right of the edition date:

5th Ed., July 11, 1970; Revised 4/12/75.

READING YOUR CHARTS

Chart Symbols and Chart No. 1

Chart Symbols are not accurate in scale or detail, but they are shown at the correct location and they present a large amount of information without congestion or confusion. The standard symbols and abbreviations which have been approved for use on regular nautical charts published in the United States are shown in Chart No. 1, "Nautical Chart Symbols and Abbreviations." Buy Chart No. 1 the same day you buy your first nautical chrart, for you *must* know the *meaning* of each chart symbol in order to fully understand and appreciate each of your charts. The symbols and abbreviations on any given chart may differ from those shown on Chart No. 1, but the meaning will still be clear. Many chart symbols warn of hidden hazards—rocks, reefs, wrecks, or shoals. Learn to recognize them at a glance; sooner or later you'll be glad you did.

Lettering

Standard lettering has been adopted for all American-produced charts:

Roman (the normal vertical) type is used for features that are dry at high water and are not affected by the movement of water, except for heights *above* water.

Italic (*slanting*) type is used for water, underwater, and floating features, except soundings.

The type of lettering may be your only way of knowing if a charted rock pokes its head above the waves or lurks just beneath the surface.

The Hard Edge

The *shoreline* shown on nautical charts represents the lines of contact between the "hard edge" of the land and the soft edge of the water. This line of contact is usually the mean high-water line. In confined coastal waters, where there is less tidal change, a mean water-level line may be used. The shoreline of interior waters (rivers and lakes) is usually a line representing a specified elevation above a selected datum. A shoreline is symbolized by a heavy line. A broken line indicates that the charted position is approximate.

Where the low-water line differs considerably from the high-water line, the low-water line may be indicated by dots in the case of mud, sand, gravel, or stones, with the kind of material indicated, and by the symbol for rock or coral. An area alternately covered and uncovered may be shown by a tint that is usually a combination of the land tint and a blue water tint. The "apparent" shoreline shows that the outer edge of marine vegetation *appears* to be the shoreline. It is shown as a light line on your chart. The inner edge is marked by a broken line when no other symbol (such as a cliff or levee) clearly marks the shore. The area between the two may be given the combined land-water tint or the land tint.

Water Depths

Soundings or depths of water are shown by numbers. These do *not* follow the general rule for lettering. They may be roman or italic, depending on when and how the survey was made. The unit of measurement used for soundings on each chart is shown in large block letters at the top and bottom of the chart as "SOUNDINGS IN METERS,"

"SOUNDINGS IN FATHOMS," or sometimes "SOUNDINGS IN FATHOMS AND FEET." Use the depth-conversion scale for converting charted depths to feet, meters, or fathoms.

Soundings are supplemented by a series of *depth contours,* lines that connect points of equal depth. These lines show the hills, valleys, and slopes beneath your keel. The types of lines used for various depths are shown in part R of Chart No. 1. On some charts depth contours are drawn as solid lines, the depth shown by numbers placed in breaks in the lines. A "swept area" that has been wire-dragged may be considered especially accurate. *A broken or indefinite contour is substituted when the reliability of the contour is questionable.* Depth contours are given in the unit of measurement of the soundings. This type of chart, presenting a detailed "picture" of the bottom, is particularly useful if your vessel is equipped with a depth sounder. The side limits of dredged channels are indicated by broken lines. The depth and the date of dredging, if known, are shown by a statement in or along the channel, but the possibility of silting should be kept in mind.

The chart scale is usually too small to permit all soundings to be shown. The *least* depths are generally chosen first, and a sounding pattern is worked out to provide safety, a practical presentation of the bottom, and a neat, uncluttered chart. Keep in mind that the state of the tide affects the depth from one minute to the next, and an isolated rock or shoal sounding should be approached with caution—if it can't be avoided altogether.

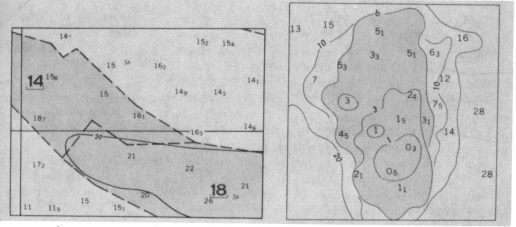

A swept area.   *Depth contours.*

The Bottom's Surface

The substance forming the bottom is shown by abbreviation. These are listed in part S of Chart No. 1. A few of the less well-known terms are given below:

Ooze is a soft, slimy, organic sediment composed principally of shells or other hard parts of minute organisms.

Marl is a crumbling, earthy deposit, particularly one of clay mixed with sand, lime, or decomposed shells. A layer of marl may be quite compact.

Shingle consists of small, rounded, water-worn stones, similar to gravel but generally larger.

Schist is crystalline rock of a finely laminated nature.

Madrepore is a stony coral.

Lava is rock in the fluid state, or after it has solidified.

Pumice is cooled volcanic glass with a great number of minute cavities. It is very light.

Tufa is a porous rocky deposit sometimes formed near the mouths of rivers.

Scoria (plural: scoriae) is rough, cinderlike lava.

Sea Tangle is any of the several species of seaweed, especially those of large size.

Spicules are the small skeletons of marine animals such as sponges.

Cirripeda (plural) are barnacles and certain other parasitic marine animals.

Fucus is a coarse seaweed growing on rocks.

Matte is a dense, twisted growth of a sea plant such as grass.

Chart Sounding Datum

All depths indicated on charts are reckoned from some selected level of the water, called the *chart sounding datum*. For National Ocean Survey charts of the Atlantic and Gulf Coasts of the United States and Puerto Rico the chart datum is *mean low water*. Pacific Coast charts of the United States, including Alaska, show *mean lower low water*. Most Defense Mapping Agency Hydrographic Center charts are based on *mean low water, mean lower low water,* or *mean lower water springs*. For charts of the Great Lakes and other areas where tidal effects are small or without significance, the datum adopted is approximately the mean water level.

Since the chart datum is generally a computed mean or average height

⊕	Sunken wreck dangerous to surface navigation (less than 11 fathoms over wreck).
⊙	Sunken rock dangerous to navigation.
③ Wk	Wreck over which depth is known.
②¹ Wk	Wreck with depth cleared by wire drag.
⁻⁸ Wk	Unsurveyed wreck over which the exact depth is unknown, but is considered to have a safe clearance to the depth shown.
⑤ Rk	Shoal sounding on isolated rock.
+Co+₃	Coral reef covered at sounding datum.
(Foul)	Foul ground, Foul bottom.
*(2) or �(2)	Rock which covers and uncovers with height above chart sounding datum.
⁰ Subm Piles	Submerged pilings.
③ Rep (1974)	Depth reported in 1974.
Reef	Reef of unknown extent.
④ Obstr	Obstruction
▫ ▪ Platform (lighted) HORN	Offshore platform (unnamed)
⌇₃⌇	Drying (or uncovering) heights, above chart sounding datum.

Danger symbols shown on Chart No. 1.

at some state of the tide, the depth of water at any particular moment may be *less* than shown on the chart. For example, if the chart datum is mean lower low water, the depth of water at lower low water will be less than the charted depth about as often as it is greater. A lower depth is indicated in the tide tables by a minus sign (−).

The shoreline shown on charts is the high-water line, generally the level of mean high water. The heights of lights, rocks, and islets are generally reckoned from this level.

Danger Signs

Learn each of the *danger* signs; they are the "enemy." The danger symbols are shown in part O of Chart No. 1. Take rocks, for example. A rock that uncovers itself at mean high water may be shown as an islet, while an offshore rock that is covered at high water but exposed at low will have its own symbol and possibly a statement such as *"Uncov 2 ft"* or the figure in feet underlined and enclosed in parentheses, (2). For a rock that does not uncover but is considered dangerous, the symbol will be enclosed by a dotted curve for emphasis.

Another unpleasant underwater hazard—a wreck—will have its own distinctive symbol. The usual symbol for a visible wreck is shown below. A sunken wreck with less than 11 fathoms of water over it is considered dangerous and its symbol is surrounded by a dotted curve. The safe clearance depth found over a wreck is indicated by a standard sounding number placed at the wreck.

As if rocks and wrecks aren't bad enough, keep in mind the shoals, reefs, fish stakes, and submerged pilings that are waiting out there for the unwary. Study their symbols in Chart No. 1 until you know them by heart.

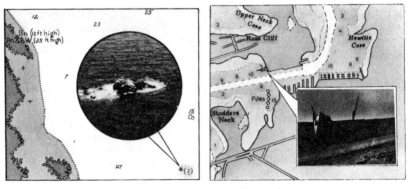

A rock awash.   A visible wreck.

Piles, dolphins (clusters of piles), snags, and stumps are shown as small circles with a label identifying the type of obstruction. If such dangers are submerged, the letters "Subm" precede the label. Fish stakes and traps are shown when they are known to be permanent or hazardous to navigation. Most dangers are emphasized with a blue tint and dotted line surrounding the danger.

Aids to Navigation

These are the "good guys" that have been placed out there by the Coast Guard or private sources to help keep you out of harm's way. Their symbols, which are also shown in Chart No. 1, are usually supplemented by abbreviations and sometimes by additional descriptive text. The size of these symbols on your charts is exaggerated for emphasis. It is important to know which part of the symbol represents the actual position of the aid. For floating aids (lightships and buoys), the position part of the symbol marks the approximate location of the anchor or sinker, the aid swinging in an orbit around this position.

The principal charted aids to navigation are lighthouses, other lights on fixed structures, beacons, lightships, radiobeacons, and buoys. The number of aids shown and the amount of information concerning them varies with the scale of the chart. Unless otherwise indicated, lights that do not alternate in color are white, and alternating lights are red and white. Light lists give complete navigational information concerning them.

Lighthouses and other lights on fixed structures are shown as black dots surrounded by nautical purple disks or as black dots with purple flare symbols. The center of the black dot is the position of the light. On large-scale charts the characteristics of lights are shown in the order shown in Table 1. The legend for this light would appear on the chart:

Gp Fl R (2) 10 sec 160 ft 19 M "6"

Table 1. **Order of Light Characteristics on Charts**

Characteristic	Example	Meaning
1. Character	Gp Fl	group flashing
2. Color	R	red
3. Period	(2) 10 sec	two flashes every 10 seconds
4. Height	160 ft	160 feet
5. Range	19M	19 nautical miles
6. Number	"6"	light number 6

On older charts this form is slightly varied. As the chart scale becomes smaller, and six items listed above are omitted in the following order: (1) height; (2) period (seconds); (3) number (of flashes, etc.) in group; (4) light number; (5) visibility. Names of unnumbered lights are shown when space permits.

When *daybeacons* are shown by small triangles, the center of the triangle marks the position of the aid. Except on Intracoastal Waterway charts and charts of state waterways, the abbreviation "Bn" is shown beside the symbol, with the appropriate abbreviation for color if known. For black beacons the triangle is solid black and there is no color abbreviation. All beacon abbreviations are in roman lettering.

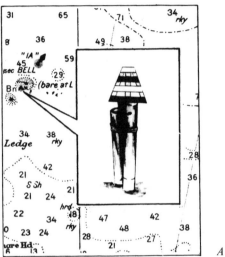

A daybeacon.

Lightships are shown by a ship symbol. The center of the small circle at the base of the symbol indicates the approximate position of the lightship's anchor. The circle is overprinted by a small purple disk or a purple flare emanating from the top of the symbol. As a floating

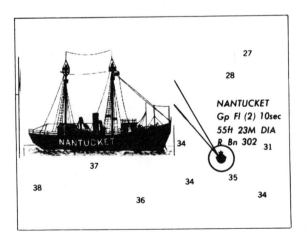

A lightship with a radiobeacon.

aid, the light characteristics and the name of the lightship are given in italic letters.

Radiobeacons are indicated on the chart by a small purple circle and an abbreviation to indicate whether it's a radiobeacon (R Bn) or a radar beacon (Racon). The same symbol is used for a radio direction finder station with the abbreviation "RDF" and a coast radar station with the abbreviation "Ra." Other radio stations are indicated by a small black circle with a dot in the center, or a smaller circle without a dot, and the appropriate abbreviation. In every case the center of the circle marks the position of the aid.

Buoys, except mooring buoys, are usually shown by a diamond-shaped symbol and a small dot or small circle at one of its points. The dot or small circle indicates the approximate position of the buoy's sinker. A mooring buoy is shown by a distinctive symbol (see part L of Chart No. 1). The small circle interrupting the symbol's baseline indicates the approximate position of the sinker.

A black buoy is shown by a solid black diamond, without abbreviation. For all other buoys, color is indicated by an abbreviation, or in full by a note on the chart. The diamond-shaped symbols of red buoys are often colored purple. A buoy symbol with a line connecting the side points (shorter axis), half of the symbol being purple or open and the other half black, indicates horizontal bands. A line connecting the upper and lower points (longer axis) represents vertical stripes. Two lines connecting the *opposite sides* of the symbol indicate a checkered buoy.

There is no significance to the angle at which the diamond shape appears on the chart. The symbol is placed to avoid interference with other features of the chart.

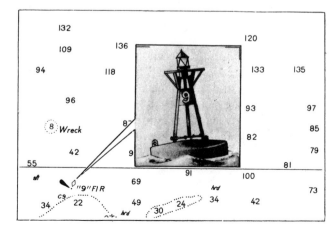

A lighted buoy.

Lighted buoys are indicated by a purple flare emanating from the buoy symbol or by a small purple disk centered on the dot or small circle indicating the approximate position of the buoy's sinker.

Abbreviations for light characteristics, type and color of buoy, number of the buoy, and any other pertinent information given near the symbol are in italic letters. The letter *C, N,* or *S* indicates a can, nun, or spar. The words "bell," "gong," and "whistle," are shown as "BELL," "GONG," and "WHIS," respectively. The number or letter designation of the buoy is given in quotation marks on NOS charts. On some other charts they may be given without quotation marks or punctuation—No 1, No 2, etc.

Aeronautical lights included in the light lists are shown by the lighthouse symbol, accompanied by the abbreviation "AERO."

Ranges are indicated by a broken or solid line. The solid line, which indicates that part of the range intended for navigation, may be broken at irregular intervals to avoid being drawn through soundings. That part of the range line drawn only to guide the eye to objects to be kept in range is broken at regular intervals. If the direction is given, it is expressed in degrees clockwise from true north.

Sound signal apparatus is indicated by the appropriate word in capital letters (HORN, BELL, GONG, etc.) or an abbreviation indicating the type of sound. Sound signals are represented by three arcs of concentric circles within an angle of 45°, oriented and placed as necessary for clarity. The letters "DFS" indicate a *distance finding station* having synchronized sound and radio signals.

Private aids, when shown, are marked "Priv maintd." Some privately maintained unlighted aids are indicated by a small circle accompanied by the word "Marker," or a larger circle with a dot in the center and the word "MARKER." The center of the circle indicates the position of the aid. A privately maintained lighted aid has the light symbol and is accompanied by the characteristics and the usual indication of its private nature. Private aids should be used with caution.

A *light sector* is the sector or area bounded by two radii and the arc of a circle in which a light is visible or in which it has a distinctive color different from that of adjoining sectors. The limited radii are indicated on the chart by dotted lines. Colors of the sectors are indicated by words spelled out if space permits, or by abbreviations (W, R, etc.) if it does not.

Land Areas

The amount of detail shown on the land areas of nautical charts depends on the scale and the intended purpose of the chart.

Contour lines connect points of equal elevation and the heights represented by the contours are indicated at suitable places along the lines. Heights are usually expressed in feet (or in meters, with means for conversion to feet). The interval between contours is uniform over any one chart.

Spot Elevations are generally given only for summits or for the tops of conspicuous landmarks. When there is insufficient space to show the heights of islets or rocks, they are indicated by italic numbers enclosed in parentheses in the water area nearby.

Cities are shown in a generalized pattern that approximates their extent and shape. Street names are generally not charted except those along the waterfront on large-scale charts. In general, only the main arteries and thoroughfares or major coastal highways are shown on small-scale charts. Buildings along or near the waterfront are shown on large-scale charts. Special symbols are used for certain kinds of buildings, as indicated in part I of Chart No. 1. Both single- and double-track railroads are indicated by a single line with crossmarks. A fence or sewer extending into the water is shown by a broken line, usually labeled. Airports are shown on small-scale charts by symbol and on large-scale charts by shape and extent of runways. Breakwaters and jetties are shown by single or double lines depending on the scale of the chart. A submerged portion and the limits of the submerged base are shown by broken lines.

Landmarks

A large circle with a dot at its center is used for selected landmarks. Capital letters are used to identify the landmark: HOUSE, FLAGPOLE, STACK, sometimes followed by "(conspic)." A small circle without a dot is used for landmarks not accurately located. Capital and lowercase letters are used to identify the landmark: Mon or Monument, Cup or Cupola, Dome. The abbreviation "PA," for "position approximate," is sometimes used as a safety feature. When only one object of a group is charted, its name is followed by a descriptive legend in parentheses, including the number of objects in the group, for example "(TALLEST OF FOUR)" or "(NORTHEAST OF THREE)."

Some chart labels are interpreted as follows:

Building or *house*. One of these terms is used when the entire structure is the landmark.

A *spire* is a slender pointed structure extending above a building. It is seldom less than two-thirds of the entire height of the structure. The term is not applied to a short pyramid-shaped structure rising from a tower or belfry.

A *cupola* is a small dome-shaped tower or turret rising from a building.

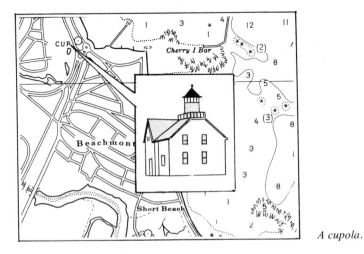

A cupola.

A *dome* is a large, rounded, hemispherical structure rising above a building, or a roof of the same shape. A prominent example is on the Capitol of the United States in Washington, D.C.

A *chimney* is a relatively small, upright structure projecting from above a building.

A *stack* is a tall smokestack or chimney. The term is used when the stack is more prominent as a landmark than accompanying buildings.

A *flagpole* is a single staff from which flags are displayed. The term is used when the pole is not attached to a building.

The term *flagstaff* is used for a flagpole rising from a building.

A *flag tower* is a scaffoldlike tower from which flags are displayed.

A *radio tower* is a tall pole or structure for elevating radio antennas.

A *radio mast* is a relatively short pole or slender structure for elevating radio antennas, usually found in groups.

A *tower* is any structure which has its base on the ground and is high in proportion to its base, or that part of a structure higher than the rest but having essentially vertical sides for the greater part of its height.

A *lookout station* or *watch tower* is a tower surmounted by a small house.

A *water tower* is a structure enclosing a tank or standpipe; the presence of the tank or standpipe may not be apparent.

A *standpipe* is a tall cylindrical structure, the height of which is several times the diameter.

The term *tank* is used for a water tank elevated high above the ground by a tall skeleton framework.

The expression *gas tank* or *oil tank* is used for the distinctive structures described by these words.

Miscellaneous

A *measured nautical mile* on the chart is accurate to within 6 feet of the correct length. Most measurements in the United States were made before 1959, when the United States adopted the International Nautical Mile. The new value is within 6 feet of the previous standard length of 6080.20 feet, adjustments not having been made.

Courses shown on charts are given in true direction.

Bearings shown are in true directions *toward* (not from) the objects.

Commercial radio braodcasting stations are shown on charts when they are of value to the mariner for radio bearings or as landmarks.

Compass roses are placed at convenient locations on Mercator charts to make it easy for you to plot your bearings and courses. The outer circle is graduated in degrees with zero at true north. The inner circle is graduated in points and degrees with the arrow indicating magnetic north.

Magnetic information. On many charts magnetic variation is given to the nearest 15′ by notes in the centers of compass roses; the annual change is given to the nearest 1′ to permit correction of the given value at a later date. When this is done, the magnetic information is updated when a new edition is issued.

Currents are sometimes shown on charts, with arrows giving the directions and figures giving the speeds. The information refers to the usual or average conditions, and it is not safe to assume that conditions at any given time will be totally accurate.

Longitudes are reckoned eastward and westward from the meridian of Greenwich, England, unless otherwise stated.

Notes on charts should be read with care. Several types of notes are used. Those in the margin give such information as the chart number and (sometimes) publication and edition notes, identification of adjoining charts, etc. Notes in connection with the chart title include such information as scale, sources of charted data, tidal information, the unit in which soundings are given, cautions, etc. Another class of notes is that given in proximity to the detail to which it refers. Examples of this type of note are those referring to a local magnetic disturbance, controlling depths of channels, measured miles, dangers, dumping grounds, anchorages, etc.

A careful skipper will select each of the charts he expects to use during a day's cruising *before* he gets underway. Then, if he's *really* careful, he'll put them in the sequence of expected usage, scanning each for hazards he may encounter later or harbors that could provide refuge if the weather turns foul. Rummaging through a confusion of charts when it's blowing half a gale is a sure cure for boredom—but it's no way to pilot a vessel.

Anchorage areas are shown within purple broken lines and are labeled as such. Anchorage berths are shown as purple circles with the number or letter assigned to the berth inscribed within the circle. Caution notes are sometimes shown when there are specific anchoring regulations.

Spoil areas, where the bottom may have been rearranged by dredging, are shown within short broken black lines. The area is tinted blue (NOS charts only) and labeled ''SPOIL AREA.''

Firing and bombing practice areas in the United States territorial and adjacent waters are shown on National Ocean Survey charts and Defense Mapping Agency Hydrographic Center charts of the same area and comparable scale. Danger areas established for short periods of time are not charted, but are announced locally. Danger areas in effect for longer periods are published in *Notice to Mariners*. Any aid to navigation established to mark a danger area or a fixed or floating target is shown on charts.

Traffic separation schemes show routes to increase safety of navigation, particularly in areas of high-density shipping. Traffic separation schemes are shown on standard nautical charts of scale 1:600,000 and larger, and are printed in purple. The arrows give the general direction of traffic only, and ships need not set their courses strictly by the arrows. Remember, these traffic lanes were laid out for *big* ships; the prudent skipper of a small vessel will stay clear whenever possible.

A *logarithmic time-speed-distance* nomogram with an explanation of its application is shown on harbor charts at scales of 1:40,000 and larger.

Tidal boxes are shown on charts of scales 1:75,000 and larger.

Tabulations of controlling depths are shown on NOS harbor charts.

Title. The chart title may be at any convenient location, usually in some area not important to navigation. It is composed of several distinctive parts, as shown.

TIDAL INFORMATION					
Place	Height referred to datum of soundings (MLLW)				
Name (Lat/Long)	Mean Higher High Water	Mean High Water	Mean Tide Level	Mean Lower Low Water	Extreme Low Water
	feet	feet	feet	feet	feet
Cape Alava (48°10′N/124°44′W)	8.2	7.4	4.4	0.0	−4.0
Cape Flattery (48°23′N/124°44′W)	8.0	7.2	4.3	0.0	−4.0
Neah Bay (48°22′N/124°37′W)	7.9	7.1	4.3	0.0	−4.0

A typical chart tidal table.

NANTUCKET HARBOR							
Tabulated from surveys by the Corps of Engineers - report of June 1972 and surveys of Nov. 1971							
Controlling depths in channels entering from seaward in feet at Mean Low Water					Project Dimensions		
Name of Channel	Left outside quarter	Middle half of channel	Right outside quarter	Date of Survey	Width (feet)	Length (naut. miles)	Depth M.L.W. (feet)
Entrance Channel	11.1	15.0	15.0	11-71	300	1.2	15
Note.–The Corps of Engineers should be consulted for changing conditions subsequent to the above.							

A typical chart tabulation of controlling depths.

GENERAL GEOGRAPHIC AREA ⟶	WEST INDIES CUBA—SOUTH COAST
SPECIFIC LOCALITY ⟶	GUANTANAMO BAY
SOURCE AND DATE(S) OF SURVEY ⟶	From U.S. Navy surveys to 1951 with additions and corrections to 1975
CHART SOUNDING DATUM ⟶	SOUNDINGS IN METERS (Under 31 in meters and half meters) reduced to the approximate level of Mean Sea Level HEIGHTS IN METERS ABOVE MEAN SEA LEVEL Contour interval 10 meters
LEGEND ⟶	For Symbols and Abbreviations, see Chart No. 1 Names and boundaries are not necessarily authoritative
PROJECTION ⟶	MERCATOR PROJECTION
HORIZONTAL DATUM ⟶	WORLD GEODETIC SYSTEM—1972 DATUM
SCALE ⟶	SCALE 1:200,000 AT LAT. 19°50′

A full chart title, showing all of the information typically provided.

CHART NUMBERING SYSTEM

Nautical charts produced and issued by the Defense Mapping Agency Hydrographic Center and National Ocean Survey are numbered according to scale and geographical area. With the exception of certain charts produced for military use only, one- to five-digit numbers are used. And with the exception of one-digit numbers, the first digit identifies the area and the number of digits establishes the scale range. The *one-digit numbers* are used for products that are not actually charts, such as Chart No. 1, "Nautical Chart Symbols and Abbreviations," or Chart No. 5, "National Flags and Ensigns."

Two- and three-digit numbers are assigned to small-scale charts that depict the major portion of an ocean basin or a large area, with the first digit identifying the ocean basin. Two-digit numbers are used for charts of scale 1 : 9,000,000 and smaller. Three-digit numbers are used for charts of scales 1 : 2,000,000 to 1 : 9,000,000.

Four-digit numbers are used for nonnavigational and special-purpose charts, such as chart 5090, "Maneuvering Board."

Five-digit numbers are assigned to charts of scale 1 : 2,000,000 and larger that cover portions of a coastline. These charts are based on the regions of the nautical chart index. The first of the five digits indicates the region; the second digit indicates the subregion; the last three digits indicate the geographical sequence of the chart within the subregion.

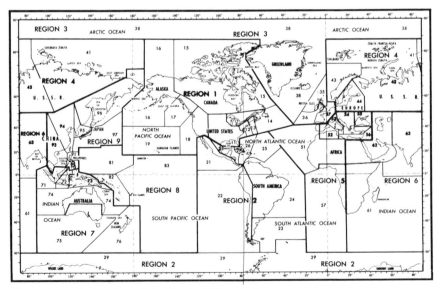

The regions of subregions of the Nautical Chart Index.

Number of Digits	Scale
1	No Scale
2	1:9,000,000 and smaller.
3	1:2,000,000 to 1:9,000,000.
4	Nonnavigational and special purpose.
5	1:2,000,000 and larger.

The scale of a chart determines the number of digits in its number.

USE OF CHARTS

Study each of your charts when you buy it—and again *before* you use it. Read the notes and be sure you understand them. Pay particular attention to soundings, noting the units in which depths are given. If you don't understand all the chart symbols, look them up in Chart No. 1. Danger areas—rocks, wrecks, and shoals—should be noted, perhaps even marked.

More than one skipper has sailed hard into a maze of fish traps because one small notation "didn't really look all that important." How many personal notations you make on your charts depends on how well you know a particular area and your overall experience. Don't clutter your charts with dire warnings and skulls and crossbones, but if you err, err on the side of caution.

Maintaining Charts

The print date in the lower left-hand corner of the chart is the date of the latest *Notice to Mariners* used to update the chart. It is your responsibility to maintain it after that date. An out-of-date or an uncorrected chart is a menace. The various issues of *Notice to Mariners* subsequent to the print date contain all the information needed for maintaining your charts.

Old, frayed, coffee-stained charts should be replaced, particularly if a new edition is available. The fact that a new edition has been prepared generally indicates that there have been substantial changes in the charted area.

Use and Stowage of Charts

Protect your charts with the care they deserve. Spread them flat when you're using them, and above all, keep them dry. Wet charts stretch, distorting lines; and vital symbols or soundings sometimes rub off, especially if a chart must be folded for stowage. Few small vessels have adequate chart-stowage space, even those with respectable chart tables. Some skippers stow their charts beneath bunk cushions, others build overhead chart bins, but most resort to a single or double fold. (Whatever you do, don't buy a chart-stowage tube; a rolled chart will *never* lie flat when you use it.) If you must fold your charts, fold them as little as possible. Some skippers fold them printed-side in; others, printed-side out. Whichever you choose, be consistent. Be sure the chart number and title are in the *same* corner when the charts are stacked for stowage. Stow them in *numerical* order, and keep a separate list (number, title, and scale) in your logbook or possibly beneath the lid of your chart table.

Permanent corrections to charts should be made in ink so that they will not be inadvertently erased. All other lines should be drawn in pencil so that they can be easily erased without removing permanent information or otherwise damaging the chart. Lines should be drawn no longer than necessary, and be neatly labeled. When a passage has been completed, your charts should be carefully erased.

Small-Craft Charts

Small-craft charts published by NOS are designed primarily for boatmen. In some cases small-craft charts provide a better presentation of navigational hazards than the standard nautical chart because of scale and detail. Small-craft charts (SC for "small craft" or PF for "pocket-fold small craft" in the various nautical chart catalogs) usually have a scale of 1:40,000, but the scale of others may range from 1:10,000 to 1:80,000. Some skippers prefer them, while others opt for flat charts if they are available. SC or PF charts are particularly useful in an open cockpit, especially if a brisk breeze is blowing.

Nautical Chart Catalogs

The five *free* nautical chart catalogs listed below may be obtained from most authorized nautical chart agents, or by writing to: Distribution Division (OA / C44), National Ocean Survey, Riverdale, MD 20737 (telephone: 301 / 436-6990). Available are:

No. 1 Atlantic and Gulf Coasts, including Puerto Rico and the Virgin Islands
No. 2 Pacific Coast, including Hawaii, Guam, and Samoa Islands
No. 3 Alaska
No. 4 Great Lakes and Adjacent Waterways
No. 5 Bathymetric Maps and Special-Purpose Charts

In addition to a complete list of the charts and prices available for each area, each catalog lists nautical chart agents, state by state; foreign agents for NOS publications; maps and charts issued by other federal agencies such as the five-volume *U.S. Coast Guard Light List;* sailing and general charts; and other publications issued by NOS— *U.S. Coast Pilots, Tide Tables, Tidal Current Tables, Tidal Current Charts,* and *Tidal Diagrams.*

A Final Look at Scale

The five chart fragments that follow show Block Island, Rhode Island, at scales ranging from 1 : 1,200,000 (small scale) to 1 : 15,000 (a large-scale view of Great Salt Pond).

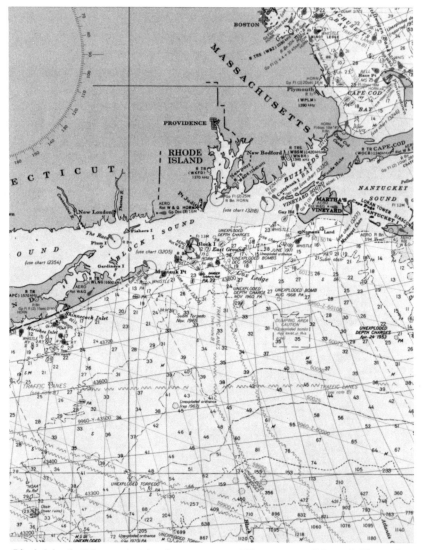

Block Island, R.I., at a scale of 1:1,200,000 (Chart 13003, "Cape Sable to Cape Hatteras").

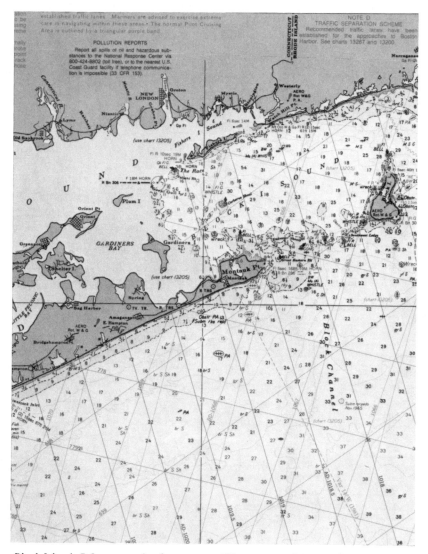

Block Island, R.I., at a scale of 1:400,000 (Chart 12300, "Approaches to New York, Nantucket Shoals to Five Fathom Bank").

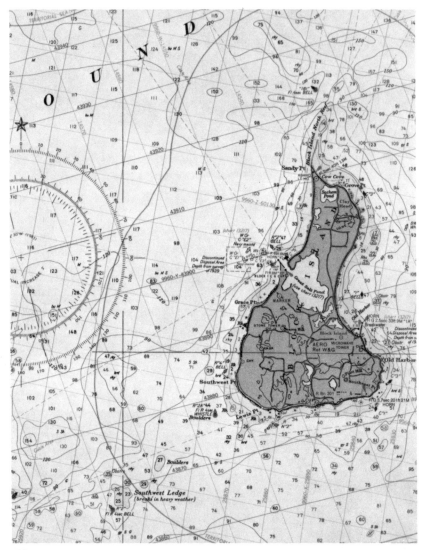

Block Island, R.I., at a scale of 1:80,000 (Chart 13205, "Block Island Sound and Approaches").

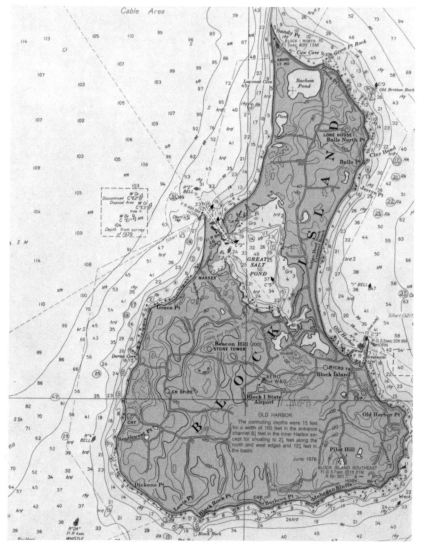

Block Island, R.I., at a scale of 1:40,000 (Chart 13215, "Block Island Sound, Point Judith to Montauk Point").

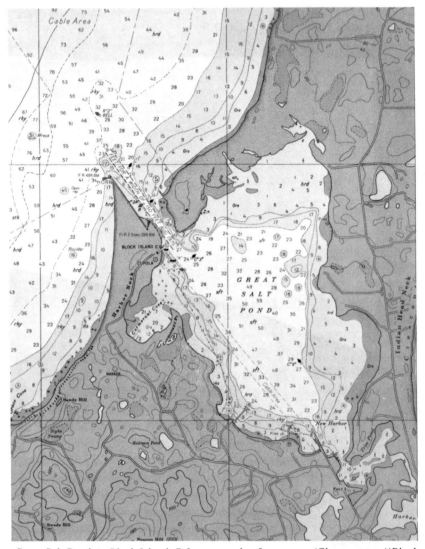

Great Salt Pond on Block Island, R.I., at a scale of 1 : 15,000 (Chart 13217, "Block Island").

2
The Tools
of the Art

You could load your little vessel to her gunnels with expensive navigation equipment—all of it impressive, much of it useful, some of it worth little more than ballast. Yet you *can* pilot your craft successfully with three simple "tools" that should cost less than twenty dollars.

If that sounds like an oversimplification, think about it for a moment. Piloting, in its purest form, is moving a vessel from here to there—successfully. You plot your course and keep track of your movement on a nautical chart. And what do you *really* need to do that? You could do the job with:

1. A pencil
2. Dividers
3. Parallel Rulers

The pencil should be sharp and not so hard that it will damage your chart; the dividers—or "pair" of dividers—should be of good quality; and the parallel rulers should be as long as you can accommodate comfortably on your piloting surface. And 12" rulers are fine, of course, but 18" rulers are better.

Although you *could* do the job with these three tools, a well-stocked navigation station will include all or most of the following:

1. *Pencils* (plural, possibly no. 2s), a pencil sharpener (or pocket-knife), *and* a soft eraser.

2. *Dividers*—two hinged legs with pointed ends, used to "step off"

or measure distances on a chart. The setting may be retained by friction at the hinge or by a set screw against a spring. Dividers come in several styles; try them all and select the one that suits you best. Some pilots prefer one-handed dividers, which have been adapted from an eighteenth-century British navy design; others prefer "professional" dividers, either 5″ or 7″. If in doubt, don't agonize over your decision—either model will do the job.

3. *Sturdy parallel rulers* that will not warp. In their most common form, parallel rulers consist of two plastic bars that are hinged in such a manner that when one bar is held in place on a flat surface, the other can be moved yet remain parallel to its original direction. Press firmly on one ruler while the other is being moved to prevent slippage. The principal use of parallel rulers in piloting is to transfer the direction of a charted line to a compass rose and vice versa.

The edges of the rulers must be truly straight. Test your parallel rulers against a straight line, such as a meridian on a chart, or by "walking" the rulers between parallel lines on opposite sides of the chart. Parallel rulers that aren't absolutely parallel are worse than useless.

Directions can also be transferred by using two drafting triangles or by one triangle and a straightedge, but why bother with triangles when inexpensive parallel rulers are such a simple and efficient tool?

4. *Protractors and plotters.* Protractors are used to measure angles on a chart. A protractor consists essentially of a graduated arc, usually 180°. Some protractors are plastic, others metal. Some have one movable plastic arm, others have three movable arms that are attached to a see-through baseplate. Although useful under certain conditions, the three-armed protractor is impractical on a small boat that has a cramped navigation station.

The plotter is a variation of the same theme—a device that has been designed to help you plot a course on a chart. In its most common form such a device consists essentially of a protractor combined with a straightedge. There are two general types: one has no movable parts; the other has a pivot at the center of the arc of the protractor. The direction of the straightedge is controlled by placing the center of the protractor arc and the desired scale graduation on the same reference line. Some fixed-type plotters have auxiliary scales that indicate true direction if a parallel is used, and most plotters also provide linear distance scales. In the movable-arm type of plotter, a protractor is aligned with a meridian, and the movable arm is rotated until it is in the desired direction.

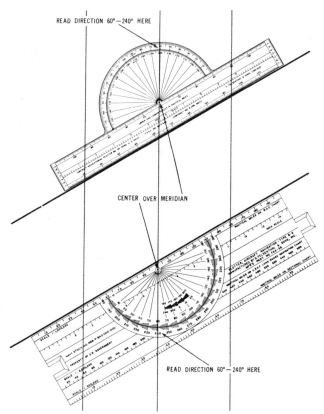

Two plotters with no movable parts.

Protractors and plotters are useful and inexpensive tools. One or the other is usually included in any basic navigator's kit, but you may prefer to study them all at a chandlery or in a marine catalog before selecting the one that suits your personal taste and individual need.

5. *A mounted Chronometer*—or simply a good waterproof watch. Old Joshua Slocum may have circumnavigated the globe with nothing more than an ancient alarm clock (or so he claimed), but a respectable quartz watch will serve all a small-boat pilot's needs. Brass chronometers are attractive when mounted on polished mahoghany; what you want is the *correct* time.

6. *The nautical slide rule.* Also known as the time-speed-distance computer, this wonderfully simple, easy-to-read device will tell you how fast you are going, how long it will take to reach your destination, or how far you've come—*if* you know *two* of the three factors: time, speed, or distance. (Ours, produced by Davis Instrument Corporation, is grimy with age, but its two rotating stiff-plastic discs work as smoothly as they did a dozen years ago when it was purchased for a very few dollars.)

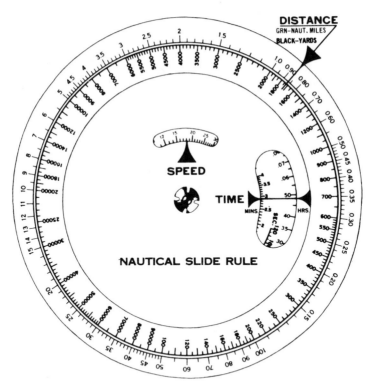

One type of nautical slide rule.

Distance, speed, and time are related by the formula

$$\text{Distance} = \text{Speed} \times \text{Time}$$

Therefore if any two of the three quantities are known, the third can be found. The units, of course, must be consistent. Thus if speed is measured in knots and time in hours, the answer is in nautical miles. Similarly, if distance is measured in yards and time in minutes, the answer is in yards per minute.

The solution of problems involving distance, speed, and time can easily be accomplished with a nautical slide rule. Several circular slide rules particularly adapted for solution of distance, speed, and time problems have been devised. One of these, called the "nautical slide rule," is shown. Several types are sold, but buy one *soon;* you'll never regret it.

We could talk here of other piloting tools—your primary compass, a hand-bearing compass, VHF, depth sounder, even the RDF—but each will be covered separately, either in the text or in Chapter 11, "Piloting Instruments." If you have a chart, a pencil, dividers, parallel rulers, a watch, and perhaps a protractor and nautical slide rule, you are ready to learn the exciting and satisfying art of piloting. If you have each of the above "tools of the art," you're a thousand leagues ahead of Christopher Columbus—he had none of them.

3

Dead Reckoning

The term "dead reckoning" has a salty ring to it. But more to the point, it is also the basis for good piloting. Dead reckoning—otherwise known as "DR"—is the determination of your *present* position by advancing a prior *known* position along a course or courses at various speeds. It really isn't very important whether the term comes from *"deduced* position" or relates to something (your boat) that *was* "dead" in the water but has now moved along a certain course for a certain distance. What *is* important is the fact that a DR position is seldom totally accurate. The reasons for this may be any or all of the following:

The water around you *also* moves.
Wind causes leeway.
Few compasses are perfect.
Fewer helmsmen are perfect.
And *no* new skippers are perfect (in fact, it's a rare *old* skipper who doesn't *over*estimate his boat's speed through the water).

Therefore your *approximate* dead reckoning position should be *corrected* from time to time, possibly with one or more bearings, or by identifying a buoy or light. Dead reckoning is basic piloting; all other methods are refinements for correcting your DR.

If a pilot or skipper can accurately judge his set, drift, and leeway, knows his compass error, keeps the helmsman awake, and admits he is really sailing at 5 knots—and not 7, his vague DR can be converted to a reasonably accurate "estimated position" (EP).

An *estimated position* may be established by applying an estimated correction to a dead reckoning position, or by estimating the course and speed being made good over the bottom. The expression "dead reckoning" is sometimes applied loosely to this "estimated reckoning," but when good information regarding current, wind, speed, and course is available, "estimated position" should be used. Estimates should be based on judgment and experience, but before adequate experience is gained, one should be cautious in applying corrections, for the estimates of the inexperienced are often wrong.

Dead reckoning also helps the pilot predict the availability of aids to navigation, interpret soundings for checking a position, predict times of making landfalls or sighting lights, estimate an arrival time, or evaluate the reliability and accuracy of other position-determining information. Because of the importance of accurate dead reckoning, a careful log should be kept of all courses and speeds, times of all changes, and compass errors. These may be recorded directly in a log or pilot's notebook. (Logs will be discussed later in this volume.)

Most small-boat skippers keep their dead reckoning by plotting directly on a chart, only rarely using big-ship plotting sheets. Lines are drawn to represent the direction and distance of travel, indicating dead reckoning and estimated positions from time to time. This method is simple and direct. Large errors are apparent as inconsistencies in an otherwise regular plot, and all hands aboard can see at a glance where they are—or at least where the skipper *thinks* they are.

PLOTTING A POSITION ON A CHART

A position is expressed at sea in units of latitude and longitude, generally to the nearest minute of a degree (0° 1') but in coastal piloting it may be expressed as bearing and distance from a known position, such as a landmark or aid to navigation.

Your Mercator charts are *conformal,* meaning that directions and angles are correctly represented. It is customary to orient the chart with 000° (north) at the top; other directions are in their correct relations to north and each other.

As an aid in measuring direction, *compass roses* are printed at convenient places on the chart or plotting sheet. A desired direction can be measured by placing a straight-edge along the line from the center of a compass rose to the circular graduation representing the desired direction. The straightedge is then in the desired direction, which may be transferred to any other part of the chart with parallel rulers or two triangles. The direction between two points is determined by transferring that direction to a compass rose, again with your parallel rulers. Plotters or protractors may also be used to plot a compass direction at a point on the chart without using the compass rose.

Measurement of direction, whether or not by compass rose, can be made at any convenient place on a Mercator chart, since meridians are parallel to each other and a line making a desired angle with any one makes the same angle with all others. Such a line is a *rhumb line*.

Compass roses for both true and magnetic directions may be given. Be sure you use the "magnetic" ring for coastal piloting, for that is what your compass shows and the course the helmsman *should* be steering. When a plotter or protractor is used for measuring an angle with respect to a meridian, the resulting direction is true and the conversion from true to magnetic must be noted.

MEASURING DISTANCE ON A CHART

The length of a line on a chart is usually measured in nautical miles, to the nearest 0.1 mile. For this purpose it is customary to use the latitude scale, considering 1 minute of latitude equal to 1 nautical mile. Therefore, always measure with your dividers on the *sides* of your chart, never at the top or the bottom. The error introduced by the assumption that 1 minute = 1 mile is not great over distances normally measured in coastal piloting.

Since the latitude scale on the side of a Mercator chart expands with increased latitude, measurement should be made at approximately your latitude or the midlatitude of your course. For a chart covering a small area, such as a harbor chart, this precaution is not important. On such charts a separate mile scale may be given, and it may safely be used over the entire chart.

For long distances the line should be broken into a number of parts or *legs,* each one being measured at its midlatitude. Most dividers will not span an excessively long distance

In measuring distance, the pilot spans with his dividers the length of the line to be measured, and then, without altering the setting, transfers this length to the latitude scale and carefully notes the reading. For a long line, the navigator sets his dividers to some convenient distance

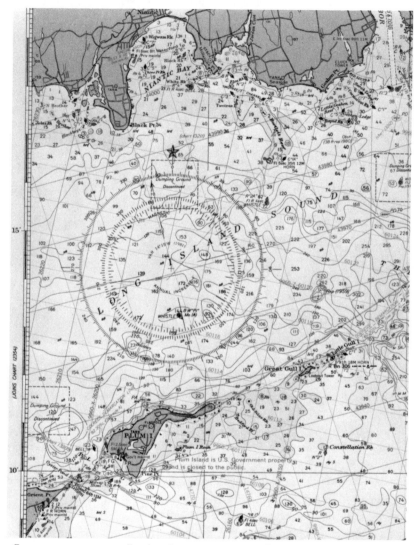

Compass roses are usually placed on open areas on charts.

on the latitude scale and steps off the line, counting the number of steps, multiplying this by the length of the step, and adding any remainder. The distance so measured is the length of the rhumb line.

PLOTTING AND LABELING THE COURSE LINE AND POSITION

Your *course* is your intended direction of travel through the water. A *course line* is a line extending in the direction of the course. From a known position of your vessel, the course line is drawn in the direction indicated by the course. It is good practice to label all lines and points of significance as they are drawn, for an unlabeled line or point may be misinterpreted later. Any simple, clear, logical system of labels is suitable. The following is widely used and might well be considered standard.

A course line with labels.

Label a course line with direction and speed. *Above* the course line place a capital *C* followed by three figures to indicate the course steered. It is customary to label and steer courses to the nearest whole degree. As mentioned before, small-boat skippers should label a course with the *magnetic* reading, for that is the course to be steered. *Below* the course line, and under the direction label, place a capital *S* followed by figures representing the speed in knots. Since the course is *always* given in degrees magnetic and the speed in knots, it is not necessary to indicate the units or reference the direction.

A point to be labeled is usually enclosed by a small circle in the case of a *fix* (an accurate position determined without reference to any former position), by a semicircle in the case of a dead reckoning position, and by a small square in the case of an estimated position. It is labeled with the time, usually to the nearest minute. Time is usually expressed in four figures without punctuation, on a 24-hour basis. Zone time (your *local* time) is usually used. A course line is a succession of an infinite number of dead reckoning positions. Only selected points should be labeled.

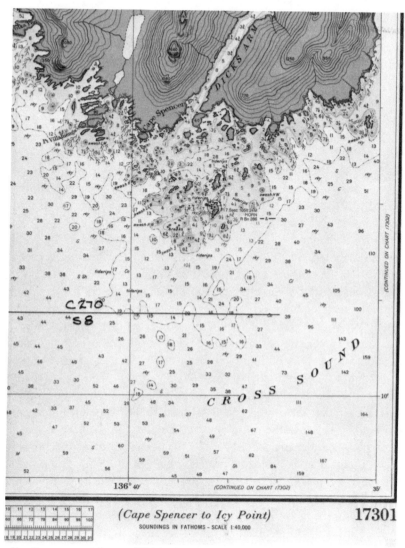

(Cape Spencer to Icy Point)
SOUNDINGS IN FATHOMS – SCALE 1:40,000

17301

Heading west at 8 knots off Dicks Arm.

The times of fixes and estimated positions are placed horizontally; the times of dead reckoning positions are customarily placed at an angle to the course line. Unfortunately most small-craft skippers aren't all that neat—but *you* should try to keep your labels consistent and simple.

DEAD RECKONING BY PLOT

As a vessel clears a harbor, the pilot should obtain one last good fix while identifiable landmarks are still available. This is called *taking departure,* and the position determined is called the *departure.* A course bearing back to the entrance of the harbor is also a wise precaution, especially if there is *any* chance that fog may close in and you may want to come about and scurry home. Your course line is drawn from your point of departure (perhaps the end of a breakwater or a big sea buoy) and labeled. The number of points selected for labeling depends primarily on the judgment and individual preference of the pilot. It is good practice to label each point where a change in course or speed occurs. If such changes are frequent, no additional points need be labeled. With infrequent changes, it is good practice to label points at some regular interval, perhaps every hour. From departure, the dead reckoning plot continues unbroken until a new well-established position is obtained, when both DR and fix are shown. The fix serves as the start of a new dead reckoning plot.

A typical dead reckoning plot is shown. It is assumed that no fix was obtained between the initial one at 0800 and the fix at 1430. Keep a neat plot and leave no doubt as to the meaning of each line and marked point. *A neat, accurate plot is the mark of a good pilot*—and it may also keep your little vessel away from nasty rocks and wicked shoals. The plot of the *intended track* or course should be kept extended to some future time. A good pilot, like a defensive driver, is always *ahead* of his vessel. In shoal water or when near the shore, aids to navigation, or dangers, it is vital to keep the plot on your chart as accurate and up to the minute as possible. Offshore, you may plot a more relaxed DR course, intensifying your efforts only when you are nearing thin water or closing with the hard edges of the land.

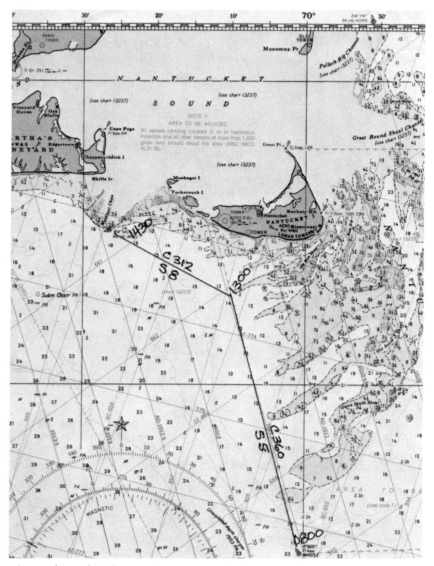

At 1300 hours this pilot turned to course 312° and increased his speed to 8 knots when he estimated he had run approximately 25 nautical miles.

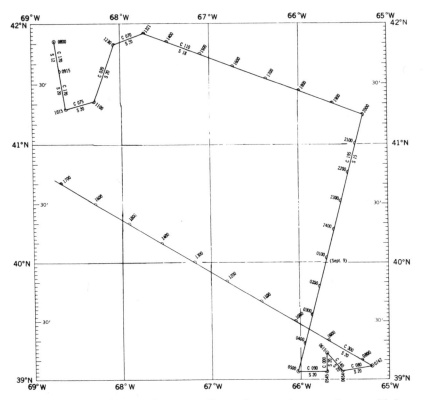

A complex dead reckoning plot at sea. Yours, in coastal waters, is more likely to progress steadily and smoothly—from here to there.

CURRENT

Water in motion over the surface of the earth is called *current*. The direction in which the water is moving is called the *set,* and the speed is called the *drift*. In piloting it is customary to use the term "current" to include all factors introducing geographical error in dead reckoning, whether their immediate effects are on the vessel or the water. When a fix is obtained, one assumes that the current has set *from* the DR position at the same time *to* the fix, and that the drift is equal to the distance in miles between these positions, divided by the number of hours since the last fix. This is true regardless of the number of changes of course or speed since the last fix.

If set and drift since the last fix are known or can be estimated, a better position can be obtained by applying a correction to that obtained by dead reckoning. This is conveniently done by drawing a straight line in the direction of the set for a distance equal to the drift, multiplied by the number of hours since the last fix. The direction of a straight line from the last fix to the EP is the estimated *course made good,* and the length of this line divided by the time is the estimated *speed made good.* The course and speed actually made good over the ground are called the *course over the ground (COG)* and *speed over the ground (SOG),* respectively. A capital *S* above the line represents the "set" and a *D* below the line is the "drift."

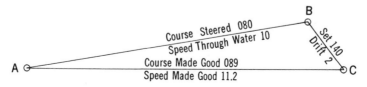

Finding course and speed made good through a current.

If a current is setting in the same direction as the course, or its reciprocal, the course over the ground is the same as that through the water. The effect on the speed can be found by simple arithmetic. If the course and set are in the same direction, the speeds are added; if in opposite directions, the smaller is subtracted from the larger. This situation is not unusual when you encounter a tidal current while entering or leaving a port or a small harbor. But watch those buoys as you enter or leave, for strange cross currents may set you on the mud or rocks, even when you are steering a perfect course. Woods Hole on the Atlantic Coast is noted for this, particularly for underpowered vessels or boats under sail.

Leeway is the leeward movement of a vessel due to wind. It may be expressed as distance, speed, or angular difference between course steered and course through the water. However expressed, its amount varies with the velocity and relative direction of the wind, type of vessel, amount of freeboard, trim, speed, state of the sea, and depth of the water. The better you know your craft, the better you can estimate her "leeway" under different conditions of speed, wind, and waves.

Leeway should be applied by adding its effect to that of the current or any other element that may introduce a geographical error to your dead reckoning plot. It is customary to consider the combined effect of all such elements as "current," and to make allowance for it when plotting your course. In sailing ship days it was common practice to consider leeway in terms of its effect on the course only, and to apply it as a correction in the same manner that variation and deviation are

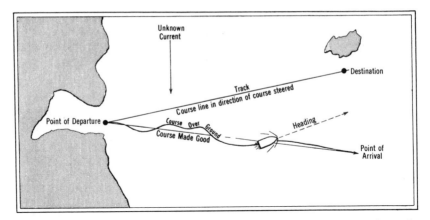

Course line, track, course over the ground, course made good, and heading—the elements of piloting your little vessel from here to there.

applied. While this method has merit even with power vessels, it is generally considered inferior to that of simply considering leeway as part of current.

DEAD RECKONING EQUIPMENT

Your compass is *essential* to dead reckoning. You *must* have one, and you *should* have the best you can afford. It's even better to have two. Nothing else aboard is as essential to the safety of your boat as is the nautical compass—not even you, the new skipper. An intelligent crew could probably bring your little ship home in a fog if you fell over the side—but could they do it without a compass? A mechanical log, either taffrail or a propeller under the hull, or an engine revolution counter is useful in determining your speed through the water. But neither is totally *essential* if you know the performance of your craft under various and varying conditions. Your vessel has *you,* and you have a *compass.* After that, the ancient and honorable art of piloting begins with your practiced skills at dead reckoning.

4

Piloting

And now let's get to the heart of the matter—piloting your vessel from here to there and back again with maximum pleasure and minimum trauma. It can be fun, and it's *supposed* to be fun! If it isn't fun, something is wrong—and that "something" is probably *you*.

Bowditch (H.O.9—*American Practical Navigator*) has this to say about piloting:

> On the high seas, where there is no immediate danger of grounding, navigation is a comparatively leisurely process. Courses and speeds are maintained over relatively long periods, and fixes are obtained at convenient intervals. Under favorable conditions a vessel might continue for several days with no positions other than those obtained by dead reckoning, or by estimate, and with no anxiety on the part of the captain or navigator. Errors in position can usually be detected and corrected before danger threatens.
>
> In the vicinity of shoal water the situation is different. Frequent or continuous positional information is usually essential to the safety of the vessel. An error, which on the high seas may be considered small, may in what are called *pilot waters* be intolerably large. Frequent changes of course and speed are common. The proximity of other vessels increases the possibility of collisions and restricts movements.

Bowditch then goes on to say a few kind words about "local knowledge" and the pilot whose "knowledge of his waters is gained not only through his own experience and familiarity, but by availing himself of all local information resources, public and private, recent and longstanding. . . ."

But a few words of caution about "local knowledge" are also

appropriate here: *Know your source!* Sooner or later you are certain to meet the "Old Salt" who calls out "Don't worry—plenty of water" moments before you go aground. Only later do you learn that Old Salt's knowledge of local waters is limited to the splash in his scotch. If in doubt, trust yourself; that's why you're reading this book.

The term "piloting" is used by *Bowditch* to mean the art of safely conducting a vessel in coastal waters that are littered with *charted* "hazards"—rocks, wrecks, reefs, and shoals. Sooner or later another Old Salt (hopefully, not the *same* Old Salt) will tell you, "If you don't go aground once in a while, you don't go anywhere."

To a degree that's true—but going aground, even *touching* bottom, is not to be taken lightly. Boats are meant to *float;* anything else is an abomination. Going aground, whether on a calm day in a quiet harbor or on a reef during a raging gale, is first a problem, then a danger, and finally a potential disaster. You don't *need* that kind of problem; you've invested too much in your boat to put her into unnecessary danger.

Even with the excellent charts that are available, there is an excuse for occasionally touching bottom; but there is *no* excuse for taking a cavalier attitude about a situation that results from carelessness or stupidity.

No other form of navigation requires the continuous alertness needed in piloting. At no other time are experience and judgment so valuable. The ability to work rapidly and to correctly interpret all available information, always keeping "ahead of the vessel," may mean the difference between safety and disaster.

PREPARATION FOR PILOTING

Because the time element is often of vital importance in piloting, adequate preparation is important. Long-range preparation includes organization and training. This organization and training should include your helmsmen, who must be granted less tolerance in straying from your charted course in "pilot waters" than when your little ship is farther offshore.

The more *immediate* preparation includes a study of the charts and publications of the area to familiarize yourself with channels, shoals, tides, currents, aids to navigation, etc. There's rarely enough time to dig out the right chart or find the right book when you're standing into danger. This preparation also includes the development of a definite "plan" for transiting hazardous waters. Prudence dictates that your crew, especially the helmsman, should also know your plan—*in advance*. You can be certain that there won't be enough time to hold a crew conference when danger is all around you. This doesn't mean that you are delegating your responsibility as skipper; the safety of your vessel, and all those aboard her, begins and ends with you.

There is no mystique to "piloting; it's as basic as good seamanship. Don't clutter your head with complex theory; above all, *keep it simple*. Whether you are daysailing or cruising, what you *really* want to know at *all times* are two simple things:

1. Where am I?
2. Where are all those other *things?*

And that starts with your "position."

POSITION

Piloting, as in celestial and radionavigation, makes extensive use of *lines of position*. You can assume that your vessel is *somewhere* along a line of position. A line of position may be highly reliable or of questionable accuracy. Lines of position are of great value, but you should always keep in mind that *they can be in error* because of imperfections in the instruments used for obtaining them and human limitations in those who use the instruments and utilize the results. Your confidence in various lines of position is a matter of judgment acquired from experience.

Two lines of position that *intersect* are better than one; three are even better.

Bearings

A bearing is the horizontal direction of one point from another. It usually expressed in degrees. In navigation, north is generally used as the reference direction, and angles are measured clockwise through 360°. It is customary to express all bearings in three digits, using preliminary zeros where needed. Thus north is 000° or 360°, a direction 7° to the right of north is 007°, east is 090°, southwest is 225°, etc.

For plotting, you will undoubtedly use magnetic compass bearings when you are marking your chart, but additional quick-reference or "eyeball" bearings can be useful as you move through hazardous

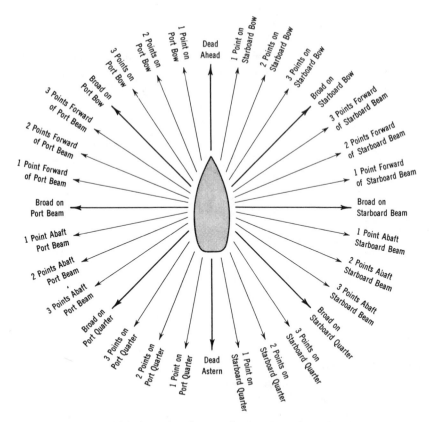

One method—a bit old-fashioned perhaps—of expressing relative bearings.

waters. These are relative to the heading of your little ship. A bearing expressed as angular distance from your heading is called the *relative bearing*. It is usually measured clockwise through 360°. A relative bearing may be expressed in still another way, as illustrated. This is especially useful if you are passing urgent information to a helmsman. Except for dead ahead and points at 45° intervals from it, this method is used principally for indicating directions obtained visually, without precise measurement. An even more general indication of relative bearing may be given by such directions as "ahead," "on the starboard bow," "on the port quarter," "astern." The term "abeam" may be used as the equivalent of either the general "on the beam" or sometimes the more precise "broad on the beam." Degrees are sometimes used instead of points to express relative bearings.

A *bearing line* in the direction of a charted object is one of the most widely used lines of position. If you know that an identified landmark has a certain bearing from your vessel, the vessel can only be *some-*

where along that line. Thus if a lighthouse is *east* of a ship, that ship is *west* of the lighthouse. If a beacon bears 156°, the observer must be on a line extending 156° + 180° = 336° from the beacon.

Bearings are usually obtained on small vessels from your primary compass, hand-bearing compass, radio direction finder, or radar. One type of bearing can be obtained by eye without measurement. When two objects appear directly in a line, one behind the other, they are said to be "in range," and together they constitute a *range*. For accurately charted objects, a range may provide the most accurate line of position obtainable, and one of the easiest to observe. Tanks, steeples, towers, cupolas, etc., sometimes form *natural ranges*. A pilot should be familiar with prominent ranges in his cruising area, particularly those that can be used to mark turning points, indicate limits of shoals, or define an approach heading. So useful is the range in marking a course that artificial ranges have been installed in line with channels in many harbors. If you keep the range marks in line, you're safely in the channel. If the *farther* beacon (customarily the higher one) appears to "open out" (move) to the right of the forward (lower) beacon, you know you are to the right of your desired track. Similarly, if it opens out to the left, you are off track to the left.

The line defined by the range is called a *range line* or *leading line*. Range daybeacons and other charted objects forming a range are often called *leading marks*. Range lights are often called *leading lights*.

Plot only a short part of a line of position in the vicinity of your vessel to avoid confusion and to reduce chart wear from erasures. Avoid drawing lines through the chart symbol indicating the landmark used. In the case of a range, a straightedge is placed along the two objects, and the desired portion of the line is plotted. A single bearing is labeled with the time above the line.

Distance

If your vessel is a certain distance from an identified point on the chart, you are somewhere on a circle with that point as the center and the distance as the radius. A single distance (range) arc is also labeled with the time above the line.

The distance from your position to a known location may be obtained by radar, range finder, or simply an eyeball "guesstimate." However, be aware that estimating the distance to a visible object—a distant buoy, a light or a converging ship—is one of your most difficult tasks. Your ability will improve with practice, so make that practice a part of your normal routine. All too often we *underestimate* the distance to a fixed object such as a distant harbor light, but *overestimate* the distance between our vessel and another, especially if the other ship is larger. As much as anything, this results from wishful thinking. Practice is the antidote.

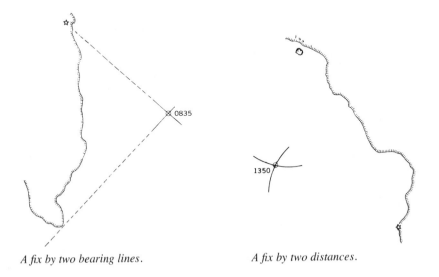

A fix by two bearing lines.   *A fix by two distances.*

The Fix

A line of position, however obtained, represents a series of possible positions, but not a single position. However, if two simultaneous, nonparallel lines of position are available, the intersection of the two lines is one form of fix. Examples of several types of fix are given in the accompanying illustrations. In the first illustration, a fix was obtained from two bearing lines. The fix of the second illustration was obtained by two distance circles. The third illustrates a fix from a range and a distance. In the fourth, a bearing and distance of a single object are used. Use a small circle to indicate the fix at the intersection of the lines of position. The time of the fix is the time when the lines of position were established. It is essential that you can *identify* two objects for a good two-bearing fix. The angle between lines of position is also important. The ideal is 90°. If the angle is small, a slight error in measuring or plotting either line results in a relatively large error in the indicated position. In the case of a bearing line, nearby objects are preferable to those at a considerable distance, because the linear (distance) error resulting from an angular error increases with distance.

Another consideration is the type of object observed. Lighthouses, spires, and flagpoles are good objects because the point of observation is well defined. A large building, nearby mountains, or a point of land may leave some reasonable doubt as to the exact point used for observation. If a headland bluff is used, as in the first illustration above,

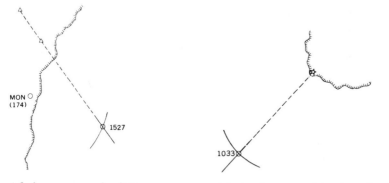

A fix by a range and a distance.   *A fix by distance and bearing of a single object.*

there is a possibility that a low spit may extend seaward from the part observed. A number of towers or chimneys, close together, require careful identification. A buoy or a lightship may drag anchor and be out of position. Most buoys are secured by a single anchor and swing as the tide, current, and wind change. But you have to trust *something,* and a government marker is reasonably reliable for a fix.

If three lines of position cross at a common point, or form a small triangle, it is reasonable to assume that the position is reliable. However, this is not an absolute, and frequent fixes are essential in crowded, cluttered waters. Because small errors are certain to occur, it is interesting to note how those small errors are magnified by distance. This is known as the "Rule of Sixty." *Bowditch* states:

A single bearing line of an accurately charted object will be offset from the observer's actual position by an amount dependent upon the net angular error of the observation and plot, and distance of the charted object from the observer. The amount of offset is expressed approximately in the "Rule of Sixty," which may be stated as follows: The offset of the plotted bearing line from the observer's actual position is 1 / 60th of the distance to the object observed for each degree of error. In the derivation of the Rule of Sixty, the assumption is made that the angular error is small, i.e., not more than the small errors normally associated with compass observations and plotting. Using this assumption, the sine function of the angular error is taken as equal to the same number of radians as the error. As shown below, the offset is equal to 1 / 60th of the distance to the charted object observed times the sine of the angular error of the bearing line as plotted. Thus, an error of 1° represents an error of about 100 feet if the object is 1 mile distant, 1000 feet if the object is 10 miles away, and 1 mile if the object is 60 miles from the observer.

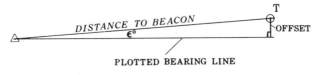

The basic principle of the Rule of Sixty.

For accurate results, observations made to fix the position of a moving vessel should be made simultaneously, or nearly so. On a slow-moving vessel, relatively little error is introduced by making several observations in quick succession. A wise precaution is to observe the objects more nearly ahead or astern first, since these are least affected by the motion of the observer. However, when you want to obtain a good estimate of the speed being made good, it may be desirable to observe the most rapidly changing bearing first, assuming that such observation can be better coordinated with the time "mark."

Sometimes it is not possible or desirable to make simultaneous or nearly simultaneous observations. Such a situation may arise when only a single object is available for observation, or when all available objects are on nearly the same or reciprocal bearings and there is no means of determining distance. Under such conditions, a period of several minutes or more may be permitted to elapse between observations to provide lines of position crossing at suitable angles. When this occurs, the lines can be adjusted to a common time to obtain a "running fix." Refer to the next four illustrations. Let's say you are charging along the coast on course 020° at a speed of 15 knots. At 1505 a lighthouse bears 310°. If the line of position is accurate, you are somewhere on it at the time of observation. Ten minutes later you will have traveled 2.5 miles in direction 020°. If you were at A at 1505, you will be at A' at 1515. However, if the position at 1505 was B, the position at 1515 will be B'. A similar relationship exists between C and C'. Thus if any point on the original line of position is moved a distance equal to the distance run, and in the direction of the motion, a line through this point, parallel to the original line of position, represents all possible positions of the ship at the later time. This process is called

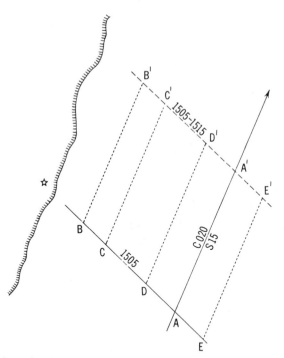

Advancing a line of position.

advancing a line of position. The moving of a line back to an earlier time is called *retiring* a line of position. You may reasonably assume that you have moved from one point to another *along* the coast, but you don't know how far you are *off* the coast.

The accuracy of an adjusted line of position depends not only on the accuracy of the original line, but also on the reliability of the information used in moving the line. If there are any changes of course or speed, these should be considered, for the motion of the line of position should reflect as accurately as possible the movement of the observer between the time of observation and the time to which the lines is adjusted. Perhaps the easiest way to do this is to measure the direction and distance between dead reckoning or estimated positions at the two times, and use these to adjust some point on the line of position. This method is shown in the next drawing. In this illustration, allowance is made for the estimated combined effect of wind and current, this effect being plotted as an additional course and distance. If courses and speeds made good over the ground are used, the separate plotting of the wind and current effect is not used. In the illustration, point *A* is the DR position at the time of observation and point *B* is the estimated position (the DR position adjusted for wind and current) at

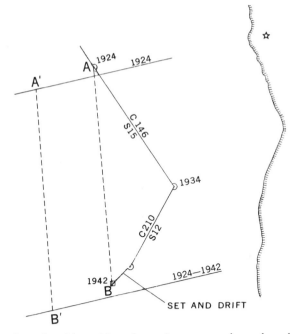

Advancing a line of position with a change in course and speed, and allowing for current.

the time to which the line of position is adjusted. Line $A'B'$ is of the same length and in the same direction as line AB.

Other techniques may be used. The position of the object observed may be advanced or retired, and the line of position drawn in relation to the adjusted position. This is the most satisfactory method for a *circle of position,* as shown in the next illustration. When the position of the landmark is adjusted, the advanced line of position can be laid down without plotting the original line, which need be shown only if it serves a useful purpose. This not only eliminates part of the work, but reduces the number of lines drawn on the chart and decreases the possibility of error.

Another method is to draw any line, such as a perpendicular, from the dead reckoning position at the time of observation to the line of position. A line of the same length and in the same direction, drawn from the DR position or EP at the time to which the line is adjusted, locates a point on the adjusted line, as shown. If a single course and speed is involved, common practice is to measure from the intersection of the line of position and the course line. If the dividers are set to the distance run between bearings and placed on the chart so that one point is on the first bearing line and the other point is on the second bearing

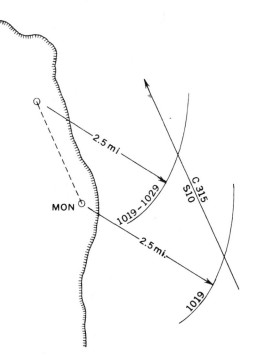

Advancing a circle of position.

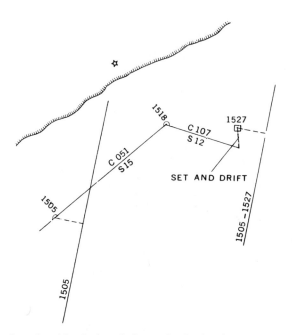

Advancing a line of position by its relation to the dead reckoning position.

line, and the line connecting the points is parallel to the course line, the points will indicate the positions of the vessel at the times of the bearings.

The Running Fix

A fix obtained by means of lines of position taken at different times and adjusted to a common time is called a *running fix*. In piloting, common practice is to *advance* earlier lines to the time of the last observation. A running fix obtained from two bearings of the same

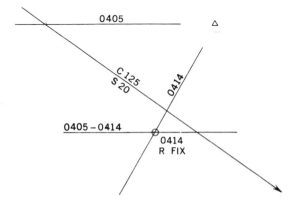

A running fix by two bearings on the same object.

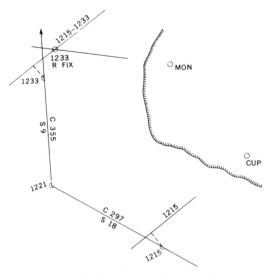

A running fix with a change of course and speed between observations on different landmarks.

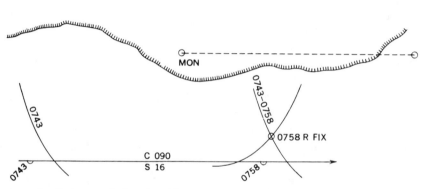

A running fix by two circles of position.

object is illustrated. In the next illustration, the boat changes course and speed between observations of two objects. A running fix by two circles of position is shown in the third illustration.

When simultaneous observations are not available, a running fix may provide the most reliable position obtainable. The time between observations should be no longer than about 30 minutes, for the uncertainty of course and distance made good increases with time. The running fix is far from perfect. You may encounter an unknown head current that will slow your estimated speed over the ground. The effect of an unknown head current is shown in the following illustration. Here, a vessel is proceeding along a coast, on course 250°, speed 12 knots. At 0920 light *A* bears 190°, and at 0930 it bears 143°. If the earlier bearing line is advanced a distance of 2 miles (10 minutes at 12 knots) in the

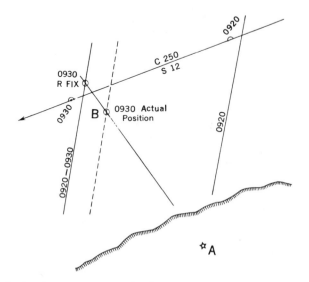

The effect of a head current on a running fix.

direction of the course, the running fix is shown by the solid lines. However, if there is a head current of 2 knots, the vessel is making good a speed of only 10 knots, and in 10 minutes will travel a distance of only 1⅔ miles. If the first bearing line is advanced this distance, as shown by the broken line, the actual position of the ship is at *B. This is nearer the beach than the running fix,* and therefore is a dangerous situation.

If there is either a head or following current, a series of running fixes based on a number of bearings of the same object will plot in a straight line parallel to the course line. The plotted line will be too close to the object observed if there is a following current, and too far out if there is a head current. The existence of the current will not be apparent unless the actual speed over the ground is known. The position of the plotted line relative to the dead reckoning course line is not a reliable guide.

A current oblique to your course will result in an incorrect position, but the direction of the error won't be known. The existence of an oblique current, but not its amount, can be detected by observing and plotting several bearings of the same object. The running fix obtained by advancing one bearing line to the time of the next one will not agree

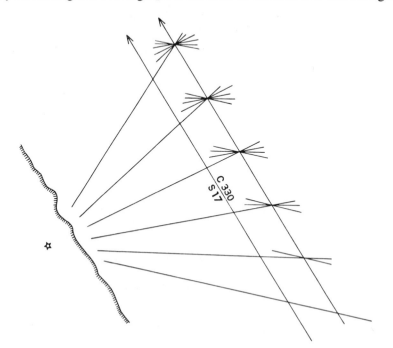

A number of running fixes with a following current.

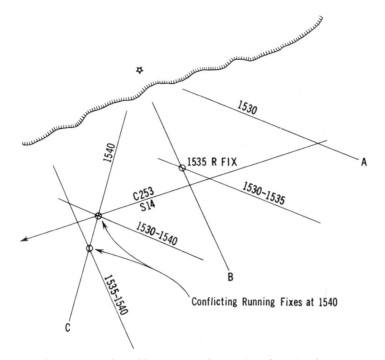

Detecting the existence of an oblique current by a series of running fixes.

with the running fix obtained by advancing an earlier line. Thus if bearings *A*, *B*, and *C* are observed at 5-minute intervals, the running fix obtained by advancing *B* to the time of *C* will not be the same as that obtained by advancing *A* to the time of *C*, as shown.

Whatever the current, the *direction* of the course made good (assuming constant current and constant course and speed) can be determined. Three bearings of a charted object *O* are observed and plotted in the next two illustrations. Through *O*, draw *XY* in any direction. Using a convenient scale, determine points *A* and *B* so that *OA* and *OB* are proportional to the time intervals between the first and second bearings and the second and third bearings, respectively. From *A* and *B*, draw lines parallel to the second bearing line, intersecting the first and third bearing lines at *C* and *D*, respectively. The direction of the line from *C* to *D* is the course being made good.

The priniciple of the method shown in the above illustration is based on the property of similar triangles. The distance of the line *CD* from the track is in error by an amount proportional to the ratio of the speed being made good to the speed assumed for the solution. If a good fix (not a running fix) is obtained at some time before the first bearing for the running fix, and the current has not changed, the track can be determined by drawing a line from the fix, in the direction of the course

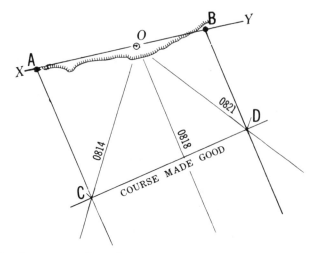

Determining the course made good.

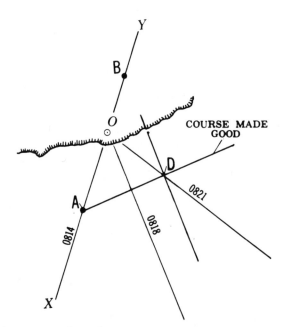

Determining the course made good.

made good. The intersection of the track with any of the bearing lines is an actual position. A frequently desirable variation of the method is to use the first bearing line as the side of triangle that is divided in proportion to the time intervals between bearings, as shown here. This method of solution of the *three-bearing problem* is presented in *The Complete Coastal Navigator* by Charles H. Cotter.

The current can be determined whenever a dead reckoning position and fix are available for the same time. The direction *from* the dead reckoning position *to* the fix is the set of the current. The distance between these two positions, divided by the time (expressed in hours and tenths) since the last fix, is the drift of the current in knots. For accurate results, the dead reckoning position must be run up from the previous fix without any allowance for current. Any error in either the dead reckoning position (such as poor steering, unknown compass error, inaccurate log, or wind) or the fix will be reflected in the determination of the current. *When the dead reckoning position and fix are close together, a relatively small error in either may introduce a large error in the apparent set of the current.*

SAFE PILOTING WITHOUT A FIX

A fix or running fix is not always necessary to ensure the safety of your vessel. If you are motoring or sailing up a dredged channel, for instance, the only knowledge needed to prevent grounding is to stay alert and steer within the limits of the dredged area. This information may be provided by a range in line with the channel or a series of channel markers. A fix is not needed except to mark the point at which a range can no longer be followed with safety.

Under favorable conditions a *danger bearing* can be used to ensure safe passage past a shoal or other danger, as in the illustration. You are proceeding along a coast on intended track *AB* and you know there is a nasty shoal off your port bow. A line *HX* is drawn from lighthouse *H*, tangent to the outer edge of the danger. As long as the bearing of light *H* is *less* than *XH*, the danger bearing, the vessel is in safe water.

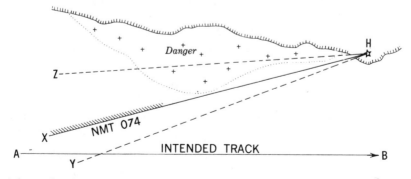

A danger bearing.

An example is *YH,* since no part of the bearing line passes through the danger area. Any bearing *greater* than *XH,* such as *ZH,* indicates a *possible* dangerous situation. If the object is passed on the port side, the safe bearing is *less* than the danger bearing, as shown in the illustration. If the object is passed on the starboard side, the danger bearing represents the minimum bearing, safe ones being *greater.* To be effective, a danger bearing should not differ greatly from the course, and the object of which bearings are to be taken should be easily identifiable and visible over the entire area of usefulness of the danger bearing. A margin of safety might be provided by drawing line *HX* through a point a short distance off the danger. In this case the danger bearing is labeled NMT 074 to indicate that the bearing of the light should be *not more than* 074°. The hazardous side of the bearing line is hatched. If a natural or artificial range is available as a danger bearing, it should be used. This method is particularly useful for racing sailors who sometimes tend to hug the beach to avoid offshore currents or to pick up offshore breezes. It may be picturesque to sail or motor close to the coast, but it's a lot *safer* offshore.

Your depth sounder, if you have one, is a useful instrument for providing a *danger sounding* in tricky shoal waters. The value selected depends on the draft of the vessel and the slope of the bottom. It should be sufficiently deep to provide adequate maneuvering room to reach deeper water before grounding, once the minimum depth is obtained. In an area where the shoaling is gradual, a smaller margin of depth can be considered than in an area of rapid shoaling. Where the shoaling is very abrupt, danger sounding is impractical. It is a good practice to mark the danger sounding prominently on your chart. A colored pencil is useful for this purpose.

If it is desired to round a point marked by a prominent landmark without approaching closer than a given minimum distance, this can be done by sailing or motoring until the minimum distance is reached and then immediately changing course to bring the landmark broad on the beam. Frequent small changes of course are then used to keep the landmark near, *but not forward of,* the beam. This method is not reliable if the vessel is being moved laterally by wind or current.

An approximation of the distance off can be found by noting the rate at which the bearing changes. If the landmark is kept abeam, the change is indicated by a change of heading. During a change of 57°, the distance off is about the same as the distance run. For a change of 28°, the distance is about twice the run; for 19° it is about three times the run; for 14° it is about five times the run. Another variation is to measure the number of seconds required for a change of 16°. The distance off is equal to this interval multiplied by the speed in knots and divided by 1000. That is, $D = ST/1000$, where D is the distance in nautical miles, S is the speed in knots, and T is the time interval in seconds.

Soundings

The most important use of soundings is to determine if the water is deep enough for safety, whether you are underway or at anchor. You know, of course, the draft of your vessel, and your charts should be studied *in advance* in order for you to spot—then skirt—thin-water areas. A lead line is adequate for anchoring, but a depth sounder is preferable when you are underway.

Under favorable conditions, soundings can be a valuable aid in establishing your position. Their value depends on the configuration of the bottom, the amount and accuracy of information given on the chart, the type and accuracy of the sounding available aboard the vessel, and the knowledge and skill of the skipper-pilot. In an area having a flat bottom devoid of distinctive features, or where detailed information is not given on the chart, little positional information can be gained from soundings. However, in an area where depth curves run roughly parallel to the shore, a sounding might indicate distance from the beach. In any area where a given depth curve is sharply defined and relatively straight, it serves as a line of position which can be used with other lines, such as those obtained by bearings of landmarks, to obtain a fix. The crossing of a sharply defined trench, ridge, shoal, or flat-topped seamount (a guyot) can provide valuable positional information.

In any such use, identification of the feature observed is important. In an area of rugged underwater terrain, identification might be difficult unless an almost continuous determination of position is maintained, for it is not unusual for a number of features within a normal radius of uncertainty to be similar. If your echo sounder produces a continuous recording of the depth, called a *bottom profile,* this can be matched to the chart in the vicinity of the course line. If no profile is available, a rough approximation of one can be constructed as follows: Record a series of soundings at short intervals, the length being dictated by the scale of the chart and the existing situation. For most purposes the interval might be each minute, or perhaps each half mile or mile. Draw a straight line on transparent material and, at the scale of the chart, place marks along the line at the distance intervals at which soundings were made. For this purpose the line might be superimposed over the latitude scale or a distance scale of the chart. At each mark, record the corresponding sounding. Then place the transparency over the chart and, by trial and error, match the recorded soundings to those indicated on the chart. Keep the line on the transparency parallel or nearly parallel to the course line plotted on the chart. A current may cause some difference between the plotted course line and the course made good. Also, speed over the bottom might be somewhat different from that used for the plot. This should be reflected in the match. This method should be used with caution, because it may be possible to fit the *line of soundings* to several places on the chart.

Exact agreement with the charted bottom should not be expected at all times. Inaccuracies in the soundings, tide, or incomplete data on the chart may affect the match, but more than one skipper has found his way home in a pea-soup fog by matching soundings to his chart. Any marked discrepancy should be investigated, particularly if it indicates less depth than anticipated. If such a discrepancy cannot be reconciled, the wise skipper will come about and haul off to deeper water or anchor and wait for more favorable conditions.

Most Probable Position (MPP)

Since information sufficient to establish an *exact* position is seldom available, you should try at all times to know your *most probable position*—your MPP. ''Most probable'' is certainly preferable to GOK—''God Only Knows!'' If three reliable bearing lines cross at a point, there is usually little doubt as to the position, and little or no judgment is needed. But when conflicting information or information of questionable reliability is received, a decision is required to establish the MPP. At such a time, your experience and judgment will be put to the test. Judgment can be improved if you try continually to account for all apparent discrepancies, even under favorable conditions. If you habitually analyze the situation whenever positional information is received, you will develop judgment as to the reliability of various types of information and will learn which should be treated with caution.

When complete positional information is lacking, or when the available information is considered of questionable reliability, the most probable position might well be considered an *estimated position* (EP).

Such a position might be determined from a single line of position, from a line of soundings, from lines of position that are somewhat inconsistent, or from a dead reckoning position with a correction for current or wind.

Whether the "most probable position" is a fix, a running fix, estimated position, or dead reckoning position, you should keep it current at all times—both *in* your head and *on* your chart. The practice of continuing a dead reckoning plot from one good fix to another is advisable, whether or not the information is available to indicate a most probable position differing from the dead reckoning position, for the DR plot provides an indication of current and leeway. A series of estimated positions may not be consistent because of the continual revision of the estimate as additional information is received. However, it is good practice to plot all MPPs, and sometimes to maintain a separate EP plot based on the best estimate of course and speed being made good over the ground, for this will help you know whether your present course is a safe one.

Piloting and Electronics

If there is no mystique to piloting, and *if* an MPP (most probable position) is preferable to a GOK (God Only Knows) position, you might say that *some* electronic equipment is preferable to *no* electronic equipment. Maybe yes; maybe no. You *should* be able to function as an able pilot with nothing more than your basic dead reckoning instruments—a pencil, dividers, parallel rulers, compass, and charts. Depend too heavily on electronic gadgetry and sooner or later it will let you down. Batteries fail, terminals corrode, and wiring deteriorates, and *when* they do, you'd better know how to pilot your little vessel from *here* to *there* with nothing more than a pencil, dividers, parallel rulers, compass, and chart—and your own good common sense.

Practical Piloting

In pilot waters navigation is primarily an art. It is essential that the principles explained in this chapter be mastered and applied intelligently. From every experience the wise pilot acquires additional knowledge and improves his judgment. Mechanically following a set of procedures should not be expected to produce perfect results.

While piloting, the successful skipper is somewhat an opportunist, fitting his technique to the situation at hand. If you are cruising in a large area having relatively weak currents and moderate traffic, such as Chesapeake Bay, fixes may be obtained at relatively long intervals with a dead reckoning plot between. In a narrow waterway with swift currents and heavy traffic, an almost continuous fix is needed. In such an area you may draw the desired track on your chart and obtain eye-ball fixes every minute or so, steering your boat back on the track as it begins to drift to one side.

If you plan to traverse unfamiliar waters, study your charts, coast pilot, tide and tidal tables, and light lists to familiarize yourself with local conditions. An experienced pilot learns to interpret the signs around him. The ripple of water around buoys and other obstructions, the direction and angle tilt of buoys, the direction at which vessels ride at anchor—these can provide meaningful information regarding currents. The wise pilot learns to interpret such signs when the position of his vessel is *not* in doubt. Then, when visibility is poor or available information is inconsistent, the ability developed at favorable times can be of great value.

With experience, you will know when a danger angle or danger bearing is useful, and what ranges are reliable and how they should be used. However familiar you are with an area, you should not permit yourself to become careless in the matter of timing lights for identification, plotting your progress on a chart, or keeping a good recent position. Fog sometimes creeps in unnoticed, obscuring landmarks before you realize its presence. A series of frequent fixes obtained while various aids are visible provides valuable information on position and current.

Practical piloting requires a thorough familiarity with principles involved and local conditions, constant alertness, and judgment. A study of avoidable groundings reveals that in most cases the problem is not a lack of knowledge, but failure to use or interpret available information. Among the most common errors are:

1. Failure to obtain or evaluate soundings.
2. Failure to identify aids to navigation.
3. Failure to *use* available navigational aids.
4. Failure to maintain a complete, up-to-date chart inventory.
5. Failure to adjust a magnetic compass.
6. Failure to check magnetic compass readings at frequent intervals.

7. Failure to keep a dead reckoning plot.
8. Failure to plot new bearings.
9. Failure to properly evaluate information received.
10. Failure to do your own navigating (following another vessel, for example).
11. Failure to obtain and use information avalable on charts and in publications.
12. Failure to "brief" your crew on your "plans."
13. Failure to "keep ahead" of your vessel.

5

The Rules of the Road

You know it's foolhardy and embarrassing to bump the bottom, and you know it's downright dangerous to bump the hard edges of the shore—but what about all those vessels around you? You don't want to bump them either. A collision—*any* boating accident—is a serious affair, even if no one is injured and no real damage occurs. It's sad but true that you can't assume that every skipper knows, understands, and will obey each Rule of the Road. If *you* know the rules, you will greatly improve your chances of avoiding a collision; then if you practice "defensive piloting," you will probably cruise for years without even a minor mishap.

The following rules—Public Law 96–591—were enacted as the Inland Navigational Rules Act of 1980 "to unify the rules for preventing collisions on the inland waters of the United States. . . ."

You may wish to obtain the full text of Public Law 96–591, but for our purposes here, the author has excerpted those portions that apply most directly to you, a new skipper. Although portions of this act have been deleted, those portions that remain have been kept intact. The act follows:

Part A—General
Rule 1
Application

• These Rules apply to all vessels upon the inland waters of the United States, and to vessels of the United States on the Canadian waters of the Great Lakes to the extent that there is no conflict with Canadian Law.

Rule 2
Responsibility

• Nothing in these Rules shall exonerate any vessel, or the owner, master, or crew thereof, from the consequences of any neglect to comply with these Rules or of the neglect of any precaution which may be required by the ordinary practice of seamen, or by the special circumstances of the case.

• In construing and complying with these Rules due regard shall be had to all dangers of navigation and collision and to any special circumstances, including the limitations of the vessels involved, which may make a departure from these Rules necessary to avoid immediate danger.

Rule 3
General Definitions

For the purpose of these Rules and this Act, except where the context otherwise requires:

• The word "vessel" includes every description of water craft, including nondisplacement craft . . . used or capable of being used as a means of transportation on water;

• The term "power-driven vessel" means any vessel propelled by machinery;

• The term "sailing vessel" means any vessel under sail provided that propelling machinery, if fitted, is not being used.

• The term "vessel engaged in fishing" means any vessel fishing with nets, lines, trawls, or other fishing apparatus which restricts maneuverability, but does not include a vessel fishing with trolling lines or other fishing apparatus which do not restrict maneuverability;

• The term "vessel not under command" means a vessel which through some exceptional circumstance is unable to maneuver as required by these Rules and is therefore unable to keep out of the way of another vessel; vessels restricted in their ability to maneuver include, but are not limited to: a vessel engaged in laying, servicing, or picking up a navigation mark, submarine cable, or pipeline; a vessel engaged in dredging, surveying, or underwater operations; a vessel engaged in replenishment or transferring of persons, provisions, or cargo while underway; a vessel engaged in the launching or recovery of aircraft; a vessel engaged in minesweeping operations; and a vessel engaged in a towing operation such as severely restricts the towing vessel and her tow in their ability to deviate from their course.

• The word "underway" means that a vessel is not at anchor, or made fast to the shore, or aground;

• The words "length" and "breadth" of a vessel mean her length overall and greatest breadth;

• Vessels shall be deemed to be in sight of one another only when one can be observed visually from the other;

• The term "restricted visibility" means any condition in which visibility is restricted by fog, mist, falling snow, heavy rainstorms, sandstorms, or any other similar causes;

• "Western Rivers" means the Mississippi River, its tributaries, South Pass, and Southwest Pass, to the navigational demarcation lines dividing the high seas from harbors, rivers, and other inland waters of the United States, and the Port Allen–Morgan City Alternate Route, and that part of the Atchafalaya River above its junction with the Port Allen–Morgan City Alternate Route including the Old River and the Red River;

• "Great Lakes" means the Great Lakes and their connecting and tributary waters including the Calumet River as far as the Thomas J. O'Brien Lock and Controlling Works (between mile 326 and 327), the Chicago River as far as the east side of the Ashland Avenue Bridge (between mile 321 and 322), and the Saint Lawrence River as far east as the lower exit of Saint Lambert Lock;

• "Inland Waters" means the navigable waters of the United States shoreward of the navigational demarcation lines dividing the high seas from harbors, rivers, and other inland waters of the United States and the waters of the Great Lakes on the United States side of the International Boundary;

• "Inland Rules" or "Rules" mean the Inland Navigational Rules and the annexes thereto, which govern the conduct of vessels and specify the lights, shapes, and sound signals that apply on the inland waters.

PART B—STEERING AND SAILING RULES
SECTION I. CONDUCT OF VESSELS IN ANY CONDITION OF VISIBILITY
Rule 4
Application

Rules in this subpart apply in any condition of visibility.

Rule 5
Lookout

• Every vessel shall at all times maintain a proper lookout by sight and hearing as well as by all available means appropriate in the prevailing circumstances and conditions so as to make a full appraisal of the situation and to the risk of collision.

Rule 6
Safe Speed

• Every vessel shall at all times proceed at a safe speed so that she can take proper and effective action to avoid collision and be stopped within a distance appropriate to the prevailing circumstances and conditions.

• In determining a safe speed the following factors shall be among those taken into account: the state of visibility; the traffic density including concentration of fishing vessels or any other vessels; the maneuverability of the vessel with special reference to stopping distance and turning ability in the prevailing conditions; at night, the presence of background lights such as from shore lights or from backscatter of her own lights; the state of wind, sea, and current, and the proximity of navigational hazards; the draft in relation to the available depth of water.

Rule 7
Risk of Collision

• Every vessel shall use all available means appropriate to the prevailing circumstances and conditions to determine if risk of collision exists. If there is any doubt, such risk shall be deemed to exist.

Rule 8
Action to Avoid Collision

• Any action taken to avoid collision shall, if the circumstances of the case admit, be positive, made in ample time and with due regard to the observation of good seamanship.

• Any alteration of course or speed to avoid collision shall, if the circumstances of the case admit, be large enough to be readily apparent to another vessel observing visually or by radar; a succession of small alterations of course or speed should be avoided.

• If there is sufficient sea room, alteration of course alone may be the most effective action to avoid a close-quarters situation provided that it is made in good time, is substantial, and does not result in another close-quarters situation.

• Action taken to avoid collision with another vessel shall be such as to result in passing at a safe distance. The effectiveness of the action shall be carefully checked until the other vessel is finally past and clear.

• If necessary to avoid collision or allow more time to assess the situation, a vessel shall slacken her speed or take all way off by stopping or reversing her means of propulsion.

Rule 9
Narrow Channels

• A vessel proceeding along the course of a narrow channel or fairway shall keep as near to the outer limit of the channel or fairway which lies on her starboard side as is safe and practicable.

• A vessel of less than 20 meters in length or a sailing vessel shall not impede the passage of a vessel that can safely navigate only within a narrow channel or fairway.

• A vessel engaged in fishing shall not impede the passage of any other vessel navigating within a narrow channel or fairway.

• A vessel shall not cross a narrow channel or fairway if such crossing impedes the passage of a vessel which can safely navigate only within that channel or fairway. The latter vessel shall use the danger signal prescribed in Rule 34 below if in doubt as to the intention of the crossing vessel.

• In a narrow channel or fairway when overtaking, the vessel intending to overtake shall indicate her intention by sounding the appropriate signal prescribed in Rule 34 and take steps to permit safe passing. The overtaken vessel, if in agreement, shall sound the same signal. If in doubt she shall sound the danger signal prescribed in Rule 34.

• A vessel nearing a bend or an area of a narrow channel or fairway where other vessels may be obscured by an intervening obstruction shall navigate with particular alertness and caution and shall sound the appropriate signal prescribed in Rule 34.

• Every vessel shall . . . avoid anchoring in a narrow channel.

SECTION II. CONDUCT OF VESSELS IN SIGHT OF ONE ANOTHER
Rule 11
Application

Rules in this subpart apply to vessels in sight of one another.

Rule 12
Sailing Vessels

• When two vessels are approaching one another, so as to involve risk of collision, one of them shall keep out of the way of the other as follows:

• When each has the wind on a different side, the vessel which has the wind on the port side shall keep out of the way of the other.

• When both have the wind on the same side, the vessel which is to windward shall keep out of the way of the vessel which is to leeward.

• If a vessel with the wind on the port side sees a vessel to windward and cannot determine with certainty whether the other vessel has the wind on the port or on the starboard side, she shall keep out of the way of the other.

• For the purpose of this Rule the windward side shall be deemed to be the side opposite to that on which the mainsail is carried or, in the case of a square-rigged vessel, the side opposite to that on which the largest fore-and-aft sail is carried.

Rule 13
Overtaking

• Notwithstanding anything contained in Rules 4 through 18, any vessel overtaking any other shall keep out of the way of the vessel being overtaken.

• A vessel shall be deemed to be overtaking when coming up with another vessel from a direction more than 22.5 degrees abaft her beam; that is, in such a position with reference to the vessel she is overtaking, that at night she would be able to see only the sternlight of that vessel but neither of her sidelights.

• When a vessel is in any doubt as to whether she is overtaking another, she shall assume that this is the case and act accordingly.

• Any subsequent alteration of the bearing between the two vessels shall not make the overtaking vessel a crossing vessel within the meaning of these Rules or relieve her of the duty of keeping clear of the overtaken vessel until she is finally past and clear.

Rule 14
Head-on Situation

• When two power-driven vessels are meeting on reciprocal or nearly reciprocal courses so as to involve risk of collision, each shall alter her course to starboard so that each shall pass on the port side of the other.

• Such a situation shall be deemed to exist when a vessel sees the other ahead or nearly ahead and by night she could see the masthead lights of the other in a line or nearly in a line or both sidelights and by day she observes the corresponding aspect of the other vessel.

• When a vessel is in any doubt as to whether such a situation exists, she shall assume that it does exist and act accordingly.

Rule 15
Crossing Situation

• When two power-driven vessels are crossing so as to involve risk of collision, the vessel which has the other on her starboard side shall keep out of the way and shall, if the circumstances of the case admit, avoid crossing ahead of the other vessel.

• On the Great Lakes [and] Western Rivers a vessel crossing a river shall keep out of the way of a power-driven vessel ascending or descending the river.

Rule 16
Action by Give-Way Vessel

• Every vessel which is directed to keep out of the way of another vessel shall, so far as possible, take early and substantial action to keep well clear.

Rule 17
Action by Stand-on Vessel

• Where one of two vessels is to keep out of the way, the other shall keep her course and speed. The latter vessel may, however, take action to avoid collision by her maneuver alone, as soon as it becomes apparent to her that the vessel required to keep out of the way is not taking appropriate action in compliance with these Rules.

• When, from any cause, the vessel required to keep her course and speed finds herself so close that collision cannot be avoided by the action of the give-way vessel alone, she shall take such action as will best aid to avoid collision.

Rule 18
Responsibilities between Vessels

• Except where Rules 9, 10, and 13 otherwise require: a power-driven vessel underway shall keep out of the way of:
a vessel not under command;
a vessel restricted in her ability to maneuver;
a vessel engaged in fishing; and
a sailing vessel.
• A sailing vessel underway shall keep out of the way of:
a vessel not under command;
a vessel restricted in her ability to maneuver; and
a vessel engaged in fishing.
• A vessel engaged in fishing when underway shall, so far as possible, keep out of the way of:
a vessel not under command; and
a vessel restricted in her ability to maneuver.

SECTION III. CONDUCT OF VESSELS IN RESTRICTED VISIBILITY
Rule 19
Conduct of Vessels in Restricted Visibility

• This Rule applies to vessels not in sight of one another when navigating in or near an area of restricted visibility.

• Every vessel shall proceed at a safe speed adapted to the prevailing circumstances and conditions of restricted visibility. A power-driven vessel shall have her engines ready for immediate maneuver.

• Except where it has been determined that a risk of collision does not exist, every vessel which hears apparently forward of her beam the fog signal of another vessel, or which cannot avoid a close-quarters situation with another vessel forward of her beam, shall reduce her speed to the minimum at which she can be kept on course. She shall if necessary take all her way off and, in any event, navigate with extreme caution until danger of collision is over.

PART C—LIGHTS AND SHAPES
Rule 20
Application

• Rules in this part shall be complied with in all weathers.

• The Rules concerning lights shall be complied with from sunset to sunrise.

Rule 21
Definitions

• "Masthead light" means a white light placed over the fore and aft centerline of the vessel showing an unbroken light over an arc of the horizon of 225 degrees and so fixed as to show the light from right ahead to 22.5 degrees abaft the beam on either side of the vessel, except that on a vessel of less than 12 meters in length the masthead light shall be placed as nearly as practicable to the fore and aft centerline of the vessel.

• "Sidelights" mean a green light on the starboard side and a red light on the port side each showing an unbroken light over an arc of the horizon of 112.5 degrees and so fixed as to show the light from right ahead to 22.5 degrees abaft the beam on its respective side. On a vessel of less than 20 meters in length the side lights may be combined in one lantern carried on the fore and aft centerline of the vessel, except that on a vessel of less than 12 meters in length the sidelights when combined in one lantern shall be placed as nearly as practicable to the fore and aft centerline of the vessel.

• "Sternlight" means a white light placed as nearly as practicable at the stern showing an unbroken light over an arc of the horizon of 135 degrees and so fixed as to show the light 67.5 degrees from right aft on each side of the vessel.

• "Towing light" means a yellow light having the same characteristics as the "sternlight."

• "All-round light" means a light showing an unbroken light over an arc of horizon of 360 degrees.

• "Flashing light" means a light flashing at regular intervals at a frequency of 120 flashes or more per minute.

• "Special flashing light" means a yellow light flashing at regular intervals at a frequency of 50 to 70 flashes per minute, placed as far forward and as nearly as practicable on the fore and aft centerline of the tow and showing an unbroken light over an arc of the horizon of not less than 180 degrees nor more than 225 degrees and so fixed as to show the light from right ahead to abeam and no more than 22.5 degrees abaft the beam on either side of the vessel.

Rule 22
Visibility of Lights

The lights prescribed in these Rules shall have an intensity as specified in Annex I to these Rules, so as to be visible at the following minimum ranges for a vessel of less than 12 meters in length:
- a masthead light, 2 miles;
- a sidelight, 1 mile;
- a sternlight, 2 miles;
- a towing light, 2 miles;
- a white, red, green, or yellow all-round light, 2 miles; and
- a special flashing light, 2 miles.

Rule 23
Power-Driven Vessels Underway

A power-driven vessel underway shall exhibit:
- a masthead light forward; except that a vessel of less than 20 meters in length need not exhibit this light forward of amidships but shall exhibit it as far forward as is practicable;
- a second masthead light abaft of and higher than the forward one; except that a vessel of less than 50 meters in length shall not be obliged to exhibit such light but may do so;
- sidelights; and
- a sternlight.
- A power-driven vessel of less than 12 meters in length may, in lieu of the lights prescribed . . . above, exhibit an all-round white light and sidelights.
- A power-driven vessel when operating on the Great Lakes may carry an all-round white light in lieu of the second masthead light and sternlight prescribed above. The light shall be carried in the position of the second masthead light and be visible at the same minimum range.

Rule 24
Towing and Pushing

- Where from any sufficient cause it is impracticable for a vessel not normally engaged in towing operations to display [proper towing or pushing lights], such vessel shall not be required to exhibit those lights when engaged in towing another vessel in distress or otherwise in need of assistance. All possible measures shall be taken to indicate the nature of the relationship between the towing vessel and the vessel being assisted. The searchlight authorized by Rule 36 may be used to illuminate the tow.

Rule 25
Sailing Vessels Underway and Vessels under Oars

• A sailing vessel underway shall exhibit: . . . sidelights and a sternlight.

• In a sailing vessel of less than 20 meters in length the lights prescribed [above] may be combined in one lantern carried at or near the top of the mast where it can best be seen.

• A sailing vessel underway may, in addition to the lights prescribed [above] exhibit at or near the top of the mast, where it can best be seen, two all-round lights in a vertical line, the upper being red and the lower green, but these lights shall not be exhibited in conjunction with the combined lantern permitted in the foregoing paragraph.

• A sailing vessel of less than seven meters in length shall, if practicable, exhibit the lights prescribed in the first two paragraphs, but if she does not, she shall have ready at hand an electric torch or lighted lantern showing a white light which shall be exhibited in sufficient time to prevent collision.

• A vessel under oars may exhibit the lights prescribed in this Rule for sailing vessels, but if she does not, she shall have ready at hand an electric torch or lighted lantern showing a white light which shall be exhibited in sufficient time to prevent collision.

Rule 30
Anchored Vessels and Vessels Aground

• A vessel at anchor shall exhibit where it can best be seen, in the fore part, an all-round white light, and at or near the stern and at a lower level than the [foreward light] an all-round white light.

• A vessel aground shall exhibit the lights prescribed above.

• A vessel of less than seven meters in length, when at anchor, not in or near a narrow channel, fairway, anchorage, or where other vessels normally navigate, shall not be required to exhibit the lights prescribed [above].

• A vessel of less than 20 meters in length, when at anchor in a special anchorage area, shall not be required to exhibit the anchor lights required by this Rule.

PART D—SOUND AND LIGHT SIGNALS
Rule 32
Definitions

• The word "whistle" means any sound signaling appliance capable of producing the prescribed blasts and which complies with specifications in these Rules.

• The term "short blast" means a blast of about one second's duration.

• The term "prolonged blast" means a blast of from four to six seconds' duration.

Rule 33
Equipment for Sound Signals

• A vessel of less than 12 meters in length shall be provided with some means of making an efficient sound signal.

Rule 34
Maneuvering and Warning Signals

• When power-driven vessels are in sight of one another and meeting or crossing, each vessel maneuvering shall indicate that maneuver by the following signals on her whistle: one short blast to mean "I intend to leave you on my port side"; two short blasts to mean "I intend to leave you on my starboard side."

Upon hearing the one or two blast signal, the other shall, if in agreement, sound the same whistle signal and take the steps necessary to effect a safe passing. If, however, from any cause, the vessel doubts the safety of the proposed maneuver, she shall sound the danger signal and each vessel shall take appropriate precautionary action until a safe passing agreement is made.

• A power-driven vessel intending to overtake another power-driven vessel shall indicate her intention by the following signals on her whistle: one short blast to mean "I intend to overtake you on your starboard side"; two short blasts to mean "I intend to overtake you on your port side."

The power-driven vessel about to be overtaken shall, if in agreement, sound a similar signal. If in doubt she shall sound the danger signal.

• When vessels in sight of one another are approaching each other and from any cause either vessel fails to understand the intentions or actions of the other, or is in doubt whether sufficient action is being taken by the other to avoid collision, the vessel in doubt shall immediately indicate such doubt by giving at least five short and rapid blasts on the whistle.

• A vessel nearing a bend or an area of a channel or fairway where other vessels may be obscured by an intervening obstruction shall sound one prolonged blast. This signal shall be answered with a prolonged blast by any approaching vessel that may be within hearing around the bend or behind the obstruction.

• When a power-driven vessel is leaving a dock or berth, she shall sound one prolonged blast.

Rule 35
Sound Signals in Restricted Visibility

In or near an area of restricted visibility, whether by day or night, the signals prescribed in this Rule shall be used as follows:

• A power-driven vessel making way through the water shall sound at intervals of not more than 2 minutes one prolonged blast.

• A power-driven vessel underway but stopped and making no way through the water shall sound at intervals of not more than 2 minutes two prolonged blasts in succession with an interval of about 2 seconds between them.

• A vessel not under command; a vessel restricted in her ability to maneuver, whether underway or at anchor; a sailing vessel; a vessel engaged in fishing, whether underway or at anchor; and a vessel engaged in towing or pushing another vessel shall, instead of the signals prescribed [above], sound at intervals of not more than 2 minutes, three blasts in succession; namely, one prolonged followed by two short blasts.

• A vessel towed or if more than one vessel is towed the last vessel of the tow, if manned, shall at intervals of not more than 2 minutes sound four blasts in succession; namely, one prolonged followed by three short blasts. When practicable, this signal shall be made immediately after the signal made by the towing vessel.

• A vessel at anchor shall at intervals of not more than 1 minute ring the bell rapidly for about 5 seconds.

• A vessel aground shall give the bell [signal] . . . and shall, in addition, give three separate and distinct strokes on the bell immediately before and after the rapid ringing of the bell. A vessel aground may in addition sound an appropriate whistle signal.

• A vessel of less than 12 meters in length shall not be obliged to give the above-mentioned signals, but, if she does not, shall make some other efficient sound signal at intervals of not more than 2 minutes.

Rule 36
Signals to Attract Attention

• If necessary to attract the attention of another vessel, any vessel may make light or sound signals that cannot be mistaken for any signal authorized elsewhere in these Rules, or may direct the beam of her searchlight in the direction of the danger, in such a way as not to embarrass any vessel.

The complete text of the new Inland Rules may be obtained from the Superintendent of Documents, U.S. Government Printing Office, Washington, DC 20402. (Order Public Law 96–591. The price *was* $2.)

6

Road Signs in the Sea

Like the nautical chart, visual and audible aids to navigation warn the pilot where *not* to go. If a series of buoys leads you along a safe channel, they also alert you that danger lurks on either side of the "road"; if a lighthouse beckons you toward a distant shore, it also warns you that you are approaching the hard edge of that shore.

The term *aid to navigation* includes lighthouses, beacons, lightships, sound signals, buoys, marine radiobeacons, racons, and the medium- and long-range radionavigation systems. This chapter is limited to the visual and audible aids in the navigable waters of the United States and its possessions. Each aid is designed to be seen or heard so that it provides the necessary system coverage to enable safe transit of a waterway. It is a good rule of thumb to *observe all government marks,* even though those marks may have been placed there to aid vessels far bigger than your own. In other words: *Don't cut corners!*

Maintenance of marine aids to navigation is one of the many functions of the United States Coast Guard. This small but hard-working service is responsible for the maintenance of lighthouses, lightships, radiobeacons, racons, Loran, sound signals, buoys, and beacons on all navigable waters of the United States and its possessions, including the Atlantic and Pacific coasts of the continental United States, the Great Lakes, the Mississippi River and its tributaries, Puerto Rico, the U.S. Virgin Islands, the Hawaiian Islands, Alaska, and Trust Territory of the Pacific Islands.

Lights on Fixed Structures

Lights on fixed structures vary from the tallest lighthouse on the coast, flashing with an intensity of millions of candlepower, to a simple battery-powered lantern on a wooden pile in a small creek. Being in fixed positions enabling accurate charting, lights provide a reliable means of determining positions with relation to land and hidden dangers during daylight and darkness. The structures are often distinctively colored to facilitate their observation during daylight.

A *major light* is a light of high intensity and reliability on a fixed structure or on a marine site (except range lights). Major lights include primary seacoast lights and secondary lights. *Primary seacoast lights* are those major lights established for the purpose of making landfalls and coastwise passages from headland to headland. *Secondary lights* are those major lights, other than primary seacoast lights, established at harbor entrances and other locations where high intensity and reliability are required. Major lights are usually located at manned or monitored automated stations.

A *minor light* is an automatic unmanned (unwatched) light on a fixed structure usually showing low to moderate intensity. Minor lights are established in harbors, along channels and rivers, and in isolated locations. They usually have the same numbering, coloring, and light and sound characteristics as the lateral system of buoyage (see below).

Lighthouses

The lighthouses along our coasts all exhibit major lights. They stand on prominent headlands, at harbor entrances, on isolated dangers, or at other points where it is necessary that mariners be warned or guided. Their principal purpose is to support a light at a considerable height above the water. In many instances sound signals, radiobeacon equipment, and operating personnel are housed in separate buildings located near the tower. Such a group of facilities is called a *light station*.

Many lighthouses that were originally tended by resident keepers are now operated automatically. There are also many automatic lights on smaller structures that are maintained through periodic visits of Coast Guard cutters or of attendants in charge of a group of such aids. The relative importance of lights cannot be judged on the basis of whether or not they have resident keepers.

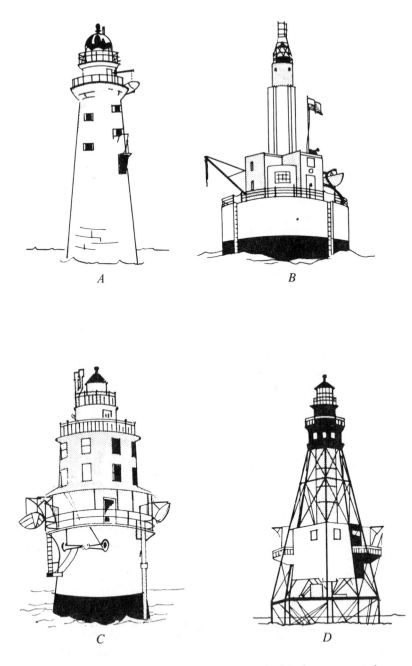

Typical light structures. A. *Masonry structure.* B. *Cylindrical tower square house on cylindrical base.* C. *Cylindrical caisson structure.* D. *Skeleton iron structure.*

Offshore Light Stations

Offshore light stations and large navigational buoys are replacing lightships where practicable. The offshore light stations in U.S. waters, such as the one shown, have helicopter landing surfaces. In the 1975 *Light List,* the Chesapeake Light Station is described as a blue tower on a white square superstructure on four black piles. "CHESAPEAKE" is on the sides; the piles are floodlit sunset to sunrise.

A typical offshore light station.

Range Lights

These lights, as illustrated, are pairs of lights so located as to form a range in line with the center of channels or an entrance to a harbor. The rear light is higher than the front light and a considerable distance in back of it, thus enabling the mariner to use the range by keeping the lights in line as he progresses up the channel. Range lights are sometimes used during daylight hours through the use of high-intensity lights.

Otherwise, the range-light structures are equipped with daymarks for ordinary daytime use. Range lights are usually white, red, or green, and display various characteristics to differentiate them from surrounding lights.

Directional Lights

A directional light is a single light that projects a beam of high intensity, separate color, or special characteristic in a given direction. It has limited use for those cases where a two-light range may not be practicable or necessary. The directional light is essentially a narrow-sector light.

Aeronautical Lights

Although they have been placed to aid aircraft, aeronautical lights of high intensity may be the first lights observed at night from vessels approaching the coast. Those situated near the coast are listed in the Defense Mapping Agency Hydrographic Center's *List of Lights* but are *not* listed in the Coast Guard's *Light List,* which you are more likely to have aboard. These lights are not designed or maintained for marine navigation.

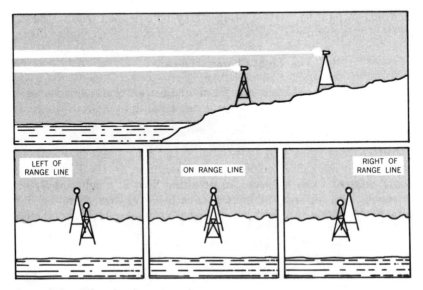

Range lights. When they line up, you're on target.

Bridges

Bridges across navigable waters of the United States are generally marked with red, green, and white lights for nighttime navigation. Red lights mark piers and other parts of the bridge. Red lights are also used on drawbridges to show when they are in a closed position. Green lights are used to mark the centerline of navigable channels through fixed bridges. The preferred channel, if there are two or more channels through the bridge, is marked by three white lights in a vertical line above the green light.

Green lights are also used on drawbridges to show when they are in the open position. Because of the variety of drawbridges, the position of green lights on the bridge will vary according to the type of structure.

Bridges that are infrequently used may be unlighted. In unusual cases the type and method of lighting may be different from what is normally found.

Drawbridges that must open for passage of vessels operate on sound and light signals given by the approaching vessel and acknowledged by the bridge tender. Effective in 1982, the following signals were established:

1. *Sound* a 4- to 6-second blast, followed by a 1-second blast—horn or whistle. The bridge should respond in kind within 30 seconds, or with five short blasts if the bridge cannot open immediately. A red flag or red light, swung back and forth horizontally, also means that the bridge cannot open.

2. *Radiotelephone*—normally Channel 13, VHF, using low power. Request an opening and await an acknowledgement from the tender. It is usually unwise to try to slip through on another boat's opening; you may find the bridge closing on your bow, with no room for you to maneuver.

LIGHT CHARACTERISTICS

Characteristics

Lights are given distinctive characteristics so that one navigational light may be distinguished from another or from the general background of shore lights or as a means of conveying certain information.

This distinctiveness may be obtained by giving each light a distinctive sequence of light and dark intervals, by having lights that burn steadily and others that flash or occult, or by giving each light a distinctive color or color sequence. In the light lists, the dark intervals are referred to as *eclipses*. An *occulting light* is a light totally eclipsed at regular intervals, the duration of light always being greater than the duration of darkness. A *flashing light* is a light that flashes at regular intervals, the duration of light always being less than the duration of darkness. An *equal-interval light* is a light that flashes at regular intervals, the duration of light always being equal to the duration of darkness. (This light is also called an *isophase light*.)

Light Phase Characteristics

The distinctive sequences of light and dark intervals or distinctive sequences in the variations of the luminous intensity of a light are its *phase characteristic*. The phase characteristics of lights that change color do not differ from those of lights that do not change color. A continuous steady light that shows periodic color change is described as an *alternating light*. The alternating characteristic is also used with other light phase characteristics, as shown in the illustration.

Most lighted aids to navigation are automatically extinguished during daylight hours. These automatic switches are not of equal sensitivity, and all lights do not come on or go off at the same time. Mariners should take this fact into account when identifying aids to navigation during twilight periods.

Sectors

"Sectors" of colored glass or plastic are placed in the lanterns of certain lights to mark shoals or to warn mariners away from nearby land. Lights so equipped show one color from most directions and a different color or colors over definite arcs of the horizon. These are indicated in the light lists and on your charts. A sector changes the color of a light when viewed from certain directions, but not the characteristic. For example, a flashing white light having a red sector, when viewed from within the sector, will appear flashing red.

Sectors may be but a few degrees in width, marking an isolated rock or shoal, or of such width as to extend from the direction of the deep water toward shore. Bearings referring to sectors are expressed in degrees as observed from a vessel toward the light.

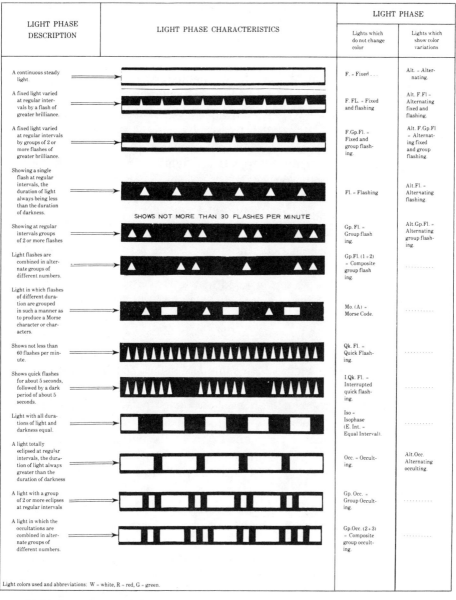

LIGHT PHASE DESCRIPTION	LIGHT PHASE CHARACTERISTICS	LIGHT PHASE	
		Lights which do not change color	Lights which show color variations
A continuous steady light.		F. = Fixed . . .	Alt. = Alternating.
A fixed light varied at regular intervals by a flash of greater brilliance.		F. Fl. = Fixed and flashing	Alt. F. Fl = Alternating fixed and flashing.
A fixed light varied at regular intervals by groups of 2 or more flashes of greater brilliance.		F. Gp. Fl. = Fixed and group flashing.	Alt. F. Gp. Fl = Alternating fixed and group flashing.
Showing a single flash at regular intervals, the duration of light always being less than the duration of darkness.		Fl. = Flashing	Alt. Fl. = Alternating flashing.
Showing at regular intervals groups of 2 or more flashes	SHOWS NOT MORE THAN 30 FLASHES PER MINUTE	Gp. Fl. = Group flashing.	Alt. Gp. Fl. = Alternating group flashing.
Light flashes are combined in alternate groups of different numbers.		Gp. Fl. (1+2) = Composite group flashing.	. . . .
Light in which flashes of different duration are grouped in such a manner as to produce a Morse character or characters.		Mo. (A) = Morse Code.	. . . .
Shows not less than 60 flashes per minute.		Qk. Fl. = Quick Flashing.	. . . .
Shows quick flashes for about 5 seconds, followed by a dark period of about 5 seconds.		I. Qk. Fl. = Interrupted quick flashing.	. . . .
Light with all durations of light and darkness equal.		Iso = Isophase (E. Int. = Equal Interval).	. . . .
A light totally eclipsed at regular intervals, the duration of light always greater than the duration of darkness		Occ. = Occulting.	Alt. Occ. Alternating occulting.
A light with a group of 2 or more eclipses at regular intervals		Gp. Occ. = Group Occulting.	. . . .
A light in which the occultations are combined in alternate groups of different numbers.		Gp. Occ. (2+3) = Composite group occulting.	. . . .

Light colors used and abbreviations: W = white, R = red, G = green.

Light phase characteristics.

In the majority of cases water areas covered by red sectors should be avoided. (Your chart will give you the exact extent of the danger.) In some cases a narrow sector may mark the best water across a shoal. A narrow sector may also mark a turning point in a channel.

The transition from one color to the other is not abrupt, but changes through an arc of uncertainty of about 2° or less.

Other Factors

A number of factors affect the visual range and apparent characteristics of lighted aids to navigation. The condition of the atmosphere has a considerable effect on the distance at which lights can be seen. Sometimes lights are obscured by fog, haze, dust, smoke, or precipitation that may be present at the light or between you and the light. On the other hand refraction may cause a light to be seen farther than under ordinary circumstances. A light of low intensity will be easily obscured by unfavorable conditions of the atmosphere. The intensity of a light should always be considered when expecting to sight it in thick weather. Haze and distance may reduce the apparent duration of the flash of a flashing light. In some conditions of the atmosphere white lights may have a reddish hue. In clear weather green lights may have a whitish hue. Keep in mind that lights on high elevations are more frequently obscured by clouds, mist, and fog than those near sea level.

In regions where ice conditions prevail in the winter, the lantern panes of unattended lights may become covered with ice or snow, which will greatly reduce their luminous ranges and may also cause them to appear of different color.

The increasing use of brilliant shore lights for advertising, illuminating bridges, and other purposes may cause navigational lights, particularly those in densely inhabited areas, to be outshone and difficult to distinguish from the background lighting. Mariners are requested by the Coast Guard to report such cases in order to attempt to improve the conditions.

The "loom" of a powerful light is often seen beyond the geographic range of the light. The loom may sometimes appear sufficiently sharp to obtain a bearing.

At short distances, some of the brighter flashing lights may show a faint continuous light between flashes.

The distance of an observer from a light cannot be estimated by its apparent intensity. *Check the characteristics of the light* carefully to avoid confusing it with a nearby low-intensity light, such as a buoy.

If lights are not sighted within a reasonable time after prediction, you may be standing into danger. In spite of the best efforts of the Coast Guard, lights occasionally go out. You should report any extinguished light you find.

The apparent characteristic of a complex light may change with distance. For example, a light that actually displays a characteristic of fixed white varied by flashes of alternating white and red (the phases having a decreasing range of detection in the order: flashing white, flashing red, fixed white) may, when first sighted in clear weather, show as a simple flashing white light. As your vessel draws nearer, the red flash will become visible and the characteristic will apparently be alternating flashing white and red. Later, the fixed white light will be seen between the flashes and the true characteristic of the light can finally be recognized—fixed white, alternating white and red (F.W.Alt.Fl. W. and R.).

LIGHTSHIPS AND LARGE NAVIGATIONAL BUOYS

Lightships

Lightships serve the same purpose as lighthouses. They are equipped with lights, sound signals, and radiobeacons. They are ships only because they are placed at points where it has been impracticable to build lighthouses. Lightships mark the entrances to important harbors or estuaries and dangerous shoals in busy waters. They also serve as leading marks for both transocean and coastwise traffic. The two lightships in United States waters are painted red with the name of the station in white on both sides. Superstructures are white; masts, lantern galleries, ventilators, and stacks are painted buff. Relief lightships are painted the same as the regular station ships, with the word "RELIEF" in white letters on the sides.

By night a lightship displays a characteristic masthead light and a less brilliant light on the forestay. The forestay indicates the direction in which the vessel is headed, and hence the direction of the current (or wind) since lightships head into the wind or current. By day a lightship displays the International Code signal of the station when requested, or if an approaching vessel does not seem to recognize it.

Lightships are anchored to a very long scope of chain and the radius of their swinging circle is considerable. The chart symbol represents the approximate location of the anchor. Under certain conditions of wind and current they are subject to sudden and unexpected sheers, so always stand clear when passing one of these lonely sentinels in heavy weather.

Because of their exposed locations, during extremely heavy weather lightships may be carried off station. A lightship known to be off station will secure her light, sound signal, and radiobeacon, and fly the

International Code signal "LO," signifying "I am not in my correct position." *Station buoys,* often called *watch buoys,* are sometimes moored near lightships to mark the approximate station should the lightship be carried away or temporarily removed. These buoys are always unlighted and in some cases are moored as much as a mile from the lightship.

Large Navigational Buoys

Large navigational buoys and offshore light stations are replacing lightships where practicable. These 40-foot-diameter buoys may show secondary lights from heights of about 36 feet above the water. In addition to the light, they may mount a radiobeacon and provide sound signals. A station buoy may be moored nearby.

A large navigational buoy.

BUOYAGE

Buoys

Buoys are used to delineate channels, indicate shoals, mark obstructions, and warn the mariner of dangers where the use of fixed aids for such purposes would be uneconomical or impracticable. By their color, shape, number, and light or sound characteristics, buoys provide indications as to how you should avoid navigational hazards.

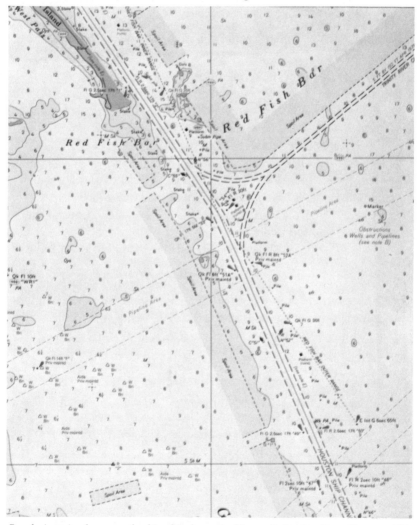

Road signs in the sea—the big-ship lanes in Upper Galveston Bay, Houston Ship Channel.

The many different sizes and types of buoys meet a wide range of environmental conditions and user requirements. The principal types of buoys used by the United States are lighted, lighted sound, unlighted sound, and unlighted. Some examples of these are illustrated here.

A *lighted buoy* consists of a floating hull with a tower on which a lantern is mounted. Batteries to power the light are contained in special pockets in the buoy hull. To keep the buoy in an upright, stable position, a large counterweight may extend from a tube below the surface of the water. A radar reflector may form part of the buoy tower.

Lighted sound buoys have the same general configuration as lighted buoys but are equipped with either a gong, bell, whistle, or electronic horn. Bells and gongs on buoys are sounded by tappers that hang from the tower and swing as the buoys roll in the sea. Bell buoys produce sound of only one tone; gong buoys produce several tones.

Whistle buoys make a loud moaning sound that is caused by the rising and falling motions of the buoy in the sea. A sound buoy equipped with an electronic horn produces a pure tone at regular intervals and operates continually regardless of the sea state.

Unlighted sound buoys have the same general appearance as lighted buoys (except for old whistles) but are not equipped with lights.

Unlighted (soundless) *buoys* have either a can or a nun shape. *Can buoys* have a cylindrical shape whereas *nun buoys* have a conical shape usually located on top of a cylindrical shape.

Buoys are *floating aids* that require moorings to hold them in position. Typically, the mooring consists of chain and a large concrete sinker. Because buoys are subjected to waves, wind, and tides, the scope of the moorings will normally be about three times the depth of the water, and the buoy can be expected to swing in a circle as the current, wind, and wave conditions change.

Fallibility of Buoys

Buoys aren't always where you expect them to be. Anything that floats in water can be moved by water, and it would be *imprudent* to expect floating aids to always maintain their charted positions and to constantly and unerringly display their advertised characteristics. The Coast Guard does its best but nobody's perfect.

The buoy symbol shown on charts indicates the approximate position of the buoy body and the sinker that secures the buoy to the seabed. The approximate position is used because of practical limitations in placing and keeping buoys and their sinkers in exact geographical loca-

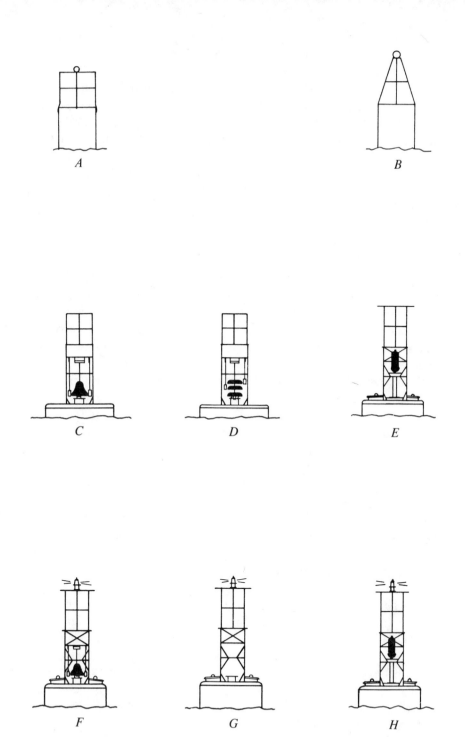

The principal types of buoys in the United States waters. A. *Can.* B. *Nun.* C. *Unlighted bell.* D. *Unlighted gong.* E. *Unlighted whistle.* F. *Lighted bell.* G. *Lighted buoy.* H. *Lighted whistle.*

tions. These limitations include inaccuracies in position-fixing methods, prevailing atmospheric and sea conditions, the slope of the seabed, the fact that buoys are moored with more chain than the water depth, and the fact that the positions of the buoys and sinkers can't be under continuous surveillance. The position of the buoy can be expected to shift inside and outside the area shown by the chart symbol—and buoys may break free and drift away. Also, lighted buoys may be extinguished or sound signals may not function because of ice, collisions, or other accidents.

The concept that a *wreck buoy* always occupies a position directly over the wreck it is intended to mark is erroneous. Buoys are placed in position by a vessel and it is usually physically impossible for these vessels to maneuver directly over a wreck. For this reason a wreck buoy is usually placed on the seaward or channelward side of a wreck. To avoid confusion in some situations, two buoys may be used, with the wreck between them. Obviously, you should *never* attempt to pass between two wreck buoys.

Sunken wrecks are sometimes moved by severe sea conditions. Just as shoals may shift, wrecks may shift away from wreck buoys.

All buoys should be regarded as warnings, guides, or aids—but not as infallible navigation marks, especially those located in exposed positions.

Buoyage Systems

Most maritime countries use either a *lateral system* of buoyage or the *cardinal system,* or both. In the lateral system, used on all navigable waters of the United States, the coloring, shape, numbering, and lighting of buoys indicate the direction to a danger relative to the course that should be followed. The color, shape, lights, and numbers of buoys in the lateral system are determined relative to a direction *from seaward.* Along the *coasts* of the United States, the *clockwise* direction around the country is considered to be the direction "from seaward." Proceeding in a westerly and northerly direction on the Great Lakes (except Lake Michigan, and in a southerly direction on Lake Michigan) is considered to be proceeding "from seaward." On the Intracoastal Waterway proceeding in a general southerly direction along the Atlantic Coast, and in a general westerly direction along the Gulf Coast, is considered as proceeding "from seaward." On the Mississippi and Ohio Rivers and their tributaries the aids to navigation characteristics are determined as proceeding from sea toward the head of navigation, although local terminology describes "left bank" and "right bank" as proceeding with the flow of the river. If that doesn't make sense, read it again—then check it against charts for your local cruising area.

In United States waters the following distinctive system of identification is used:

Red nun buoys mark the *right* side of channels for an inbound vessel and obstructions which should be kept to starboard. They have *even* numbers, which increase from seaward.

Black or green can buoys mark the *left* side of channels for an inbound vessel and obstructions which should be kept to port. They have *odd* numbers, which increase from seaward. The Coast Guard has been experimenting for a number of years with various shades of green to replace the familiar basic black and now has begun the changeover.

Red-and-black horizontally banded buoys mark junctions of channels or wrecks or obstructions that can be passed on either side. The color (red or black) of the *top* band and the shape (nun or can) indicate the side on which the buoy should be passed by a vessel proceeding along the primary channel. If the top most band is black, the primary channel will be followed by keeping the buoy on the port hand of an *inbound* vessel. If the topmost band is red, the primary channel will be followed by keeping the buoy on the starboard hand of an *inbound* vessel. If in doubt, rely on your chart.

Black-and-white vertically striped buoys mark the fairway or midchannel and should be passed close aboard. These midchannel or fairway buoys may have any shape.

Lighted buoys, spar buoys, and sound buoys are not differentiated by shape to indicate the side on which they should be passed. Their purpose is indicated only by their coloring, numbering, or light characteristics.

All *solid red* and *solid black* buoys are numbered. The red buoys bear even numbers and the black buoys bear odd numbers. The numbers for each increase from seaward. The numbers are kept in approximate sequence on both sides of the channel by omitting numbers where required. Buoys of other colors are not numbered, but a buoy of another color may be lettered for identification.

Lights. Red lights are used only on red buoys and buoys with a red band at the top, green lights are used only on black buoys and buoys with a black band at the top. White lights are used without any color significance. Lights on red or black buoys are always regularly flashing or regularly occulting. Quick-flashing lights are used when a light of distinct cautionary significance is desired, as at a sharp turn or constriction in the channel. Interrupted quick-flashing lights are used on red-and-black horizontally banded buoys. White Morse A flashing lights are used on midchannel buoys—that is: *dit dah!*

Special-purpose buoys. White buoys mark anchorages. Yellow buoys mark quarantine anchorages. White buoys with green tops are used in dredging and survey operations. Black-and-white horizontally banded buoys mark fish net areas. Yellow-and-black vertically striped buoys mark seadromes. Buoys banded with white and international orange, either horizontally or vertically, are used for special purposes to which neither the lateral system colors nor the other special-purpose colors apply. The shape of special-purpose buoys has no significance. They are not numbered but may be lettered. They may display any color light except red or green. Only fixed, occulting, or slow-flash A characteristics are used.

Station buoys are placed close to some lightships and important buoys to mark the approximate position of the station. Such buoys are colored and numbered the same as the regular aid, lightship station buoys having the letters "LS" above the initials of the station.

Minor lights and daybeacons used to mark the sides of channels are given numbers and characteristics in accordance with the lateral system of buoyage.

Note: Certain aids to navigation are fitted with light-reflecting material (reflectors) to assist in their location in darkness. The colors of such reflectors have the same lateral significance as the color of lights. Some aids to navigation may be fitted with, or have incorporated in their design, radar reflectors.

BEACONS, DAYBEACONS, AND DAYMARKS

Beacons are fixed aids to navigation placed on shore or on marine sites. If unlighted, the beacon is referred to as a *daybeacon.* A daybeacon is identified by its color and the color, shape, and number of its daymark. The simplest form of daybeacon consists of a single pile with a daymark at or near its top, as illustrated. Daybeacons may be used instead of range lights to form a range.

Daymarks serve to make aids to navigation readily visible and easily identifiable. For example, the distinctive color pattern and shape of a lighthouse aid identification during the daytime as does the color and shape of a buoy. The size of the daymark that is required to make the aid conspicuous depends on how far the aid must be seen. On struc-

A daybeacon.

tures that can't be seen at a required distance, a daymark is added to
the structure. The daymark's shape and color will depend on its purpose. Most daymarks also display numbers or letters that identify the
aid. The numbers and letters, as well as portions of most daymarks
(and portions of unlighted buoys), are reflective.

Increasing amounts of information are conveyed by a daymark as
you approach it. At the detection distance the daymark will only tell
you that it exists; it will be just detectable from its background. At the
recognition distance the daymark can be recognized as an aid to navigation. At this distance the distinctive shape or color pattern is recog-
nizable. At the identification distance, when the number or letter can
be read, the daymark can be identified as a particular aid.

Detection, recognition, and identification distances vary widely for
any particular daymark and depend on the viewing conditions. This in
an inherent limitation of any visual signal, but is especially true for
visual signals that depend heavily on sunlight. The angle of the sun
and the position of a daymark will greatly affect its visibility. When in
doubt, proceed with caution; the water around a daymark is usually
pretty thin.

SOUND SIGNALS

Types of Sound Signals

Most lighthouses, light platforms, and lightships, and some minor
light structures and buoys, are equipped with sound-producing instru-

ments to aid the mariner during periods of low visibility. Charts and light lists of the area should be consulted for positive identification. *Caution:* Buoys fitted with a bell, gong, or whistle and actuated by wave motion may produce no sound when the sea is calm.

Any sound-producing instrument operated in time of fog—lighthouses, lightships, or buoys—serves as a useful fog signal. If it is to be effective as an aid to navigation, you must be able to identify it and to know from what point it is sounded. All lighthouses and lightships equipped with sound signals activate their distinctive signals during periods of low visibility. The characteristics of mechanized signals are varied blasts and silent periods. The various types of sound signals differ in tone:

Diaphones produce sound by means of a slotted piston moved back and forth by compressed air. Blasts may consist of two tones of different pitch, in which case the first part of the blast is of a high and the last of a low pitch. These alternate-pitch signals are called "two-tone."

Diaphragm horns produce sound by means of a disc diaphragm vibrated by compressed air or electricity. Duplex or triplex horn units of differing pitch produce a chime signal.

Sirens produce sound by means of either a disc or a cup-shaped rotor actuated by compressed air, steam, or electricity.

Whistles produce sound by compressed air emitted through a circumferential slot in a cylindrical bell chamber.

Bells are sounded by means of a hammer actuated by a descending weight, compressed gas, or electricity.

Limitations of Sound Signals

Sound signals depend on the transmission of sound through air. As aids to navigation they have limitations, for sound travels through the air in a variable and frequently unpredictable manner.

It has been established that:

1. Sound signals are heard at greatly varying distances and that the distance at which a signal can be heard may vary with the bearing of the signal from the listener.
2. Under certain conditions, when a sound signal has a combination high and low tone, it is not unusual for one of the tones to be inaudible. In the case of sirens, which produce a varying tone, portions of the blast may not be heard.

3. There are occasionally areas close to the signal in which it is wholly unaudible. This is particularly true when the sound signal is screened by intervening land or the signal is on a high cliff.
4. A fog may exist a short distance from a station but not be observable from it, and the station's signal may not be in operation.
5. Some sound signals cannot be started at a moment's notice.
6. A sound signal that may not be heard from a vessel in motion may be heard when the ship is stopped.
7. A sound signal may be louder at a distance than in the immediate proximity of the signal.

Again, nothing is perfect in this world. A sound signal is only reliable if it is *there,* if it is *working,* and if you can *hear* it. Blind faith is foolhardy—especially near land in a fog. If you have any doubt of your position, sound the depth and place a lookout on the bow if you can. Sound signals are an "aid," not an absolute.

Also, *don't assume:*

1. That you are out of hearing distance because you don't hear the signal.
2. That if you hear a sound signal faintly, you are a great distance from it.
3. That you are near to it because you hear the sound plainly.
4. That the distance from and the intensity of a sound on one occasion is a guide for any future occasion.
5. That the sound signal is not sounding because you can't hear it.
6. That the signal is in the direction the sound seems to come from.

INTRACOASTAL WATERWAY AIDS

The Intracoastal Waterway (ICW) runs parallel to the Atlantic and Gulf Coasts from Manasquan Inlet on the New Jersey shore to the Mexican border. Aids marking these waters have some portion of them marked with yellow, as shown in Chart No. 1. Otherwise the coloring and numbering of buoys and beacons follow the same system as that in other U.S. waterways.

In order that vessels may readily follow the Intracoastal Waterway route where it coincides with another marked waterway such as an important river, special markings are employed. These special markings are applied to the buoys or other aids that already mark the river or waterway for other traffic. Such aids are referred to as *dual-purpose aids*. The marks consist of a yellow square or a yellow triangle, placed on a conspicuous part of the dual-purpose aid. The yellow square, in outline similar to a can buoy, indicates that the aid on which it is placed should be kept on the left hand when following the Intracoastal Waterway down the coast. The yellow triangle has the same meaning as a nun; it should be kept on the right side. Where such dual-purpose marking is employed, the mariner following the Intracoastal Waterway disregards the color and shape of the aid on which the mark is placed, being guided solely by the shape of the yellow mark.

MISSISSIPPI RIVER SYSTEM

Aids to navigation on the Mississippi River and its tributaries in the Second Coast Guard District and parts of the Eighth Coast Guard District generally conform to the lateral system of buoyage. The following differences are significant:

1. Buoys are not numbered.
2. The numbers on lights and daybeacons do not have lateral significance; they indicate the mileage from a designated point downstream, normally the river mouth.
3. Flashing lights on the left side proceeding upstream show single green or white flashes while those on the right side show double (group flashing) red or white flashes.
4. "Crossing daymarks" are used to indicate where the channel crosses from one side of the river to the other.

THE UNIFORM STATE WATERWAY MARKING SYSTEM (USWMS)

The USWMS was developed by the Coast Guard and various state boating authorities to assist small-craft operators in those states. The USWMS consists of two categories of aids to navigation. One is a system of aids that is generally compatible with the federal lateral system of buoyage. The other is a system of regulatory markers to warn small-craft operators of dangers or to provide general information and directions.

On a well-defined channel, including a river or other relatively narrow, natural or improved waterway, solid-colored red and black buoys are established in pairs (called "gates"), one on each side of the navigable channel they mark and opposite to each other, to inform the user that the channel lies between the buoys. The buoy that marks the left side of the channel viewed looking upstream or toward the head of navigation is colored black; the buoy that marks the right side of the channel is colored red.

On an irregularly defined channel, solid-colored buoys may be staggered on alternate sides of the channel but spaced at sufficiently close intervals to inform the user that the channel lies between the buoys and that he should pass between the buoys.

When there is no well-defined channel or when a body of water is obstructed by objects that can be approached from more than one direction, aids to navigation having cardinal meaning may be used. The aids conforming to the *cardinal system* consist of three distinctly colored buoys:

1. A white buoy with a red top indicates that a vessel must pass to the south or west of the buoy.
2. A white buoy with a black top indicates that a vessel must pass to the north or east of the buoy.
3. A buoy showing alternate vertical red-and-white stripes indicates that an obstruction to navigation extends from the nearest shore to the buoy and that a vessel must not pass between the buoy and the nearest shore.

The shape of buoys has no significance in the USWMS.

Regulatory buoys are colored white with international orange horizontal bands completely around the buoy circumference. One band is at the top of the buoy with a second band just above the waterline of the buoy so that both orange bands are clearly visible.

Geometric shapes are placed on the white portion of the buoy body and are colored international orange. The authorized *geometric shapes and meanings* associated with them are as follows:

1. A vertical open-faced diamond shape means danger.
2. A vertical open-faced diamond shape having a cross centered in the diamond means that vessels are excluded from the marked area.
3. A circular shape means that vessels in the marked area are subject to certain operating restrictions.

4. A square or rectangular shape indicates that directions or information are contained inside.

Regulatory markers are square- and rectangular-shaped signs that are displayed from fixed structures. Each sign is white with an international orange border. Geometric shapes with the same meanings as those displayed on buoys are centered on the signboards. The geometric shape on a regulatory marker is intended to tell a skipper if he should stay well clear of the marker or may safely approach to read any wording on the marker.

PRIVATE AIDS TO NAVIGATION

Private aids are those aids not established and maintained by the Coast Guard. Private aids include those established by other federal agencies with Coast Guard approval; aids on marine structures or other works which the owners are legally obligated to establish, maintain, and operate as prescribed by the Coast Guard: and aids that are merely desired, for one reason or another, by a private body that has established the aid with Coast Guard approval.

Although private aids to navigation are inspected periodically by the Coast Guard, the prudent mariner should exercise special caution when using them for general navigation. You never know—Old Salt may have placed them there.

II

Waves, Wind, and Weather

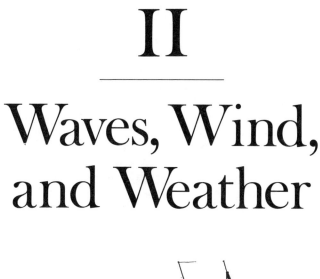

7

Tides and Tidal Currents

Water moves.

This is hardly surprising, since water is by definition a "wet liquid."

Your job as a small-boat skipper-pilot would be a lot easier if all that wet liquid around your boat would stand as still as a millpond on a sultry summer day. But it doesn't, and it won't. Water moves constantly—it ebbs and flows, it floods and swirls, it ripples, rolls, and rages. Water can be placid or downright nasty, but no tidal water is ever *completely* still. Maybe it's more fun that way.

A prudent pilot soon learns to respect and understand the sea in its many moods, but it is a wise small-boat pilot who learns to "read" the moving water around him and make that movement work to *his* advantage. The rewards are great—shorter, faster, easier passages; more pleasure, less trauma.

TIDE AND CURRENT PREDICTIONS

The daily rise and fall of the tide, with its attendant flood and ebb of tidal current, is familiar to every mariner. He is aware that at *high water* and *low water* the depth of the water is momentarily constant, a condition called *stand*. Similarly, there is a moment of *slack water* as a tidal current reverses direction. As a general rule, the change in height or the current speed is at first very slow, increasing to a maximum about midway between the two extremes, and then decreasing again.

Although tides and tidal currents are caused by the same phenomena, the time relationship between them varies considerably from place to place. For instance, if an estuary has a wide entrance and does not extend far inland, the time of maximum speed of current occurs at about the midtime between high water and low water. However, if an extensive tidal basin is connected to the sea by a small opening, the maximum current may occur at about the time of high water or low water outside the basin, when the difference in height is maximum.

The *height of tide* should not be confused with *depth of water*. For reckoning the tides, a reference level is selected. Soundings shown on the largest scale charts are the vertical distances from this level to the bottom. At any given time the actual depth is this charted depth *plus* the height of tide. In most places the reference level is some form of low water. But all low waters at a place are not the same height, and the selected reference level is seldom the *lowest* tide that occurs at the place. When lower tides occur, these are indicated by a negative sign. Thus at a spot where the charted depth is 15 feet, the actual depth is 15 feet plus the height of the tide. When the tide is 3 feet, the depth is $15 + 3 = 18$ feet. When it is -1 foot, the depth is $15 - 1 = 14$ feet. It is well to remember that *the actual depth can be less than the charted depth*. In an area where there is considerable range of tide (the difference between high water and low water), the height of tide might be an important consideration in using soundings to assist in determining position, or whether you are in safe water.

You should remember that heights given in the tide tables are *predictions,* and that when conditions vary considerably from those used in making the predictions, the heights shown may be considerably in error. Heights lower than predicted are particularly to be anticipated when the atmospheric pressure is higher than normal, or when there is a persistent strong offshore wind. Along coasts where there is a large inequality between the two high or two low tides during a tidal day, the height predictions are less reliable than elsewhere.

The current encountered in pilot waters is due primarily to tidal action, but other causes are sometimes present. The tidal current tables give the best prediction of total current, regardless of cause. The predictions for a river may be considerably in error following heavy rains or a drought. Currents can alter your course and change your speed over the bottom. Due to the configuration of land (or shoal areas) and water, the set and drift may vary considerably over different parts of a harbor. Strong currents are particularly to be anticipated in narrow passages connecting larger bodies of water. Currents of more than 5 knots are encountered from time to time in the Golden Gate at San

Francisco and regularly at the Race at the eastern gateway to Long Island Sound. Currents of more than 13 knots sometimes occur at Seymour Narrows, British Columbia.

In straight portions of rivers and channels the strongest currents usually occur in the middle, but in curved portions the swiftest currents (and deepest water) usually occur near the outer edge of the curve. Countercurrents and eddies may occur on either side of the main current of a river or narrow passage, especially near obstructions and in bights.

In general, the range of tide and the speed of tidal current are at a minimum on the open ocean or along straight coasts. The greatest tidal effects are usually encountered in rivers, bays, harbors, inlets, and bights. A pilot cruising along a coast can expect to encounter stronger sets toward or away from the shore while passing an indentation than when the coast is straight.

Tidal and current predictions for various places are published annually by the National Ocean Survey. These are supplemented by eleven sets of tidal current charts. Each set consists of charts for each hour of the tidal cycle. On these charts, the set of the current at various places in the area is shown by arrows and the drift is shown by numbers. Since these are *average* conditions, they indicate in a general way the tidal conditions on any day during any year. They are designed to be used with tidal current diagrams or the tidal current tables (except those for New York Harbor and Narragansett Bay, which are used with the tide tables). These charts are available for Boston Harbor, Narragansett Bay to Nantucket Sound, Narragansett Bay, Long Island Sound and Block Island Sound, New York Harbor, Delaware Bay and River, Upper Chesapeake Bay, Charleston (S.C.) Harbor, San Francisco Bay, Puget Sound (northern part), and Puget Sound (southern part). Current arrows are sometimes shown on nautical charts. These represent average conditions and should not be considered reliable predictions of the conditions to be encountered at any given time. When a strong current sets over an irregular bottom, or meets an opposing current, ripples may occur on the surface. These are called *tide rips*. Areas where they occur frequently are shown on charts.

If tide and current tables are not available, you may be able to obtain locally the *mean high water lunitidal interval* or the *high water full and change*. The approximate time of high water can be found by adding either interval to the time of transit (either upper or lower) of the moon. Low water occurs approximately one-quarter tidal day (about

6 hours and 12 minutes) before and after the time of high water. The actual interval varies somewhat from day to day, but approximate results can be obtained in this manner.

Tide Tables for various parts of the world are published in four volumes by the National Ocean Survey. Each volume is arranged as follows:

Table 1 contains a complete list of the predicted times and heights of the tide for each day of the year at a number of reference stations.

Table 2 gives differences and ratios which can be used to modify the tidal information for the reference stations to make it applicable to a relatively large number of subordinate stations.

Table 3 provides information for use in finding the approximate height of the tide at any time between high water and low water.

Table 4 is a sunrise-sunset table at five-day intervals for various latitudes from 76°N to 60°S.

Table 5 provides an adjustment to convert the local mean time of Table 4 to zone or standard time.

Table 6 gives the zone time of moonrise and moonset for each day of the year at certain selected places.

One volume covers the East Coast and another the West Coast of North America. The various volumes, with current prices, are listed in the nautical charts catalogs.

Tidal Current Tables are somewhat similar to tide tables, but the coverage is less extensive, being given in two volumes. The two volumes—East Coast and West Coast—are arranged as follows:

Table 1 contains a complete list of predicted times of maximum currents and slack, with the velocity (speed) of the maximum currents, for a number of reference stations.

Table 2 gives differences, ratios, and other information related to a relatively large number of subordinate stations.

Table 3 provides information for use in finding the speed of the current at any time between the tabulated entries in Tables 1 and 2.

Table 4 gives the number of minutes the current does not exceed stated amounts, for various maximum speeds.

Table 5 (Atlantic Coast of North America only) gives information on rotary tidal currents.

These tables are also listed in your chart catalogs.

Tidal current charts present a comprehensive view of the hourly speed and direction of the current in eleven bodies of water: Boston Harbor, Narragansett Bay, Long Island Sound and Block Island Sound, New York Harbor, Delaware Bay and River, Upper Chesapeake Bay,

Charleston (S.C.) Harbor, Tampa Bay, San Francisco Bay, and Puget Sound. These handy charts provide a means for determining the speed and direction of the current at various localities throughout these bodies of water. The arrows show the direction of the current; the figures give the speed in knots at the time of spring tides, that is, the time of new or full moon when the currents are stronger than average. When the current is given as weak, the speed is less than 0.1 knot.

The charts depict the flow of the tidal current under normal weather conditions. Strong winds and freshets, however, bring about nontidal currents which may modify considerably the speed and direction shown on the charts.

The speed of the tidal currents varies from day to day principally in accordance with the phase, distance, and declination of the moon. To obtain the speed for any particular day and hour, the spring speeds shown on the charts can be modified by using a correction table provided on the charts.

The *tidal currents diagrams* are a series of twelve monthly diagrams to be used with the tidal current charts. There is one diagram for each month of the year, and a new set of diagrams must be used each year. The diagrams are computer-constructed lines that locate each chart throughout all hours of every month. The diagrams indicate directly the chart and the speed correction factor to use at any desired time.

A *current diagram* is a graph showing the speed of the current along a channel at different stages of the tidal current cycle. The current tables include such diagrams for Vineyard and Nantucket Sounds (one diagram); East River, New York; New York Harbor; Delaware Bay and River (one diagram); and Chesapeake Bay. The current diagrams are a convenient means of determining the current flow on a particular day.

TIDES

The tidal phenomenon is the periodic motion of the waters of the sea due to differences in the attractive forces of various celestial bodies, principally the moon and to a lesser degree the sun, on different parts of the rotating earth. It can help you or hinder you; you can ride it or buck it; it can make or break your day. The water's rise and fall may provide enough depth to clear a bar—or prevent you from leaving a harbor. Currents caused by the rise and fall of the tide can add knots to your speed—or can make a long, slow day seem like an eternity.

The flow of the current may set you toward dangers or away from them. By understanding this phenomenon and by making intelligent use of predictions published in the tide and tidal current tables, you can set your course and schedule your passage to make the tide serve you.

In its rise and fall, the tide is accompanied by a periodic horizontal movement of the water called *tidal current*. The two movements, tide and tidal current, are intimately related, forming parts of the same phenomenon brought about by the tide-producing forces of the sun and the moon.

The relation between tide and tidal current is not a simple one, nor is it everywhere the same. To avoid misunderstanding, adopt the technical usage: *tide* for the vertical rise and fall of the water, and *tidal current* for the horizontal flow. The tide rises and falls; the tidal current floods and ebbs.

Tides are the most accurately predictable oceanographic phenomena. You might assume that oceanographers truly understand them, but this is not true; significant gaps remain. You needn't fully understand them, but you should *respect* them, and some understanding is useful if you hope to make them work for you.

The principal tide-generating forces on the surface of the earth result from the differential gravitational forces of the moon and sun. The moon is the main tide-generating body. Due to its greater distance, the effect of the sun is only 46 percent of the effect due to the moon.

Observed tides will differ considerably from the tides predicted by theory since size, depth, and configuration of the basin or waterway, friction, landmasses, inertia of watermasses, acceleration, and other factors come into play. Tides are also affected by the phase of the moon and the relative position of the earth, moon, and sun. It is more important that you, the pilot of a small vessel, know *what* happens than *why* it happens. (Chapter 31 of *American Practical Navigator* describes the "equilibrium theory" of the tidal phenomenon in wonderful detail. It's fascinating reading, but it won't help you get "from here to there.") More urgent for you at this point is a recognition and respect for the *different* tides you will encounter and the currents (or streams) those tides will generate.

Spring and Neap Tides

A combined lunar-solar effect is obtained by adding the sun's gravitational forces to the moon's gravitational forces. The resultant tide

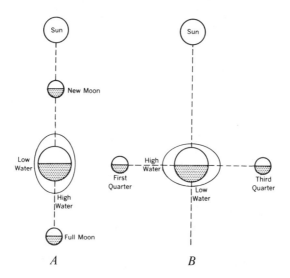

Diagram of spring and neap tides. A. Spring tides occur at times of new and full moon. The range of the tide is greater than average because solar and lunar tractive forces act in the same direction. B. Neap tides occur at times of first and third quarters. The range of tide is less than average because solar and lunar forces act at right angles to each other.

bulge will be predominantly lunar with modifying solar effects on both the height of the tide and the direction of the tidal bulge. When the earth, moon, and sun are lying approximately on the same line, the forces of the sun are acting in the same direction as the moon's forces. Because the moon is new or full, the results are tides whose ranges are greater than average. These are *spring tides,* but have nothing to do with the season.

When the moon is at first and third quarters, the forces of the sun are acting at approximately right angles to the moon's forces. The results are tides called *neap tides,* whose ranges are less than average.

With the moon in positions between quadrature and new and full moon, the effect of the sun is to cause the tidal bulge to either lag or precede the moon. These effects are called *priming* and *lagging* the tides.

At most places the rise and fall of the tides occurs twice each day. The tide rises until it reaches a maximum height, called *high tide* or *high water,* and then falls to a minimum level called *low tide* or *low water.* The rate of rise and fall is not uniform. From low water the tide begins to rise, slowly at first but at an increasing rate, until it is about halfway to high water. The rate of rise then decreases until high water is reached and the rise ceases. The falling tide behaves in a similar manner. The period at high or low water during which there is no apparent change of level is called *stand*. The difference in height between consecutive high and low waters is the *range*.

Types of Tide

A body of water has a natural period of oscillation that is dependent on its dimensions. The oceans are made up of a number of oscillating basins. As such basins are acted on by the tide-producing forces, some respond more readily to daily or diurnal forces, others to semidiurnal forces, and others almost equally to both. Hence tides at a given place are classified as one of three types—semidiurnal, diurnal, or mixed—according to the characteristics of the tidal pattern occurring at the place.

In the *semidiurnal* type of tide, there are two high and two low waters each tidal day, with relatively small inequality in the high- and low-water heights. Tides on the Atlantic Coast of the United States are representative of the semidiurnal type. The illustration shows the tide curve at Boston.

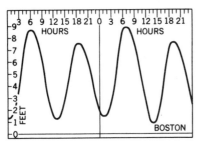

Semidiurnal type of tide at Boston.

In the *diurnal* type of tide, only a single high and low water occur each tidal day. Tides of the diurnal type occur along the northern shore of the Gulf of Mexico, in the Java Sea, the Gulf of Tonkin (off the Vietnam-China coast), and in a few other localities.

In the *mixed* type of tide, the diurnal and semidiurnal oscillations are both important factors and the tide is characterized by a large inequality in the high-water heights, low-water heights, or both. There are usually two high and two low waters each day, but occasionally the tide may become diurnal. Such tides are prevalent along the Pacific Coast of the United States. Examples of the mixed types of tide are shown. At Los Angeles it is typical that the inequalities in the high and low waters are about the same. At Seattle the greater inequalities are typically in the low waters, while at Honolulu it is the high waters that have the greater inequalities.

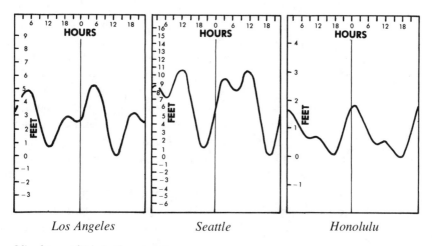

| Los Angeles | Seattle | Honolulu |

Mixed type of tide in three locations.

Special Effects

As a progressive wave enters shallow water, its speed is decreased. Since the trough is shallower than the crest, its retardation is greater, resulting in a steepening of the wavefront. Therefore in many rivers the duration of rise is considerably less than the duration of fall. In a few estuaries the advance of the low water trough is so much retarded that the crest of the rising tide overtakes the low and advances upstream as a churning, foaming wall of water called a *bore*. Bores that are large and dangerous at times of large tidal ranges may be mere ripples at those times of the month when the range is small. An example is the bore that occurs in the Petitcodiac River in the Bay of Fundy. The tide tables indicate where bores occur.

Other special features are the *double low water* (as at Hoek Van Holland) and the *double high water* (as at Southampton, England). At such places there is often a slight fall or rise in the middle of the high- or low-water period. The practical effect is to create a longer period of stand at high or low tide. The tide tables direct attention to these and other peculiarities where they occur.

Variations in Range

Though the tide at a particular place can be classified as to type, it exhibits many variations during the month. The range of the tide varies in accordance with the intensity of the tide-producing force, though there may be a lag of a day or two (*age of tide*) between a particular astronomic cause and the tidal effect. Therefore when the moon is at the point in its orbit nearest the earth (at *perigee*), the lunar semidiurnal range is increased and *perigean* tides occur; when the moon is farthest from the earth (at *apogee*), the smaller *apogean* tides occur. And as mentioned above, when the moon and sun are in line and pulling together, as at new and full moon, *spring* tides occur, and when they oppose each other, as at the quadratures, the smaller *neap* tides occur. When certain of these phenomena coincide, great perigean spring tides or small apogean neap tides occur.

It should be noted that when the range of tide is increased, as at spring tides, there is more water available only at high tide; at low tide there is less, for the high waters rise higher and the low waters fall lower at these times. There is more water at neap low water than at spring low water. While it is desirable to know the meaning of these terms, the best way of determining the height of the tide at any place and time is to read your tide tables. The diagram illustrates the variation of the ranges and heights of tides as they are related to the charted depth of the water.

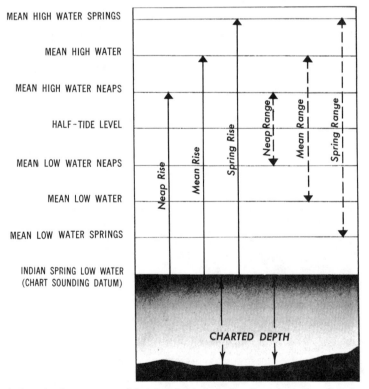

Variations in the ranges and height of tide in a locality where the chart sounding datum is Indian spring low water.

Tidal Cycles

Tidal oscillations go through a number of cycles. The shortest cycle, completed in about 12 hours and 25 minutes for the semidiurnal tide, extends from any phase of the tide to the next occurrence of the same phase. During a lunar day (averaging 24 hours and 50 minutes) there are two highs and two lows (two of the shorter cycles) for a semidiurnal tide. The moon revolves around the earth with respect to the sun in about 29½ days, commonly called the lunar month. The effect of the phase variation is completed in about two weeks as the moon varies from new to full or full to new. The effect of the moon's declination is also repeated about each two weeks. The cycle involving the moon's distance requires about 27½ days. The sun's declination and distance cycles are respectively a half year and a year in length. An important lunar cycle, called the nodal period, is 18.6 years (usually expressed in round figures as 19 years). For a tidal value, particularly a range, to be considered a true mean, it must either be based on observations extended over this period of time or adjusted to variations during the cycle.

Time of Tide

Since the lunar force has the greater effect in producing tides at most places, the tides "follow the moon." Because of the rotation of the earth, high water lags behind meridian passage (upper and lower) of the moon. The *tidal day,* which is also the *lunar day,* is the time between consecutive transits of the moon, or 24 hours and 50 minutes on the average.

In the ocean, the tide may be of the nature of the progressive wave with the crest moving forward, a stationary or standing wave which oscillates in a seesaw fashion, or a combination of the two. Caution should be used in inferring the time of tide at a place from tidal data for nearby places. In a river or estuary, the tide enters from the sea and is usually sent upstream as a progressive wave, so that the tide occurs progressively later at various places upstream.

The Tidal Datum

A tidal datum (plural: data) is a level from which heights and depths are measured. There are a number of such levels of reference that are important to the mariner. The most important reference is the datum of soundings on charts. Since the tide rises and falls continually while soundings are being taken during a hydrographic survey, the tide should be observed during the survey so that sounding taken at all stages of the tide can be reduced to a common *chart sounding datum.* Soundings on charts show depths below a selected low-water datum (occasionally mean sea level), and tide predictions in tide tables show heights above the same level. The depth of water available at any time is obtained by adding the height of the tide at the time in question to the charted depth, or by subtracting the predicted height if it is negative. The following are some of the data in general use.

The highest low water datum in considerable use is *mean low water* (*MLW*), which is the average height of all low waters at a place. About half of the low waters fall below it. *Mean low-water springs* (*MLWS*), usually shortened to *low-water springs,* is the average level of the low waters that occur at the times of spring tides. *Mean lower low water* (*MLLW*) is the average height of the lower low waters of each tidal day. *Indian spring low water* (*ISLW*) is a low-water datum that includes the spring effect of the semidiurnal portion of the tide and the tropic effect of the diurnal portion. It is about the level of lower low water of mixed tides at the time that the moon's maximum declination coincides with the time of new or full moon. *Mean lower low-water springs* is the average level of the lower of the two low waters on the days of spring tides.

In some areas where there is little or no tide, such as the Baltic Sea, *mean sea level* (*MSL*) is used as the chart datum. This is the average height of the surface of the sea for all stages of the tide over a 19-year period. This may differ slightly from *half-tide level,* which is the level midway between mean high water and mean low water.

Large-scale charts usually specify the datum of soundings, and may contain a tide note giving mean heights of the tide at one or more places on the chart. These heights are intended merely as a rough guide to the change in depth to be expected under the specified conditions. They should not be used for the prediction of heights on any particular day. Such predictions should be obtained from tide tables.

High-Water Data

Heights of land features on nautical charts are usually referenced to a high-water datum. The one used on charts of the United States, its territories and possessions, and widely used elsewhere, is *mean high water* (*MHW*), which is the average height of all high waters over a

19-year period. Any other high-water datum used on charts is likely to be higher than this. Other high-water data are *mean high water springs (MHWS), mean higher high water (MHHW),* and *tropic higher high water (TcHHW).*

Tide tables are published annually by most of the maritime nations of the world. They consist primarily of two parts. One contains predictions of the time and height of each high and low water for every day of the year for many important ports called *reference stations.* The other part contains tidal differences and ratios for thousands of other places, called *subordinate stations,* and specifies the reference station to which the differences are to be applied in order to obtain time and height of tide for any day at the subordinate station. The type of tide at a subordinate station is the same as at its reference station. Tides are affected by wind and atmospheric pressure. Keep in mind that onshore winds raise the level of the tide while offshore winds lower it.

TIDAL CURRENT

Tidal and Nontidal Currents

Horizontal movement of the water is called *current.* It may be classified as "tidal" and "nontidal." *Tidal current* is the periodic horizontal flow of water accompanying the rise and fall of the tide. *Nontidal current* is any current not due to the tidal movement. Nontidal currents include the permanent currents in the general circulatory system of the oceans as well as temporary currents arising from meteorological conditions. The current experienced at any given time is usually a combination of tidal and nontidal currents.

In piloting, the effect of the tidal current is usually more important than the changing depth due to the tide. Many mariners speak of "the tide" when they have in mind the flow of the tidal current. Ride the current—or "tide," if you prefer—whenever it's possible. Leave early, or late if it's better, but ride the current whenever you can.

Offshore, where the direction of flow is not restricted by any barriers, the tidal current is rotary; that is, it flows continuously, with the direction changing through all points of the compass during the tidal period. The tendency for the rotation in direction has its origin in the deflecting force of the earth's rotation, and unless modified by local conditions, the change is clockwise in the northern hemisphere.

In rivers or straits, or where the direction of flow is more or less restricted to certain channels, the tidal current is *reversing;* that is, it flows alternately in approximately opposite directions with an instant or short period of little or no current, called *slack water,* at each reversal of the current. During the flow in each direction the speed varies from zero at the time of slack water to a maximum, called *strength of floor* or *ebb,* about midway between the slacks. A slight departure from the sine form is exhibited by the reversing current in a strait, such as New York's East River, which connects two tidal bodies of water. The tides at two ends of a strait are seldom in phase or equal in range, and the current, called *hydraulic current,* is generated largely by the continuously changing difference in height of water at the two ends. The speed of a hydraulic current varies nearly as the square root of the difference in height. The speed reaches a maximum quickly and remains at strength longer, and the period of weak current near the time of slack is considerably shortened. Hell Gate in the East River is typical of hydraulic current at its nastiest, and most small-boat skippers breathe a sigh of relief when they've cleared that tricky stretch of racing, roiling, choppy water.

The current *direction* or *set* is the direction *toward* which the current flows. The *speed* is sometimes called the *drift.* The term *velocity* is often used as the equivalent of "speed" when referring to current, although strictly speaking velocity implies direction as well as speed. The term *strength* is also used to refer to speed, but more often to greatest speed between consecutive slack waters. The movement away from shore or downstream is the *flood;* the movement away from shore or downstream is the *ebb.* In a purely semidiurnal type of current unaffected by nontidal flow, the flood and ebb each last about 6 hours and 13 minutes.

Types of Tidal Current

Tidal currents may be of the semidiurnal, diurnal, or mixed types, corresponding to the type of tide at the place, but often with a stronger semidiurnal tendency.

The tidal currents in tidal estuaries along the Atlantic Coast of the United States are examples of the semidiurnal type of reversing current. At Mobile Bay entrance they are almost purely diurnal. At most places, however, the type is mixed to a greater or lesser degree. At Tampa and Galveston entrances there is only one flood and one ebb each day when the moon is near its maximum declination, and two floods and two ebbs each day when the moon is near the equator.

Along the Pacific Coast there are generally two floods and two ebbs every day, but one of the floods or ebbs has a greater speed and longer duration than the other, the inequality varying with the declination of the moon. The inequalities in the current often differ considerably from place to place even within limited areas, such as adjacent passages in Puget Sound and various passages between the Aleutian Islands. The diagram shows several types of reversing current.

Variations and Cycles

Tidal currents have periods and cycles similar to those of the tides and are subject to simpler variations, but flood and ebb of the current

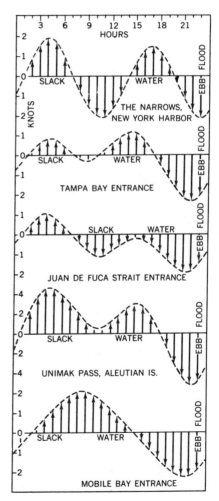

Several types of reversing current. The pattern changes gradually from day to day, particularly for mixed types.

do not necessarily occur at the same times as the rise and fall of the tide. The speed at strength increases and decreases during the two-week period, month, and year with the variations in the range of tide. Thus the stronger *spring* and *perigean currents* occur near the times of new and full moon and near the times of the moon's perigee, or at times of spring and perigean tides; the weaker *neap* and *apogean currents* occur at the times of neap and apogean tides; and *tropic currents* with increased diurnal speeds or with larger diurnal inequalities in speed occur at times of tropic tides.

As with the tide, a *mean value* represents an average obtained from a 19-year series. Since a series of current observations is usually limited to a few days, and seldom covers more than a month or two, it is necessary to adjust the observed values, usually by comparison with tides at a nearby place, to obtain such a mean.

Effect of Nontidal Flow

The current at any time is seldom purely tidal, but usually includes also a nontidal current that is due to drainage, oceanic circulation, wind, or other cause.

The speed of the current flowing in the direction of a nontidal current, such as a river, is increased by an amount equal to the magnitude of the nontidal current, and the speed of the current flowing in the opposite direction is decreased by an equal amount. In a reversing current, the effect is to advance the time of one slack and to retard the following one. If the speed of the nontidal current exceeds that of the reversing tidal current, the resultant current flows continuously in one direction without coming to a slack.

Time and Tide

At many places where current and tide are both semidiurnal there is a definite relationship between times of current and times of high and low water in the locality. Current atlases and notes on nautical charts often make use of this relationship by presenting for particular locations the direction and speed of the current at each succeeding hour after high and low water at a place for which tide predictions are available. In localities where there is considerable diurnal inequality in tide or current, or where the type of current differs from the type of tide, the relationship is not constant, and it may be hazardous to try to predict the times of current from times of tide.

Since the relationship between times of tidal current and tide is not everywhere the same, and may be variable at the same place, you must exercise extreme caution in using general rules. The belief that slacks occur at local high and low tides and that the maximum flood and ebb occur when the tide is rising or falling most rapidly may be approximately true at the seaward entrance to, and in the upper reaches of, an inland tidal waterway. But generally this is not true in other parts of inland waterways. This inconsistency can be tricky if there are lift bridges along your route and you have hoped to time your arrival during a period of slack water. More than one underpowered boat has been slammed by a swift current into the pilings of a slow-to-open bridge. When an inland waterway is extensive or its entrance constricted, the slacks in some parts of the waterway often occur midway between the times of high and low tide. Usually in such waterways the relationship changes from place to place as one progresses upstream, slack water getting progressively closer in time to the local tide maximum until at the head of tidewater (the inland limit of water affected by a tide) the slacks occur at about the times of high and low tide.

Speed and Tide

The variation in the speed of the tidal current from place to place is not necessarily consistent with the range of tide. It may be the reverse. For example, currents are weak in the Gulf of Maine where the tides are large, and strong near Nantucket Island and in Nantucket Sound where the tides are small. At any one place, however, the speed of the current at strength of flood and ebb varies during the month in about the same proportion as the range of tide, and one can use this relationship to determine the relative strength of currents on any day.

Variation across an Estuary

In inland tidal waterways the *time* of tidal current varies across the channel from shore to shore. On the average, the current turns earlier near shore than in midstream, where the speed is greater. Differences of half an hour to an hour are not uncommon, but the difference varies and the relationship may be nullified by the effect of nontidal flow. The *speed* of the current also varies across the channel, usually being greater in midstream or midchannel than near shore, but in a winding river or channel the strongest currents occur near the concave shore. Near the opposite (convex) shore the currents are weak or may eddy.

Racing sailboat skippers "play the current" if they can; a cruising skipper-pilot should also learn to take advantage of this extra speed, even if it is only a fraction of a knot.

Tidal Current Publications

The small-boat pilot should not attempt to predict currents without specific information for the locality in which he is cruising. Such information is contained in various forms in many navigational publications.

Tidal Current Tables, issued annually, list daily predictions of the times and strengths of flood and ebb currents, and of the times of intervening slacks or minima. Due to lack of observational data, coverage is considerably more limited than for the tides. The tidal current tables do include supplemental data by which tidal current predictions can be determined for many places in addition to those for which daily predictions are given. The predictions are made by computers, using current harmonic constants that are obtained by analyzing current observations in the same manner as for tides. Tables are available for the Atlantic and Pacific Coasts.

Coastal Pilots issued by maritime nations include general descriptions of current behavior in various localities throughout the world. United States *Coast Pilots* are available for the following areas:

Atlantic Coast:
    No. 1. Eastport to Cape Cod, 1981
    No. 2. Cape Cod to Sandy Hook, 1981
    No. 3. Sandy Hook to Cape Henry, 1980
    No. 4. Cape Henry to Key West, 1980
    No. 5. Gulf of Mexico, Puerto Rico, and the Virgin Islands, 1980
Great Lakes
    No. 6. Lakes Ontario, Erie, Huron, Michigan, Superior, and the
    St. Lawrence River, 1981
Pacific Coast
    No. 7. California, Oregon, Washington, and Hawaii, 1980
Alaska
    No. 8. Dixon Entrance to Cape Spencer, 1980
    No. 9. Cape Spencer to Beaufort Sea, 1981

Tidal Current Charts. A number of important harbors and water-ways are covered by sets of tidal current charts showing geographically the hourly current movement. The following charts are available:

Boston Harbor
Narragansett Bay to Nantucket Sound
Narragansett Bay
Long Island Sound and Block Island Sound
New York Harbor
Delaware Bay and River
Upper Chesapeake Bay
Charleston Harbor, S.C.
Tampa Bay
San Francisco Bay
Puget Sound—Northern Part
Puget Sound—Southern Part

Note: The Narragansett Bay tidal current charts are to be used with the annual tide tables. The other charts require the annual current tables.

Tidal Current Diagrams are a series of monthly diagrams used with tidal current charts. The diagrams directly indicate the chart to use and the speed correction factor to apply to each chart. Four diagrams are currently available:

Tidal Current Diagrams for Long Island Sound and Block Island Sound
Tidal Current Diagrams for Boston Harbor
Tidal Current Diagrams for Upper Chesapeake Bay
Tidal Current Diagrams for New York Harbor

8

Ripples and Waves

The surface of the water is seldom flat, and you wouldn't like it if it were. Water moves sideways in currents and tides, but it also jumps up and down. Flat, oily, mirrorlike calms occur from time to time—usually on hot, sultry midsummer days. Happily, close to shore they seldom last long; but when a flat calm has you locked in a furnace, don't be surprised if you start daydreaming of ice-cream parlors and air-conditioned movies. Don't worry; sooner or later a breeze will come up—and you'll be back where you belong.

OCEAN WAVES

The undulation of the surface of the water—*waves*—is one of the best known but least understood phenomena at sea. A knowledge of some basic facts concerning waves will help you avoid or minimize their danger. Above all, don't view them casually, for waves, like the wind, can be a powerful and destructive force.

Waves on the surface of the sea are caused principally by wind, but other factors, such as submarine earthquakes, volcanic eruptions, and the tide, also cause waves. If a breeze of less than 2 knots starts to blow across smooth water, small wavelets called *ripples* form almost instantaneously. When the breeze dies, these ripples disappear as suddenly as they formed, and the level surface is restored by the surface tension of the water. If the wind speed exceeds 2 knots, *gravity waves* gradually form and progress with the wind.

While the wind blows, the resulting waves are referred to as *sea*. When the wind stops or changes direction, the waves that continue without relation to local winds are called *swell*.

Unlike wind and current, waves are not deflected appreciably by the rotation of the earth, but move in the direction in which the generating wind blows. When this wind ceases, friction and spreading cause the waves to be reduced in height as they move across the surface. This reduction takes place so slowly that swell continues until it reaches an obstruction, such as the shore.

Ocean waves are very nearly the shape of an inverted *cycloid,* the figure formed by a point inside the rim of a wheel rolling along a level surface. The highest parts of waves are called *crests,* and the intervening lowest parts, *troughs*. Since the crests are steeper and narrower than the troughs, the mean or still water level is a little lower than halfway between the crests and troughs. The vertical distance between trough and crest is called *wave height*. The horizontal distance between successive crests, measured in the direction of travel, is called *wavelength*. The time interval between passage of successive crests at a stationary point is called the *wave period*. Wave height, length, and period depend on a number of factors, such as the wind speed, the length of time it has blown, and its *fetch* (the straight distance it has traveled over the surface). The accompanying table indicates the relationship between wind speed, fetch, length of time the wind blows, wave height, and wave period in deep water.

Waves can be friendly and pleasantly exhilarating when they behave themselves, but when they rear up, curl over, and break, they can be downright scary. Caution, not fear, might be a better reaction; breaking waves command respect. Most of us tend to exaggerate the height of waves that are buffeting us, much as we tend to overestimate our speed through the water.

In reporting "average" wave heights, the "average" mariner has a tendency to neglect the lower ones. It has been found that the reported value is about the average for the highest one-third. This is sometimes called the *significant* wave length. The approximate relationship between this height and others is shown in Table 2.

Table 2. **Relationship between Wave Heights**

Wave	Relative Height
Average	0.64
Significant	1.00
Highest 10 percent	1.29
Highest	1.87

The minimum time (T, *in hours*) that the wind must blow to form waves of significant height (H, *in feet*) and period (P, *in seconds*). Fetch is in nautical miles.

BEAUFORT NUMBER

Fetch	11 P	11 H	11 T	10 P	10 H	10 T	9 P	9 H	9 T	8 P	8 H	8 T	7 P	7 H	7 T	6 P	6 H	6 T	5 P	5 H	5 T	4 P	4 H	4 T	3 P	3 H	3 T
10	5.0	10.0	1.8	4.2	10.0	1.9	4.1	8.0	2.0	3.9	7.3	2.3	3.4	6.0	2.5	3.1	5.0	2.7	2.8	3.5	3.2	2.4	2.6	3.7	2.1	1.8	4.4
20	5.5	16.0	3.0	6.0	14.0	3.2	5.5	12.0	3.5	4.0	10.0	3.9	4.3	8.6	4.5	3.8	7.0	4.7	3.3	4.3	5.4	2.9	3.2	6.3	2.5	2.0	7.1
30	6.3	19.8	4.1	6.3	18.0	4.4	5.9	15.7	4.7	4.4	12.0	5.2	4.6	10.0	5.8	4.4	8.0	6.2	3.7	4.8	7.2	3.3	3.8	8.3	2.8	2.0	9.8
40	6.7	22.5	5.1	6.7	21.0	5.4	6.3	19.8	5.7	4.5	14.7	6.1	4.9	11.2	7.1	4.8	9.8	7.8	4.1	6.2	8.9	3.6	3.9	10.3	3.0	2.0	12.0
50	7.1	25.0	6.1	7.0	23.0	6.4	6.5	21.0	6.9	4.6	15.7	6.7	5.2	12.2	8.4	5.1	10.3	9.1	4.4	6.5	11.0	4.0	4.0	12.4	3.2	2.0	14.0
60	7.5	27.5	7.0	7.7	25.0	7.4	6.8	22.5	8.0	6.0	17.0	8.9	5.5	13.2	9.6	5.4	10.8	10.2	4.6	6.8	12.0	4.1	4.0	14.0	3.5	2.0	16.0
70	7.7	29.5	7.8	7.9	26.5	8.3	7.1	24.0	9.0	6.4	18.0	9.7	5.7	13.9	10.5	5.6	11.0	11.0	4.8	7.0	13.5	4.3	4.0	15.2	3.7	2.0	18.0
80	7.9	31.5	8.6	8.1	28.0	9.3	7.4	26.5	10.0	6.6	18.9	11.0	6.0	14.5	12.0	5.8	11.2	13.0	4.9	7.3	15.6	4.4	4.0	18.4	3.8	2.0	20.0
90	8.2	34.0	9.5	8.4	30.0	10.0	7.6	27.5	10.9	6.7	20.0	12.0	6.3	15.5	13.0	6.0	11.4	14.1	5.1	7.3	16.5	4.7	4.0	18.8	4.0	2.0	23.6
100	8.5	35.5	10.3	8.8	32.0	11.0	7.9	29.0	13.1	6.9	20.5	12.8	6.5	15.5	14.0	6.2	11.7	15.1	5.3	7.3	17.5	4.9	4.1	20.0	4.2	2.0	27.1
120	8.8	37.5	11.5	9.1	33.5	12.3	8.3	30.5	14.8	7.3	21.5	14.5	6.7	16.0	15.9	6.4	12.0	17.0	5.4	7.8	20.5	5.2	4.2	22.4	4.5	2.0	31.1
140	9.2	40.0	13.0	9.8	35.5	13.9	8.7	31.5	16.4	7.6	22.0	16.0	7.0	16.5	17.6	6.6	12.1	19.1	5.5	7.8	22.5	5.4	4.3	25.8	4.9	2.0	36.2
160	9.6	42.5	14.5	10.1	37.5	15.1	8.9	32.5	18.0	8.0	23.0	18.0	7.3	16.5	19.5	6.8	12.2	21.1	6.0	8.0	24.3	5.6	4.3	28.4	4.4	2.0	43.0
180	10.0	44.5	15.8	10.5	38.5	16.1	9.2	34.0	19.3	8.3	23.0	19.9	7.5	17.0	21.3	7.1	12.3	23.1	6.2	8.0	27.0	5.8	4.4	30.9			50.0
200	10.3	46.0	17.1	10.6	40.0	16.5	9.6	34.5	20.9	8.5	23.5	21.5	7.7	17.5	23.1	7.2	12.4	25.4	6.4	8.0	29.0	5.9	4.4	33.5			
220	10.6	47.5	18.2	10.9	41.0	19.1	9.8	35.0	22.0	8.8	24.0	22.9	8.0	17.9	25.0	7.3	12.6	27.2	6.6	8.0	31.1	6.0	4.4	36.5			
240	10.8	49.0	19.9	11.1	43.0	20.5	10.0	35.0	23.5	9.0	24.0	24.4	8.2	17.9	26.8	7.5	12.9	29.0	6.8	8.0	33.1	6.2	4.4	39.2			
260	11.1	50.5	20.9	11.4	44.0	21.8	10.2	35.5	25.0	9.2	25.0	26.0	8.4	18.0	28.5	7.8	13.1	30.5	6.9	8.0	34.9	6.3	4.4	41.9			
280	11.3	51.5	22.0	11.6	44.5	23.0	10.4	36.5	26.3	9.4	25.0	27.0	8.5	18.0	29.5	8.0	13.3	32.4	7.0	8.0	36.8			47.0			
300	11.6	53.0	23.2	11.8	45.0	24.3	10.6	37.0	27.6	9.5	25.0	28.2	8.7	18.0	31.5	8.1	13.4	34.1	7.1	8.0	38.5						
320	11.8	54.0	24.5	12.0	45.5	25.5	10.8	37.0	29.0	9.6	25.0	30.2	8.9	18.0	33.0	8.3	13.5	36.0	7.2	8.0	40.5						
340	12.0	55.0	25.5	12.1	46.5	26.7	10.9	37.5	30.0	9.8	25.0	31.6	9.0	18.1	34.2	8.4	13.5	38.0	7.3	8.0	42.4						
360	12.2	55.5	26.6	12.3	47.0	27.9	11.1	37.5	31.3	9.9	25.5	33.0	9.1	18.1	36.0	8.5	13.5	38.2	7.4	8.0	44.6						
380	12.4	55.5	27.7	12.5	47.5	29.1	11.2	37.5	32.5	10.0	25.5	34.2	9.3	18.2	37.1	8.6	13.6	40.2	7.5	8.0	46.1						
400	12.6	56.0	28.9	12.7	47.5	30.2	11.4	38.0	33.7	10.2	25.5	35.9	9.5	18.4	38.8	8.7	13.7	42.2	7.7	8.0	48.0						
420	12.7	56.5	29.6	13.0	47.5	31.5	11.5	38.5	34.8	10.3	26.5	36.9	9.6	18.7	40.0	8.8	13.7	43.5	7.8	8.0	50.0						
440	12.9	57.0	30.9	13.2	48.5	32.5	11.7	39.0	36.0	10.4	27.0	38.1	9.7	18.8	41.3	8.8	13.7	44.7	7.9	8.0	52.0						
460	13.1	57.5	31.8	13.5	49.0	33.5	11.8	39.5	37.0	10.6	27.5	39.5	9.8	19.0	42.8	8.9	13.8	46.2	8.0	8.0	54.0						
480	13.2	57.5	32.7	13.7	49.0	34.5	11.9	40.0	38.3	10.8	27.5	41.0	9.9	19.0	44.0	9.1	13.8	47.8	8.1	8.0	56.0						
500	13.4	58.0	33.9	14.2	50.0	35.5	12.2	40.0	41.6	10.9	27.5	42.1	10.1	19.1	45.5	9.3	13.8	49.2	8.2	8.0	58.0						
550	13.7	59.0	36.5	14.5	50.0	38.2	12.5	40.0	43.8	11.1	27.5	44.9	10.3	19.5	48.5	9.5		53.0									
600	14.0	60.0	38.7	14.6	50.5	40.3	13.1	40.0	46.4	11.3	27.5	47.7	10.5	19.7	51.8			56.3									
650	14.2	60.5	41.0	14.9	51.0	43.0	13.3		49.0	11.6	27.5	50.3	10.7	19.8	55.0												
700	14.5	60.5	43.5	15.1	51.5	45.5	13.5		51.0	11.8	27.5	53.2	11.0	19.8	58.5												
750	14.8	61.0	45.8	15.3	52.0	48.0	14.0		53.8	12.1	27.5	56.2															
800	15.0	61.5	47.8			50.6			56.2	12.3	27.5	59.2															
850	15.5	62.5	50.0			52.5			58.2																		
900	15.7	62.5	52.0			54.6																					
950	16.0	63.0	54.2			57.2																					
1000			56.3			59.3																					

Many independent wave systems often exist at the same time, and the sea surface acquires a complex and irregular pattern. Also, since the longer waves outrun the shorter ones, the resulting interference adds to the complexity of the pattern. This interference is duplicated many times in the sea, and is the principal reason that successive waves are not of the same height. The irregularity of the surface may be further accentuated by the presence of wave systems crossing at an angle to each other, producing peaklike rises.

A single particle or drop of water on the surface of the sea follows a somewhat circular orbit as a wave passes, but moves very little in the direction of motion of the wave. The common wave producing this action is called an *oscillatory wave*. As the crest passes, the particle moves forward, giving the water the appearance of moving with the wave. As the trough passes, the motion is in the opposite direction. The radius of the circular orbit decreases with depth. In shallower water the orbits become more elliptical, and in very shallow water, as at a beach, the vertical motion disappears almost completely.

Since the speed is greater at the top of the orbit than at the bottom, the particle is not at exactly its original point following passage of a wave, but has moved slightly in the direction of motion of the wave. Since this advance is small in relation to the vertical displacement, a floating object is raised and lowered by passage of a wave, but moved little from its original position. If this were not so, a slow-moving vessel would experience considerable difficulty in making way against a wave train.

A following current increases wave lengths and decreases wave heights. An opposing current has the opposite effect, decreasing the length and increasing the height. A strong opposing current may cause the waves to break. Moderate ocean currents running at oblique angles to wave directions appear to have little effect, but strong tidal currents perpendicular to a system of waves can destroy them in a short period of time. Ice crystals in seawater increase friction and smoothe the surface of the sea. The effect of pack ice is even more pronounced, even when a gale is blowing. Hail is also effective in flattening the sea, even in a high wind.

Waves and Shallow Water

When a wave encounters shallow water, the movement of the individual particles of water is restricted by the bottom, resulting in reduced wave speed. In deep water, wave speed is a function of period. In shallow water, wave speed becomes a function of depth. The shallower the water, the slower is the speed of the wave. As the wave speed slows, the period remains the same so the wavelength becomes shorter. Since the energy in the waves remains the same, the shortening of wavelengths results in increased heights. This process is called *shoaling*.

As each wave slows, the next wave behind it, still in deeper water, tends to catch up. As the wavelength decreases, the height generally becomes greater. The lower part of a wave, being nearest the bottom, is slowed more than the top. This may cause the wave to become unstable, the faster moving top falling or *breaking*. Such a wave is called a *breaker,* and a series of breakers, *surf.* Surf is for brawny young men on little plastic boards—not for you and your boat. (We'll get to that later.)

Swell passing over a shoal but not breaking undergoes a decrease in wavelength and speed, and an increase in height. Such *ground swell* may cause heavy rolling if it is on the beam and its period is the same as the period of roll of your vessel, even though the sea may appear relatively calm. Ground swell in an open anchorage can be maddening, especially after a long, hard day. Sometimes, if one exists, it would be better to sail or motor just a bit farther to another harbor, where you can anchor in comfort behind a point of land or a breakwater.

The Energy of Waves

The *potential energy* of a wave is related to the vertical distance of each particle from its still-water position, and it moves with the wave. In contrast, the *kinetic energy* of a wave is related to the speed of the particles, and is distributed evenly along the entire wave.

The amount of kinetic energy in even a moderate wave is tremendous. A 4-foot, 10-second wave striking a coast expends more than 35,000 horsepower per mile of beach. For each 56 miles of coast, the energy expended equals the power generated at Hoover Dam.

You won't encounter them on Long Island or Puget Sounds, but there are numerous reliable accounts of ocean waves 75–80 feet high, or even higher, although waves more than 55 feet high are rare. The highest wave ever reliably reported was 112 feet, observed from the U.S.S. *Ramapo* in 1933.

Don't concern yourself with estimating the height of 75- or 80-foot waves; the first one you encounter will probably be your last, and you won't be coming back to tell anyone about it anyway. However, you *can* estimate with reasonable accuracy the height, length, period, and speed of the waves you *will* encounter by comparing them to the freeboard and length of your vessel, and by timing the passage of successive wave crests past a patch of foam or an object that is floating in the water. Practice will improve your accuracy; just hope you don't get too much of it.

Tsunamis are ocean waves produced by a sudden, large-scale motion of a portion of the ocean floor or the shore, as by volcanic eruption, earthquake (sometimes called *seaquake* if it occurs at sea), or landslide. If they are caused by a submarine earthquake, they are usually called *seismic sea waves*. The point directly above the disturbance is called the *epicenter*. Either a tsunami or a storm tide that overflows the land is popularly called a *tidal wave,* although it bears no relation to the tide.

If a volcanic eruption occurs below the surface of the sea, the escaping gases cause a quantity of water to be pushed upward in the shape of a dome or mound. The same effect is caused by the sudden rising of a portion of the bottom. As this water settles back, it creates a wave which travels at high speed across the surface of the ocean.

Tsunamis are a series of waves. Near the epicenter, the first wave may be the highest. At greater distances, the highest wave usually occurs later in the series, commonly between the third and the eighth wave. Following the maximum, they again become smaller, but the tsunami may be detectable for several days.

In deep water the wave length of a tsunami is probably never greater than 2 or 3 feet. Since the wavelength is usually considerably more than 100 miles, the wave is not conspicuous at sea. In the Pacific, where most tsunamis occur, the wave period varies between about 15 and 60 *minutes,* and the speed in deep water is more than 400 knots.

When a tsunami enters shoal water, it undergoes the same changes as other waves. Because of the great speed of a tsunami when it is in relatively deep water, the slowing is much greater than that of an ordinary wave crested by wind. The increase in height is also much greater. The size of the wave depends on the nature and intensity of the disturbance. The height and destructiveness of the wave arriving on your figurative doorstep depend on your distance from the epicenter, topography of the ocean floor, and the coastline. The angle at which the wave arrives, the shape of the coastline, and the topography along the coast and offshore all have their effect. The position of the shore is also a factor, as it may be sheltered by intervening land.

Tsunamis 50 feet in height or higher have reached the shore, inflicting widespread damage. On April 1, 1946, seismic sea waves originating at an epicenter near the Aleutians spread over the entire Pacific. Scotch Cap Light on Unimak Islands, 57 feet above sea level, was completely destroyed. Traveling at an average speed of 490 miles per hour, the waves reached the Hawaiian Islands in 4 hours and 34 minutes, where they arrived as waves 50 feet above the high-water level and flooded long strips of the coast. They left a death toll of 173, and property damage of $25 million. Less destructive waves reached the shores of North and South America, and Australia, 6700 miles from the epicenter. After this disaster, a tsunami warning system was set up in the Pacific, even though destructive waves are relatively rare (averaging about one in 20 years in the Hawaiian Islands).

Earthquakes below the surface of the sea may produce a longitudinal wave that travels toward the surface at the speed of sound. The sudden shock may be so severe that the crew of a vessel above the quake will think they've struck bottom. Because of such reports, some older charts indicated shoal areas at places where the depth is now known to be 1000 fathoms or more.

Storm Tides

In relatively tideless seas such as the Baltic and Mediterranean, winds cause the chief fluctuations in sea level. Elsewhere, the astronomical tide usually masks these variations. However, under exceptional conditions, either severe extratropical storms or tropical cyclones can produce changes in sea level that exceed the normal range of tide. Low sea level is of little concern except to shipping, but a rise above the ordinary high-water mark, particularly when it is accompanied by high waves, can result in a catastrophe.

Like tsunamis, these *storm tides* or *storm surges* are popularly called "tidal waves," although they are not associated with the tide. They consist of a single wave crest and hence have no period or wavelength.

Three effects in a storm induce a rise in sea level. The first is wind stress on the sea surface, which results in a piling-up of water (sometimes called "wind set-up"). The second effect is the convergence of wind-driven currents, which elevates the sea surface along the convergence line. In shallow water, bottom friction and the effects of local topography cause this elevation to persist, and may even intensify it. The low atmospheric pressure that accompanies severe storms causes the third effect, which is sometimes referred to as the "inverted barometer." An inch of mercury is equivalent to about 13.6 inches of water and the adjustment of the sea surface to the reduced pressure can amount to several feet at equilibrium.

All three of these causes act independently, and if they happen to occur simultaneously their effects are additive. In addition, the wave can be intensified or amplified by the effects of local topography. Storm tides may reach heights of 20 feet or more, and it is estimated that they cause three-fourths of the deaths attributed to hurricanes.

Tide Waves

As discussed earlier, there are, in general, two regions of high tide separated by two regions of low tide, and these regions move progressively westward around the earth as the moon revolves in its orbit. The high tides are the crests of these *tide waves* and the low tides are the troughs. The wave is not noticeable at sea, but becomes apparent along the coasts, particularly in funnel-shaped estuaries. In certain river mouths or estuaries, the incoming wave of high water overtakes the preceding low tide, resulting in a high-crested, roaring wave which progresses upstream in one mighty surge called a *bore*. Whether it's in the Bay of Fundy or the clubhouse bar, bores, like Old Salts, should be approached with caution—if they can't be avoided altogether.

Waves and Your Vessel

The effects of waves on your little ship vary considerably with her type, your course and speed, and the condition of the sea. A short vessel has a tendency to ride up one side of a wave and down the other side, while a larger vessel tends to ride *through* the waves on an even keel. If the waves are of such length that the bow and stern of a vessel are alternately in successive crests and successive troughs, a larger vessel is subject to heavy sagging and hogging stresses, and under extreme conditions may break in two. A change of heading may reduce the danger. Because of the danger from sagging and hogging, a small vessel such as yours is sometimes better able to ride out a storm than a large one.

If successive waves strike the side of a vessel at the same phase of successive rolls, relatively small waves can cause heavy rolling. The effect is similar to that of pushing a child on a swing—the strength of the push is not as important as its timing. The same effect, if applied to the bow or stern in time with the pitch, can cause heavy pitching. A change of either heading or speed may reduce the effect.

A wave having a length twice that of a ship places that ship in danger of falling off into the trough of the sea, particularly if it is a slow-moving vessel. The effect is especially pronounced if the sea is broad on the bow or broad on the quarter. An increase of speed, if an increase is possible, reduces the hazard.

Oil on Troubled Waters

Oil has proved effective in modifying the effects of breaking waves, and has proved useful to vessels at sea, whether making way or hove-to. Its effect is greatest in deep water, where a small quantity suffices if the oil can be made to spread to windward. In shallow water where the water is in motion over the bottom, oil is less effective but may be of some value.

The heaviest oils, notably animal and vegetable oils, are the most effective. Crude petroleum is useful, but who carries barrels of crude oil aboard a pleasure boat? However, you *should* have a few spare cans of engine oil on board, and its effectiveness can be improved by mixing it with vegetable oils. Gasoline or kerosene are too thin and are of little value. Oil spreads slowly. In cold weather it may need some thinning to hasten the process and produce the desired spread before the vessel is too far away for the effect to be useful.

At sea, the best results can be expected if the vessel drifts or runs slowly before the wind, with the oil being discharged through a sink drain, the out-go in your head, or an oil bag over the side. This is a messy business, but *Bowditch* and some Old Salts swear by it. If it's any consolation, *this* old salt has been sailing since 1943, both coastal and offshore, and he has never seen oil used to tame breaking water.

OCEAN CURRENTS

The movement of the water comprising the oceans is one of the principal sources of discrepancy between the dead reckoning and the actual positions of a vessel. Water in horizontal motion is called a current, the direction *toward* which it moves being the set, and its speed the drift. A well-defined current extending over a considerable region of the ocean is called an ocean current. Although this volume deals primarily with coastal cruising, to some degree ocean currents affect each of us, whether we're on the Atlantic or Pacific Coast—Maine to Florida, Alaska to California.

A *coastal current* flows roughly parallel to a coast, outside the surf zone, while a *longshore current* is one parallel to a shore, inside the surf zone, and generated by waves striking the beach at an angle. Any current some distance from the shore may be called an *offshore* current, and one close to the shore an *inshore* current.

The strongest ocean currents consist of relatively narrow, high-speed streams that follow winding, shifting courses. Often associated with these currents are secondary *countercurrents* flowing adjacent to them but in the opposite direction, and somewhat local, roughly circular, *eddy currents*. A relatively narrow, deep, fast-moving current is sometimes called a *stream* current, and a broad, shallow, slow-moving one a *drift* current. The main generating forces of ocean currents are wind and the density differences in the water. In addition, such factors as depth of water, underwater topography, shape of the basin in which the current is running, extent and location of land, and deflection by the rotation of the earth all affect oceanic circulation.

A number of ocean currents flow with great persistence, setting up a circulation that continues with relatively little change throughout the year. Because of the influence of wind in creating current, there is a relationship between this oceanic circulation and the general circulation of the atmosphere. The oceanic circulation is shown on the chart. Some differences in opinion exist regarding the names and limits of some, but those shown are representative. The spacing of the lines is a general indication of speed, but conditions vary somewhat with the season.

Atlantic Ocean Currents

The trade winds, which blow with great persistence, set up a system of equatorial currents which extends over as much as 50° of latitude or even more. There are two westerly flowing currents conforming generally with the areas of trade winds—the North Equatorial Current, which originates to the northward of the Cape Verde Islands and flows almost due west at an average speed of about 0.7 knot; and the South Equatorial Current, which starts off the west coast of Africa, south of the Gulf of Guinea, and flows in a generally westerly direction at an average speed of about 0.6 knot. Its speed gradually increases until it may reach 2.5 knots or more off the east coast of South America. As the current approaches Cabo de São Roque, the eastern extremity of South America, it divides, the northern part being deflected by the continent of South America toward the north, where some of it unites

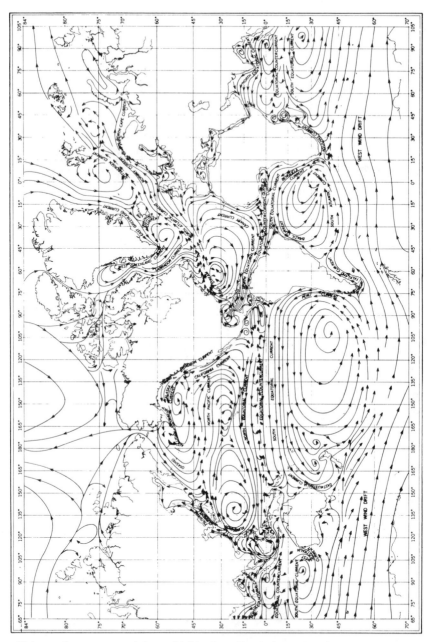

Major surface currents of the world (Northern Hemisphere winter).

with the North Equatorial Current. The combined current flows through various passages between the Windward Islands and into the Caribbean Sea. It sets toward the west, and then somewhat north of west, finally arriving off the Yucatán peninsula. From here, some of the water curves toward the right, flowing some distance off the shore of the Gulf of Mexico, and part of it curves more sharply toward the east and flows directly toward the north coast of Cuba. These two parts reunite in the Straits of Florida to form the most remarkable of all ocean currents— the Gulf Stream. Off the southeast coast of Florida this magnificent current is augmented by a current flowing along the northern coasts of Puerto Rico, Hispaniola, and Cuba. Another current flowing eastward of the Bahamas joins the stream north of these islands.

The Gulf Stream follows generally along the east coast of North America, flowing around Florida, northward and then northeastward toward Cape Hatteras, and then curving toward the east and becoming broader and slower. After passing the Grand Banks, it turns more toward the north and becomes a broad drift current flowing across the North Atlantic. That part in the Straits of Florida is sometimes called the Florida Current.

A tremendous volume of water flows northward in the Gulf Stream. It can be distinguished by its deep indigo-blue color, which contrasts sharply with the dull green of the surrounding water. It is accompanied by frequent squalls. When the Gulf Stream encounters the cold water of the Labrador Current, principally in the vicinity of the Grand Banks, there is little mixing of the waters. Instead, the junction is marked by a sharp change in temperature. The line or surface along which this occurs is called the *cold wall*. When the warm Gulf Stream water encounters cold air, evaporation is so rapid that the rising vapor may be visible as frost smoke. The stream also carries large quantities of gulfweed from the tropics to higher latitudes.

The maximum current off Florida ranges from about 2 to 4 knots. To the northward the speed is generally less, and decreases further after the current passes Cape Hatteras. As the stream meanders and shifts position, eddies sometimes break off and continue as separate, circular flows until they dissipate. Boats in the Bermuda Race have been known to be within sight of each other yet be carried in opposite directions by different parts of the same current. As the current shifts position, its extent does not always coincide with the area of warm, blue water. When the sea is relatively smooth, the edges of the current are marked by ripples.

Information is not yet available to permit prediction of the position and speed of the current at any future time, but it has been found that tidal forces apparently influence the current, which reaches its daily maximum speed about three hours after transit of the moon. The current generally is faster at the time of neap tides than at spring tides. When the moon is over the equator, the stream is narrower and faster than at maximum northerly or southerly declination. Variations in the trade winds also affect the current.

As the Gulf Stream continues eastward and northeastward beyond the Grand Banks, it gradually widens and decreases speed until it becomes a vast, slow-moving drift current known as the North Atlantic Current. In the eastern part of the Atlantic it divides, but unless we are Norwegians or British, the Gulf Stream has then drifted out of our lives until some of the Southern Drift curves south to rejoin the North Equatorial Current to start around again.

Pacific Ocean Currents

Ocean currents in the Pacific follow the general pattern of those in the Atlantic. The North Equatorial Current flows westward in the general area of the northeast trades, and the South Equatorial Current follows a similar path in the region of the southeast trades. Between these two, the weaker Equatorial Countercurrent sets toward the east, just north of the equator.

After passing the Mariana Islands in the Western Pacific, the major part of the North Equatorial Current curves somewhat toward the northwest, past the Philippines and Taiwan. Here it is deflected farther toward the north, where it becomes known as the Kuroshio, and then toward the northeast past the Nansei Shoto and Japan, and on in a more easterly direction. The limits and volume of the Kuroshio are influenced by the monsoons, being augmented during the season of southwesterly winds and diminished when the northeasterly winds are prevalent.

The Kuroshio (Japanese for "Black Stream") is so named because of the dark color of its water. It is sometimes called the Japan Stream. In many respects it is similar to the Gulf Stream of the Atlantic. Like that current, it carries large quantities of warm tropical water to higher latitudes, and then curves toward the east as a major part of the general clockwise circulation in the northern hemisphere. As it does so, it widens and slows. A small part of it curves to the right to form a weak clockwise circulation west of the Hawaiian Islands. The major portion continues on between the Aleutians and the Hawaiian Islands, where it becomes known as the North Pacific Current.

As this current approaches the North American continent, most of it is deflected toward the right to form a clockwise circulation between the west coast of North America and the Hawaiian Islands. This part of the current has become so broad that the circulation is generally weak. A small part near the coast, however, joins the southern branch of the Aleutian Current and flows southeastward as the California Current. The average speed of this current is about 0.8 knot and it is strongest near land. Near the southern end of Baja (Lower) California, this current curves sharply to the west and broadens to form the major portion of the North Equatorial Current.

During the winter, a weak countercurrent flows northwestward along the west coast of North America from southern California to Vancouver Island, inshore of the southeasterly flowing California Current. This is called the Davidson Current.

As in the Atlantic, there is in the Pacific a counterclockwise circulation to the north of the clockwise circulation. Cold water flowing southward through the western part of Bering Strait between Alaska and Siberia is joined by water circulating counterclockwise in the Bering Sea to form the Oyahio. As the current leaves the strait, it curves toward the right and flows southwesterly along the coast of Siberia and the Kuril Islands. This current brings quantities of sea ice, but no icebergs. When it encounters the Kuroshio, the Oyashio curves southward and then eastward, the greater portion joining the Kuroshio and North Pacific Current. The northern portion continues eastward to join the curving Aleutian Current. As this current approaches the west coast of North America, west of Vancouver Island, part of it curves toward the right and is joined by water from the North Pacific Current, to form the California Current. The northern branch flows in a counterclockwise direction to form the Alaska Current, which generally follows the coast of Canada and Alaska.

Ocean Currents and Climate

Ocean currents exert a marked influence on the climate of coastal regions along which they flow. Warm water from the Gulf Stream arrives off the southwest coast of Iceland, warming it to the extent that Reykjavik has a higher average winter temperature than New York City, far to the south. The west coast of the United States is cooled in the summer by the California Current and warmed in the winter by the

Davidson Current. Partly as a result of this condition, the range of monthly average temperatures is comparatively small.

BREAKERS AND SURF

Few things are more thrilling—and dangerous—than trying to cross a breaking bar or negotiate a narrow inlet in an underpowered boat when the surf is running high. Old Salt might give this sage bit of advice: "When in doubt—don't." And in this case Old Salt would be right.

It's fun to sail or motor close inshore—but there are hazards. The view is good and you seem to move faster, but if you don't blunder into a fish trap or bump over a submerged rock, the surf just may get you and toss you someplace above the high-water mark. Only a fool would flirt with this disaster; unfortunately there are some fools on the water.

Shoal Waters

In deep water, swell generally moves across the surface as somewhat regular, smooth undulations. When it reaches shoal water, the wave period remains the same but the speed decreases. The amount of decrease is negligible until the depth of water becomes about one-half the wavelength, when the waves begin to "feel" bottom. There is a slight decrease in wave height followed by a rapid increase, if the waves are traveling perpendicular to a straight coast with a uniformly sloping bottom. As the waves become higher and shorter, they also become steeper, and the crest becomes narrower. When the speed of individual particles at the crest becomes greater than that of the wave, the front face of the wave becomes steeper than the rear face. This process continues at an accelerating rate as the depth of water decreases. At some point the wave may become unstable, toppling forward to form a *breaker*.

There are three classes of breakers: a *spilling breaker* that breaks gradually over a considerable distance, a *plunging breaker* that tends to curl over and break with a single crash, and a *surging breaker* that peaks up, but surges up the beach without spilling or plunging. (The latter is classed as a breaker even though it does not actually break.) The type of breaker is determined by the steepness of the beach and

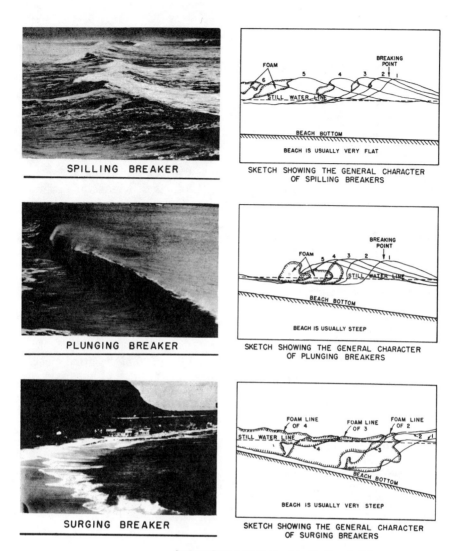

SPILLING BREAKER

SKETCH SHOWING THE GENERAL CHARACTER
OF SPILLING BREAKERS

PLUNGING BREAKER

SKETCH SHOWING THE GENERAL CHARACTER
OF PLUNGING BREAKERS

SURGING BREAKER

SKETCH SHOWING THE GENERAL CHARACTER
OF SURGING BREAKERS

Courtesy of Robert L. Wiegel, Council on Wave Research, University of California.

Three types of breakers.

the steepness of the wave before it reaches shallow water, as shown in the illustration.

Longer waves break in deeper water and have a greater breaker height. The effect of a steeper beach is also to increase breaker height. The height of breakers is less if the waves approach a beach at an acute angle. With a steeper beach slope there is greater tendency of the breakers to plunge or surge. Following the uprush of water onto a beach after the breaking of a wave, the seaward backrush occurs. The returning water is called *backwash*. It tends to further slow the bottom of a wave, thus increasing its tendency to break. This effect is greater as either the speed or depth of the backwash increases. The still-water depth at the point of breaking is approximately 1.3 times the average breaker height.

Surf varies with both position along the beach and time. At the same point, the height and period of waves vary considerably from wave to wave. A group of high waves is usually followed by several lower ones. Therefore passage through surf can usually be made most easily immediately following a series of higher waves. There will come a time when you simply must run a narrow inlet or between breakwaters to reach a snug harbor inside. If possible, lay off until you can watch another boat run in (to see if it makes it safely, and *where* it goes when it's inside), and then time your run during the smaller waves that are almost certain to come.

Since surf conditions are directly related to the height of the waves approaching a beach and the configuration of the bottom, the state of the surf at any time can be predicted if you understand the principles involved. Height of the sea and swell can be predicted from the wind, and information on bottom configuration can generally be obtained from the nautical chart.

Currents in the Surf Zone

In and adjacent to surf, currents are generated by waves approaching the bottom contours at an angle, and by irregularities in the bottom.

Waves approaching at an angle produce a *longshore current* parallel to the beach, within the surf zone. Longshore currents are most common along straight beaches, and they can be tricky near the mouth of an inlet. Their speeds increase with increasing breaker height, decreasing wave period, increasing angle of breaker line with the beach, and increasing beach slope. Their speed seldom exceeds 1 knot, but sustained speeds as high as 3 knots have been recorded. Fortunately, longshore currents are usually constant in direction.

Wavefronts advancing over nonparallel bottom contours cause convergence or divergence of the energy of the waves. Energy concentrations in areas of convergence form barriers to the returning backwash, which is deflected *along* the beach to areas of less resistance. Backwash accumulates at weak points and returns seaward in concentrations, forming *rip currents* through the surf. At these points the large volume of returning water has a retarding effect on the incoming waves, thus adding to the rip current. The waves on one or both sides of the rip, having greater energy and not being retarded by the concentration of the backwash, advance faster and farther up the beach. From here, they move along the beach as *feeder currents*. At some point of low resistance, the water flows seaward through the surf, forming the *neck* of the rip current. Outside the breaker line the current widens and slackens, forming the head.

If you pilot your boat with the care she deserves, stay off lee shores in heavy weather, and don't flirt with the surf line (especially at night), you'll probably cruise for years with no real danger from breakers. But like 80-foot waves on the open sea, once is one time too many.

9
Wind and the Weather

"The weather is of considerable interest to the mariner."

No, Old Salt didn't say that—*Bowditich* did. And that is probably the Number One understatement in *American Practical Navigator,* a book that has understatements sprinkled through its pages like rocks along the coast of Maine.

". . . those who go to sea for pleasure must do so in the full knowledge that they may encounter dangers of the highest order."

That laconic line was written by a British board of inquiry after a gale hit the Fastnet Race sailboat fleet, taking 15 lives. Twenty-four boats were abandoned in heavy seas, and 136 yachtsmen had to be rescued. You may pilot your boat for years without experiencing a killer storm, but sooner or later you are almost certain to get "caught out" in a sudden screaming summer squall.

Nothing affects the skipper-pilot's work more than the weather—not even a tired, inexperienced, or mutinous crew.

This section, therefore, deals with the weather—your adversary or your friend.

WEATHER ELEMENTS

Weather is the state of the earth's atmosphere with respect to temperature, humidity, precipitation, visibility, cloudiness, etc. All weather may be traced to the effect of the sun on the earth and the lower portions of the atmosphere. Most changes in weather involve the large-scale horizontal motion of air. Air in motion is called *wind*. This motion is produced by differences of atmospheric pressure, which are attributable to differences of temperature and the nature of motion itself.

The wind and state of the sea affect dead reckoning. Reduced horizontal visibility limits piloting. The state of the atmosphere affects electronic navigation and radio communication. If the wind is your primary motive power, knowledge of winds is of special importance.

More than a century ago Matthew Fontaine Maury sought information from ships' logs to establish speed and direction of prevailing winds over the various trade routes of the world. The information gathered was shown on pilot charts. By using these charts, mariners could select a suitable route for a favorable passage. Even power vessels are affected considerably by wind and sea. Less fuel consumption and a more comfortable passage are to be expected if winds are moderate and favorable. Pilot charts are fascinating, but are not usually of great value to coastal cruisers. More important to the new skipper-pilot-weatherwatcher are the *Marine Weather Services Charts,* which are published by the National Weather Service (NWS). This series of fifteen charts covers the coastal waters of the United States and Puerto Rico. Each lists NWS radio stations and telephone numbers, commercial stations that broadcast marine weather information, and the locations of visual storm warnings. The series is sold by the Distribution Division (OA44), National Ocean Survey, Riverdale, MD 20737.

THE AIR AROUND US

The *atmosphere* is a relatively thin shell of air, water vapor, dust, and smoke surrounding the earth. The air is a mixture of transparent gases and, like any gas, is elastic and highly compressible. Although extremely light, it has a definite weight. A cubic foot of air at standard sea-level temperature and pressure weighs 1.22 ounces, or about 1/817th part of the weight of an equal volume of water. Because of this weight, the atmosphere exerts a pressure upon the surface of the earth amounting to about 15 pounds per square inch.

As altitude increases, pressure decreases. With less pressure, density decreases. More than three-fourths of the air is concentrated within a layer averaging about 7 statute miles thick, called the *troposphere.* This is the region of most "weather," as the term is commonly understood. The top of the troposphere is marked by a thin transition zone called the *tropopause,* above which is the *stratosphere.* Beyond this lie several other layers. The average height of the tropopause ranges from about 5 miles or less at high latitudes to about 10 miles at low latitudes.

The *standard atmosphere* is a vertical structure of the atmosphere with a standard sea-level pressure of 29.92 inches of mercury (1013.25 millibars) and a sea-level temperature of 59°F (15°C). The rate of temperature decreases with height—3.6°F (2°C) per thousand feet to 11 kilometers (36,089 feet) and thereafter a constant temperature of −69.7°F (−56.5°C).

With the aid of weather satellite observations, meteorologists in recent years have learned more of the atmospheric processes in the troposphere and stratosphere as they affect weather at sea. Only recently have weather "forecasters" discovered that the *jet stream* is important to the sequence of weather. The jet stream refers to strong winds concentrated within a restricted layer of the atmosphere. Although jet-stream winds can occur at any level and geographic location, and from any direction, the term is most often associated with midlatitude winds from 225° to 315° with polar winds that average 90 knots, but may have speeds of 200 knots in the winter.

The heat required for warming the air is supplied by the sun. As radiant energy from the sun arrives at the earth, about 29 percent is reflected back into space, 19 percent is absorbed by the atmosphere, and the remaining 52 percent is absorbed by the surface of the earth. The atmosphere acts much like the glass on the roof of a greenhouse. It allows part of the incoming solar radiation to reach the surface of the earth, but is heated by the terrestrial radiation passing outward. Over the entire earth and for long periods of time, the total outgoing energy must be equivalent to the incoming energy or the temperature of the earth, including its atmosphere, would steadily increase or decrease. In local areas, or over relatively short periods of time, such a balance is not required, and in fact does not exist, resulting in changes such as those occurring from one year to another in different seasons and in different parts of the day.

If the earth had a uniform surface and did not rotate on its axis, with the sun following its normal path across the sky (solar heating increasing with decreasing latitude), a simple circulation would result. However, the surface of the earth is bumpy and much of it is covered with water; the earth rotates about its axis once in approximately 24 hours; and the axis of rotation is tilted so that as the earth moves along its orbit about the sun, seasonal changes occur. These factors, coupled with others, result in constantly changing large-scale movements of

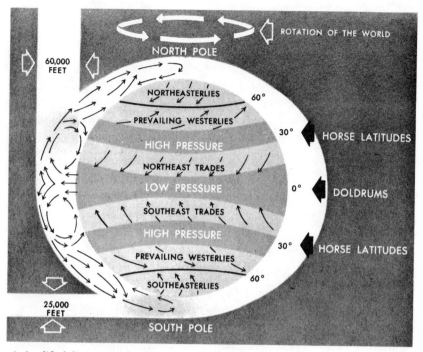

A simplified diagram of the general circulation of the atmosphere.

air. For example, the rotation of the earth exerts a force that diverts the air from a direct path between high- and low-pressure areas. The diversion of the air is toward the right in the northern hemisphere and toward the left in the southern hemisphere. Near the surface of the earth, friction tends to divert the wind from the isobars (lines of equal atmospheric pressure) toward the center of low pressure. At sea, where there is less friction than on land, the wind follows the isobars more closely. A simplified diagram of the general circulation pattern is shown in the illustration.

Air Masses

Because of large differences in the physical characteristics of the earth's surface, particularly the oceanic and continental contrasts, the air overlying these surfaces acquires differing values of temperature and moisture. The processes of radiation and convection in the lower portions of the troposphere act in differing characteristic manners for a number of well-defined regions of the earth. The air overlying these regions acquires characteristics common to the particular area.

Air masses are named according to their source regions. Four such regions are generally recognized: (1) *equatorial (E)*, the doldrum area between the north and south trades; (2) *tropical* (*T*), the trade-wind and lower temperate regions; (3) *polar* (*P*), the higher temperate latitudes; and (4) *arctic* or *antarctic* (*A*), the north or south polar regions of ice and snow. This classification is a general indication of relative temperature, as well as latitude origin. Air masses are further classified as maritime (*m*) or continental (*c*), depending on whether they form over water or over land. This classification is an indication of the relative moisture content of the air mass.

Fronts

As air masses move within the general circulation, they travel from their source regions and invade other areas dominated by air having different characteristics. Such a process leads to a zone of separation between the two air masses. The gradients of thermal and moisture properties are maximized in the zone.

Indicative of the differences in the motion of adjacent air masses, the front takes a wavelike character, hence the term *frontal wave*. Before formation of frontal waves, the isobars tend to run parallel to the fronts. As a wave is formed, the pattern is distorted somewhat, as shown in Part A of the diagram. In this illustration, colder air is north of warmer air. In this and the following illustrations, isobars are drawn at 4-millibar intervals.

The wave tends to travel in the direction of the general circulation, which in the temperate latitudes is usually in a general easterly and slightly poleward direction.

Along the leading edge of the wave, warmer air is replacing colder air. This is called the *warm front*. The trailing edge is the *cold front*, where colder air is underrunning and displacing warmer air.

The warm air, being less dense, tends to ride up over the colder air it is replacing. The slope is gentle. Partly because of the replacement of cold, dense air with warm, light air, the pressure decreases. Since the slope is gentle, the upper part of a warm frontal surface may be many hundreds of miles ahead of the surface portion. The decreasing pressure, indicated by a "falling barometer," is often an indication of the approach of such a wave. In a slow-moving, well-developed wave, the barometer may begin to fall several *days* before the wave arrives. Thus the amount and nature of the change of atmospheric pressure between observations is of assistance in predicting the approach of such a system.

The advancing cold air, being denser, tends to cut under the warmer

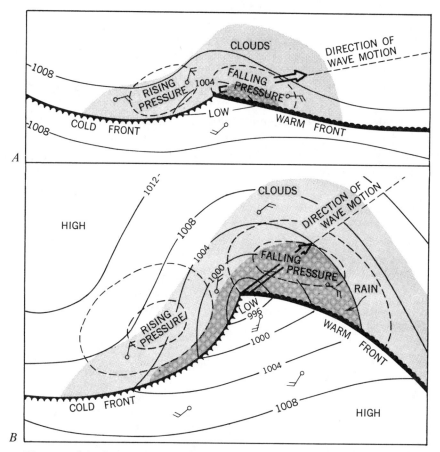

Diagram of the formation of a frontal wave (top view). A. First stage. B. A fully developed frontal wave.

air at the cold front, lifting it to greater heights. After a cold front has passed, the pressure increases—a "rising barometer."

In the first stages these effects are not marked, but as the wave continues to grow they become more pronounced, as shown in Part B of the diagram. As the amplitude of the wave increases, pressure near the center usually decreases and the "low" is said to "deepen." As it deepens, its forward speed generally decreases. The approach of a well-developed warm front is usually heralded not only by falling pressure but also by a more-or-less regular sequence of clouds. First, cirrus appear. These give way successively to cirrostratus, altostratus, alto-cumulus, and nimbostratus. Brief showers may precede the steady rain accompanying the nimbostratus.

As the warm front passes, the temperature rises, the wind shifts clockwise (in the northern hemisphere), and the steady rain stops.

Drizzle may fall from low-lying stratus clouds, or there may be fog for some time after the wind shift. During passage of the warm sector between the warm front and the cold front, there is little change in temperature or pressure. However, if the wave is still growing and the low deepening, the pressure might slowly decrease. In the warm sector the skies are generally clear or partly cloudy, with cumulus or strato-cumulus clouds most frequent. The warm air is usually moist, and haze or fog may often be present.

As the faster moving, steeper cold front passes, the wind shifts clockwise in the northern hemisphere (counterclockwise in the south-ern hemisphere), the temperature falls rapidly, and there are often brief and sometimes violent showers, frequently accompanied by thunder and lightning. Clouds are usually of the convective type. A cold front usually coincides with a well-defined wind-shift line (a line along which the wind shifts abruptly from southerly or southwesterly to northerly or northwesterly in the northern hemisphere). At sea a series of brief showers accompanied by strong, shifting winds may occur along or some distance (up to 200 miles) ahead of a cold front. These are called *squalls* (in common nautical use, the term "squall" may be addition-ally applied to any severe local storm accompanied by gusty winds, precipitation, thunder, and lightning), and the line along which they occur is called a *squall line*.

Because of its greater speed and steeper slope, which may approach or even exceed the vertical near the earth's surface (due to friction), a cold front and its associated weather passes more quickly than a warm front. After a cold front passes, the pressure rises, often quite rapidly, the visibility usually improves, and the clouds tend to diminish.

As the wave progresses and the cold front approaches the slower moving warm front, the low becomes deeper and the warm sector becomes smaller. This is shown in Part A of the next diagram.

Finally, the faster moving cold front overtakes the warm front, as shown in Part B, resulting in an *occluded front* at the surface, and an *upper front* aloft. When the two parts of the cold air mass meet, the warmer portion tends to rise above the colder part. The warm air con-tinues to rise until the entire frontal system dissipates. As the warmer air is replaced by colder air, the pressure gradually rises, a process called "filling." This usually occurs within a few days after an occluded front forms. Finally, a cold low, or simply a low-pressure system results across which little or no gradient in temperature and moisture can be found.

The sequence of weather associated with a low depends greatly on location with respect to the path of the center. The sequence described

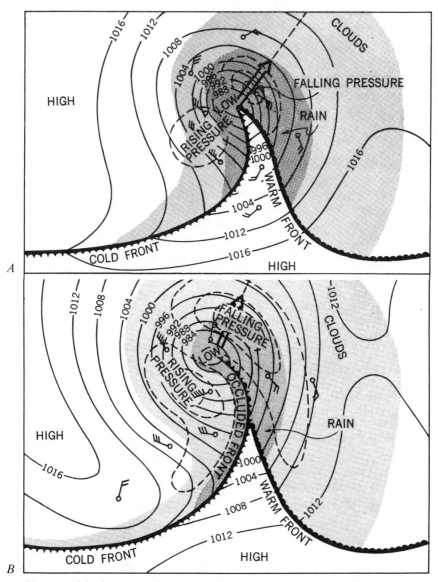

Diagram of the formation of an occluded front (top view). A. *A frontal wave nearing occlusion.* B. *An occluded front.*

above assumes that the observer is so located that he encounters each part of the system. If he is poleward of the path of the center of the low, the abrupt weather changes associated with the passage of fronts are not experienced. Instead the change from the weather characteristically found ahead of a warm front to that behind a cold front takes place gradually, the exact sequence being dictated somewhat by distance from the center, as well as by severity and age of the low.

Although each low generally follows the pattern given above, no two are ever exactly alike. Other centers of low pressure and high pressure and the air masses associated with them, even though they may be 1000 miles or more away, influence the formation and motion of individual low centers and their accompanying weather. Particularly, a high stalls or diverts a low.

Cyclones and Anticyclones

An area of relatively low pressure, generally circular, is called a *cyclone* Its counterpart for high pressure is called an *anticyclone*. These terms are used particularly in connection with the winds associated with such centers. Wind tends to blow from an area of high pressure to one of low pressure, but due to rotation of the earth, they are deflected toward the right in the northern hemisphere and toward the left in the southern hemisphere.

Because of the rotation of the earth, the circulation tends to be counterclockwise around areas of low pressure and clockwise around areas of high pressure in the northern hemisphere, the speed being proportional to the spacing of isobars. (In the southern hemisphere, the direction of circulation is reversed.) Based on this condition, a general rule (Buys-Ballot Law) can be stated thus:

If an observer in the northern hemisphere faces the surface wind, the center of low pressure is toward his right, somewhat beh nd him; and the center of high pressure is toward his left and somewhat in front of him.

If an observer in the southern hemisphere faces the surface wind, the center of low pressure is toward his left and somewhat behind him; and the center of high pressure is toward his right and somewhat in front of him.

In a general way, these relationships apply in the case of temporary local systems. The reason for the wind shift along a front is that the isobars have an abrupt change of direction. Since the direction of wind is directly related to the direction of the isobars, any change in the latter results in a shift in the wind direction.

In the northern hemisphere, the wind shifts toward the right (clockwise or veering) when either a warm or cold front passes. In the southern hemisphere, the shift is toward the left (counterclockwise or backing). When an observer is on the poleward side of the path of a frontal wave, wind shifts are reversed (i.e., backing in the northern hemisphere and veering in the southern hemisphere).

In an anticyclone, successive isobars are relatively far apart, resulting in light winds. In a cyclone, the isobars are more closely spaced and the winds are stronger. Since an anticyclonic area is a region of outflowing winds, air is drawn into it from aloft. Descending air is warmed, and as air becomes warmer, its capacity for holding uncondensed moisture increases. Therefore clouds tend to dissipate. Clear skies are characteristic of an anticyclone, although scattered clouds and showers are sometimes encountered.

In contrast, a cyclonic area is one of converging winds. The upward movement of air results in cooling, a condition favorable to the formation of clouds and precipitation. More or less continuous rain and generally stormy weather are usually associated with a cyclone.

Local Winds

In addition to the winds of the general circulation and those associated with migratory cyclones and anticyclones, there are numerous local winds that influence the weather in various places.

The most common of these are the *land* and *sea breezes,* caused by alternate heating and cooling of land adjacent to water. The effect is on a small scale and for short periods. By day the land is warmer than the water and by night it is cooler. This effect occurs along many coasts during the summer. Between about 0900 and 1100 the temperature of the land becomes greater than that of adjacent water. The lower levels of air over the land are warmed and the air rises, drawing in cooler air from the sea. This is the *sea breeze.* Late in the afternoon, when the sun is low in the sky, the temperature of the two surfaces equalizes and the breeze stops. After sunset, as the land cools below the sea temperature, the air above it is also cooled. The contracting cool air becomes denser, increasing the pressure near the surface. This results in an outflow of winds to the sea. This is the *land breeze,* which blows during the night and dies away near sunrise. Since the atmospheric pressure changes associated with this cycle are not great, the accompanying winds do not exceed gentle to moderate breezes. The circulation is usually of limited extent, reaching a distance of perhaps 20 miles inland and not more than 5 or 6 miles offshore, and to a height of a few hundred feet.

Varying conditions of topography produce a large variety of local winds. Winds tend to follow valleys, and to be deflected from high banks and shores. In mountain areas, wind flows in response to temperature distribution and gravity. An *anabatic wind* is one that blows up an incline, usually as a result of surface heating. A *katabatic wind* is one that blows down an incline.

A dry wind with a downward component, warm for the season, is called a *foehn*. The foehn occurs when horizontally moving air encounters a mountain barrier. As it blows upward to clear the barrier, it is cooled below the dew point, resulting in loss of moisture by cloud formation and perhaps rain. As the air continues to rise, its rate of cooling is reduced because condensing water vapor gives off heat to the surrounding atmosphere. After crossing the mountain barrier, the air flows downward along the leeward slope, being warmed by compression as it descends to lower levels. Thus, since it loses less heat on the ascent than it gains during the descent, and since it loses moisture during ascent, it arrives at the bottom of the mountains as very warm, dry air. It may occur at any season of the year, at any hour of the day or night, and have speed from a gentle breeze to a gale. It may last for several days or for a very short period. Its effect is most marked in winter, when it may cause the temperature to rise as much as 20°F to 30°F within 15 minutes, and cause snow and ice to melt within a few hours. On the West Coast of the United States, a foehn wind, given the name Santa Ana, blows through a pass and down a valley by that name in southern California. This wind may blow with such a force that it endangers small craft immediately off the coast.

A cold wind blowing down an incline is called a *fall wind*. Although it is warmed somewhat during descent, as is the foehn, it remains cold relative to the surrounding air. It occurs when cold air is dammed up in great quantity on the windward side of a mountain and then spills over suddenly, usually as an overwhelming surge down the other side. It is usually quite violent, sometimes reaching hurricane force.

"Local" winds have distinctive names, but only a few are important to you. A *blizzard* is a violent, intensely cold wind laden with snow (and you might ask yourself, "What am I doing out in *snow?*"). A *gust* is a sudden, brief increase in wind speed, followed by a slackening, or the violent wind or squall that accompanies a thunderstorm. A *cat's paw* is a puff of wind or a light breeze that affects a small area, causing patches of ripples on the surface of the water.

Fog

Fog is a cloud whose base is low enough to restrict visibility. (*Bowditch* means that the cloud is down on the water and you can't see the bow of your boat, let alone that buoy you're looking for.) Fog is composed of droplets of water or ice crystals that are formed by condensation or crystallization of water vapor in the air.

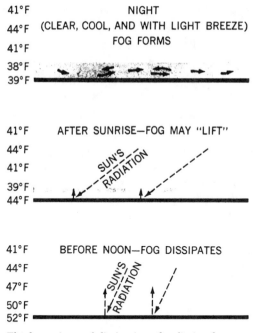

41°F	NIGHT
44°F	(CLEAR, COOL, AND WITH LIGHT BREEZE)
41°F	FOG FORMS
38°F	
39°F	

41°F	AFTER SUNRISE—FOG MAY "LIFT"
44°F	
41°F	SUN'S RADIATION
39°F	
44°F	

41°F	BEFORE NOON—FOG DISSIPATES
44°F	
47°F	SUN'S RADIATION
50°F	
52°F	

The formation and dissipation of radiation fog.

Radiation fog forms over low-lying land on clear, calm nights. As the land radiates heat and becomes cooler, it cools the air immediately above the surface. If the air is cooled to its dew point, fog forms. Often, cooler and denser air drains down surrounding slopes to heighten the effect. Radiation fog is often quite shallow, and is usually densest at the surface. After sunrise the fog may "lift" and gradually dissipate, usually being entirely gone by noon. At sea the temperature of the water undergoes little change between day and night and so radiation fog is seldom encountered more than 10 miles from shore.

Farther offshore you may encounter *advection* fog, which forms when warm, moist air blows over a colder surface and is cooled below its dew point. This type may be quite dense and often persists over relatively long periods. Advection fog is common over cold ocean currents. If the wind is strong enough to thoroughly mix the air, condensation may take place at some distance above the surface of the earth, forming low stratus clouds rather than fog. Off the coast of California, seasonal winds create an offshore current that displaces the warm surface water, causing an upwelling of colder water. Moist Pacific air is transported along the coast in the same wind system and is cooled by the relatively cold water. Advection fog results.

When very cold air moves over warmer water, wisps of visible water vapor may rise from the surface as the water "steams." In extreme cases this *frost smoke,* or *arctic sea smoke,* may rise to a height of several hundred feet, the portion near the surface constituting a dense fog that obscures the horizon and surface objects, but usually leaves the sky relatively clear.

Haze consists of fine dust or salt particles in the air, too small to be individually apparent but in sufficient number to reduce visibility and cast a bluish or yellowish veil over the landscape, subduing its colors and making objects appear indistinct. This is sometimes called *dry haze* to distinguish it from *damp haze,* which consists of small water droplets or moist particles in the air, smaller and more scattered than light fog.

Mist is synonymous with *drizzle* in the United States, and a mixture of smoke and fog is called *smog.*

Sky Coloring

White light is composed of light of all colors. Color is related to wavelength and the characteristics of each color are related to its wavelength. Thus the shorter the wavelength, the greater the amount of bending when light is refracted. This principle permits the separation of light from celestial bodies into a spectrum that ranges from red, through orange, yellow, green, and blue, to violet.

Light from the sun and moon is white, containing all colors. As it enters the earth's atmosphere, a certain amount of it is scattered. The blue and violet, being of shorter wavelength than other colors, are scattered most. Most of the violet light is absorbed in the atmosphere. Thus the scattered blue light is most apparent, and the sky looks blue. When the sunis near the horizon, its light passes through more of the atmosphere than when it is higher in the sky, resulting in greater scattering and absorption of blue and green light, so that a larger percentage of the red and orange light penetrates to the observer. For this reason the sun and moon appear redder at this time, and when this light falls on clouds they appear colored. This accounts for the colors at sunset and sunrise. As the setting sun approaches the horizon, the sunset colors first appear as faint tints of yellow and orange. As the sun continues to set, the colors deepen. Contrasts occur, due principally to differences in the height of clouds. As the sun sets the clouds become a deeper red, first the lower clouds and then the higher ones, and finally they fade to a gray.

You've heard it before, and you'll hear it again—but don't bet your boat on it: *"Red sky at night, sailor's delight;/ red sky in morning, sailor take warning."*

A green or blue moon is most likely to occur when the sun is slightly below the horizon and the longer wavelength light from the sun is absorbed, resulting in green or blue light on the atmosphere in front of the moon. The effect is most apparent if the moon is on the same side of the sky as the sun.

Rainbows

The familiar arc of concentric colored bands seen when the sun shines on rain, mist, or spray is caused by refraction, internal reflection, and diffraction of sunlight by the drops of water. A rainbow's colors are visible because of the difference in the amount of refraction of the different colors making up white light, the light being spread out to form a spectrum. Red is on the outer side and blue and violet on the inner side, with orange, yellow, and green in between, in that order from red. But no matter: rainbows are beautiful, and always welcome; a rainbow is guaranteed to lift your spirits after a rough day—and there's always the chance of a pot of gold (or a snug anchorage) at the other end.

The Corona

When the sun or moon is seen through altostratus clouds, its outline is indistinct and it appears surrounded by a glow of light called a *corona*. This is somewhat similar in appearance to the corona seen around the sun during a solar eclipse. When the effect is due to clouds, the glow may be accompanied by one or more rainbow-colored rings of small radii, with the celestial body at the center. A corona is caused by diffraction of light by tiny droplets of water. The radius of a corona is inversely proportional to the size of the water droplets. A large corona indicates small droplets. If a corona decreases in size, the water droplets are becoming larger and the air more humid. A corona, like a rainbow, may be a beautiful thing—but it's likely to mean that it's time to dig out your foul-weather gear since a rainstorm is coming your way.

Atmospheric Electricity

Most spectacular, of course, is atmospheric electricity—violent charges of electrical energy that crack and boom, flash and flicker, and make you wonder if spelunking isn't *really* the right sport for you.

Let's look at lightning first. *Lightning* is the discharge of electricity from one part of a thundercloud to another, or between such a cloud and the earth or a terrestrial object. Enormous electrical stresses build up within thunderclouds, and between such clouds and the earth. At some point the resistance of the intervening air is overcome. At first the process is a progressive one, probably starting as a *brush discharge* (St. Elmo's fire). The breakdown follows an irregular path along the line of least resistance. A hundred or more individual discharges may be necessary to complete the path between points of opposite polarity. When this "leader stroke" reaches its destination, a heavy "main stroke" immediately follows in the opposite direction. This main stroke is the visible lightning. And it's at this point that you start hoping your mast isn't the tallest mast in the harbor.

You *see* the flashes, but you *listen* to the thunder—the noise that accompanies lightning. Thunder is caused by the heating and ionizing of the air by lightning. This results in rapid expansion of the air along its path and the sending out of a compression wave. Thunder may be heard at a distance of as much as 15 miles. The elapsed time between the flash of lightning and reception of the accompanying sound of thunder is an indication of the distance, because of the difference in travel time of light and sound. Since the former is comparatively instantaneous and the speed of sound is about 1117 feet per second, the approximate distance in nautical miles is equal to the elapsed time in seconds, divided by 5.5. If the thunder accompanying lightning cannot be heard due to its distance, the lightning is called *heat lightning,* a phenomenon not unusual during "hot spells" and on quiet, sultry summer nights.

Waterspouts

A waterspout is a small, whirling storm over the ocean or inland waters. Its chief characteristic is a funnel-shaped cloud; when fully developed it extends from the surface of the water to the base of a cumulus-type cloud. The water in a spout is mostly confined to its lower portion. The air in waterspouts may rotate clockwise or counter-clockwise, depending on the manner of formation. Waterspouts are not common in higher latitudes. Many waterspouts are no stronger than dust whirlwinds, which they resemble; at other times they are strong enough to destroy small craft.

TROPICAL CYCLONES

Cyclone Classes

"Tropical cyclones" come in all shapes and sizes, but they have these things in common: they are nasty, ill-tempered, and can be destructive; they are born in the tropics or subtropics; and they are universally unloved—the unlucky mariner who has met one has no desire to meet another.

Bowditch puts it this way: "Because of their fury, and the fact that they are predominantly oceanic, they merit the special attention of all mariners, whether professional or amateur."

On his second voyage to the New World, Columbus encountered a severe tropical storm. Although his vessels suffered no damage, this experience proved valuable during his fourth voyage when his vessels were threatened by a fully developed hurricane. Columbus read the signs of an approaching storm from the appearance of a southeasterly swell, the direction of the high cirrus clouds, and the hazy appearance of the atmosphere. He directed his vessels to shelter. The commander of another group, who did not heed the signs, lost most of his ships and more than 500 of his men.

Tropical cyclones are classified by form and intensity. In successive stages of instensification, the tropical cyclone may be classified as a tropical disturbance, tropical depression, tropical storm, and hurricane or typhoon:

A *tropical disturbance* is generally 100–300 miles in diameter, has a nonfrontal migratory character, and maintains its identity for 24 hours or more. It has no strong winds and no closed isobars, i.e., isobars that completely enclose the low.

Tropical depressions have one or more closed isobars and some rotary circulation at the surface. The highest sustained (1-minute mean) surface wind speed is 33 knots.

Tropical storms have closed isobars and a distinct rotary circulation. The highest sustained (1-minute mean) surface wind speed is 34–63 knots.

A *hurricane* or a *typhoon* has closed isobars, a strong and very pronounced rotary circulation, and a sustained (1-minute mean) surface wind speed of 64 knots or higher.

Tropical cyclones occur almost entirely in six global areas, four of them in the northern hemisphere. Two of these may affect you if your cruising areas are on the southern West Coast, Hawaii, or the Gulf and East Coasts of the continental United States.

Tropical cyclones have different names in different places. Along the west coast of Mexico (or in the Atlantic) you would call this mighty monster of storms a "hurricane," but if you were sailing off Guam the same storm would be a "typhoon."

The author survived—yes, that's the right word—a typhoon aboard a destroyer off the Philippines in 1944. Possibly because he was 20 years old, and probably because 1944 is a long time ago, he doesn't recall being scared, although the ship had lost all electrical power and had to be steered by brute strength for most of a long day. However, he does recall the message that flashed through Task Force 38 that day: "Watch the *Wedderburn*." This, presumably, meant: ". . . so you can wave good-bye when she goes under."

In the North Atlantic or eastern North Pacific, a tropical cyclone with winds of 64 knots or greater is called a hurricane. That 64 knots— that's the key. And *that's* a lot of wind.

North Atlantic tropical cyclones can affect the entire North Atlantic Ocean in any month, but they are mostly a threat south of about 35°N from June through November; August, September, and October are the months of highest incidence. About nine or ten tropical cyclones (tropical storms and hurricanes) form each season; five or six reach hurricane intensity (winds of 64 knots and higher). A few hurricanes have generated winds estimated as high as 200 knots. Early- and late-season storms usually develop west of 50°W; during August and September, this spawning ground extends to the Cape Verde Islands. These storms usually move westward or west-northwestward at speeds of less than 15 knots in the lower latitudes. After moving into the northern Caribbean or Greater Antilles regions, they will usually either move toward the Gulf of Mexico or recurve and accelerate in the North Atlantic. Some will recurve after reaching the Gulf of Mexico, while others will continue westward to landfall.

The *Eastern North Pacific* hurricane season is from June through October, although a storm can form in any month. An average of fifteen tropical cyclones (tropical storms and hurricanes) forms each year with about six reaching hurricane strength. The most intense storms are often the early- and late-season ones; these form close to the coast

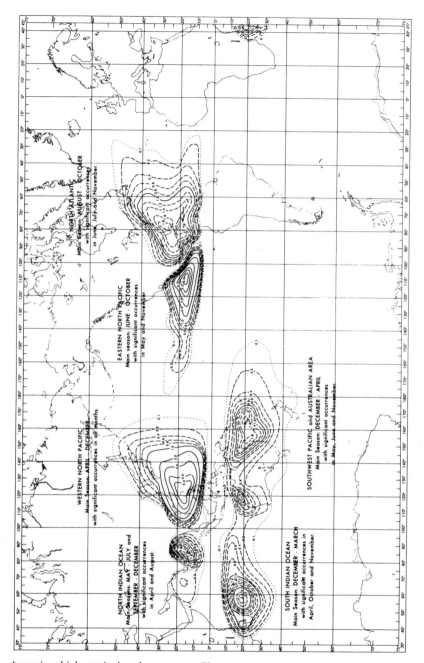

Areas in which tropical cyclones occur. The average number of tropical cyclones per 5° square has been analyzed for this drawing. The main season for intense tropical storms is shown for each major basin.

and far south. Midseason storms form anywhere in a wide band from the Mexican–Central American coast to the Hawaiian Islands. August and September are the months of highest incidence. These storms differ from their North Atlantic counterparts in that they are usually smaller in size. However, they can be just as intense.

Portrait of a Hurricane

In the early life of a hurricane, the spiral covers an area averaging 100 miles in diameter with winds of 64 knots or greater, and spreads gale-force winds over a 400-mile diameter. The cyclonic spiral is marked by heavy cloud bands from which torrential rains fall, separated by areas of light rain or no rain at all. These spiral bands ascend in decks of cumulus and cumulonimbus clouds to the limit of cloud formation, where condensing water vapor is swept off as ice-crystal wisps of cirrus clouds. Thunderstorm electrical flashes light the sky, both as lightning and as tiny electrostatic discharges.

In the lower few thousand feet, air flows in through the cyclone and is drawn upward through ascending columns of air near the center. The size and intensity decrease with altitude, the cyclonic circulation being gradually replaced above 40,000 feet by an anticyclonic circulation centered hundreds of miles away—the enormous high-altitude pump that is the exhaust system of the hurricane heat engine.

At lower levels, where the hurricane is more intense, winds on the rim of the storm follow a wide pattern, like the slower currents around the edge of a whirlpool; and like those currents, these winds accelerate as they approach the center of the vortex. The outer band has light winds at the rim of the storm, perhaps no more than 25 knots; within 30 miles of the center, winds may have velocities exceeding 130 knots. The inner band is the region of maximum wind velocity, where the storm's worst winds are felt and where ascending air is chimneyed upward, releasing heat to drive the storm. In most hurricanes these winds reach 85 knots, and more than 170 knots in the more memorable ones.

In the hurricane, winds flow toward the low pressure in the warm, comparatively calm core. There, converging air is whirled upward by convection, the mechanical thrusting of other converging air, and the pumping action of high-altitude circulations. This spiral is marked by the thick cloud walls curling inward toward the storm center, releasing heavy precipitation and enormous quantities of heat energy. At the

Satellite photograph of a hurricane. Note the clear eye.

center, surrounded by a band in which this strong vertical circulation is greatest, is the eye of the hurricane.

The eye, like the spiral rainbands, is unique to the hurricane—no other atmospheric phenomenon has this calm core. On the average, the diameter of the eye is about 14 miles, although diameters of 25 miles are not unusual. From the heated tower of maximum winds and cumulonimbus clouds, winds diminish rapidly to something less than 15 miles per hour in the eye; at the opposite wall, winds increase again, but come from the opposite direction because of the cyclonic circulation of the storm. This transformation of storm into comparative calm and then calm into violence from another quarter is spectacular. The eye's abrupt existence in the midst of opaque rain squalls and hurricane winds, the intermittent bursts of blue sky and sunlight through light clouds in the core of the cyclone, and the galleried cumulus and cumulonimbus clouds are unforgettable.

That is how an average hurricane is structured. But every hurricane is an individual, and the more or less orderly circulation described here omits the extreme variability and instability within the storm system. Pressure and temperature fluctuate wildly across the storm as the hurricane maintains its erratic life in the face of forces that will ultimately destroy it. If it is an August storm, its average life expectancy is 12 days; if a July or November storm, it lives an average of 8 days.

During those 8–12 days you may pray that the hurricane goes someplace else—Mexico, Cuba, even Panama, just as long as it's not to *your* cruising area. There really isn't anything else you can do while the navy, National Oceanic and Atmospheric Administration, and air force track the storm—except to watch or listen to the evening news and check your boat insurance policy.

Bowditch has a few more cogent words to say about hurricanes:

The safest procedure with respect to tropical cyclones is to avoid them.

Old Salt couldn't have said it better.

WEATHER FORECASTING

There's more to the art of forecasting the weather than reciting "Red sky at night . . ." or wetting your finger and holding it above your head. The prediction of weather at some future time is based on an understanding of weather processes and observations of present conditions. You will soon learn that when there is a certain sequence of cloud types, rain usually can be expected to follow within a certain period. If the sky is cloudless, more heat will be received from the sun by day and more heat will be radiated outward from the warm earth by night than if the sky is overcast. If the wind is in such a direction that warm, moist air will be transported over a colder surface, fog can be expected. A falling barometer indicates the approach of a "low," probably accompanied by stormy weather. Thus before meteorology passed from an "art" to a "science," many individuals learned to interpret certain atmospheric phenomena in terms of future weather, and to make reasonably accurate forecasts for short periods into the future. And you can do it too—especially for the *near* future and for *local* conditions. For long-range predictions and the "big picture," turn to the experts.

Continuous and accurate weather information first become available when the first observation stations were established. As such observations expanded, and as communications facilities improved, knowledge of simultaneous conditions over wider areas became available. This made possible the collection of these "synoptic" reports at forecast centers. Individual observations are made at government-operated stations on shore and aboard vessels at sea. Symbols and numbers are used to indicate on a *synoptic chart*—popularly called a *weather map*—the conditions at each observation station. Isobars are drawn through lines of equal atmospheric pressure, fronts are located and symbolically marked, areas of precipitation and fog are indicated, temperatures are noted, and the professionals decide whether it's "fair" or "foul" out there. More important, though, their input forms a picture

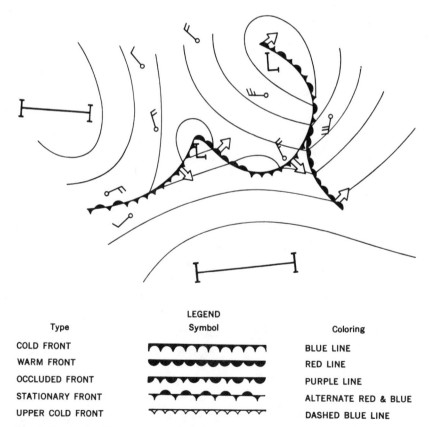

LEGEND		
Type	Symbol	Coloring
COLD FRONT		BLUE LINE
WARM FRONT		RED LINE
OCCLUDED FRONT		PURPLE LINE
STATIONARY FRONT		ALTERNATE RED & BLUE
UPPER COLD FRONT		DASHED BLUE LINE

The designations of fronts on weather maps.

that will tell other forecasters—and you—whether it's going to be fair or foul in *your* area.

Ordinarily, weather maps for surface observations are prepared every 6 (sometimes 3) hours. In addition, synoptic charts for selected heights are prepared every 12 (sometimes 6) hours. Knowledge of conditions aloft is of value in establishing the three-dimensional structure and motion of the atmosphere as input to the forecast.

Highly sophisticated computers have been developed to analyze and prognosticate weather patterns. The civil and military weather centers prepare and disseminate vast numbers of weather charts (analyses and prognoses) daily to assist local forecasters in their efforts to provide accurate, predicted weather parameters. The accuracy of a forecast decreases with the length of the forecast period. Long-term forecasts for two weeks or a month in advance are limited to "general statements" (another *Bowditch* understatement if you've ever read one)!

The factors that determine weather are numerous and varied. Ever-increasing knowledge regarding them makes possible a continually improving weather service. However, your ability to forecast the weather in *your* future will come only from observation and practice. It is sometimes as important to know the various types of weather that *might* be experienced as it is to know which of several possibilities is *most likely* to occur. You might keep in mind that you're "out there" because you chose to be, and it's always best to know your friend from your adversary; *you're going to have weather*—whether or not.

THE WIND AS A FORCE

Let's consider briefly the wind as a "force"—a force of incredible and frightening power, a force that can build giant combers on open water or whip a placid harbor into a maelstrom. The wind in its ultimate fury can overpower many small vessels, blowing out sails and making otherwise powerful engines seem like toys.

The following isn't meant to scare you off the water, but there are some lessons here. This fragment has been taken directly from *Lady Brett*'s log—August 11, 1980 (Great Salt Pond, Block Island, Rhode Island):

> Hot ashore when we went in for ice, but a pleasant SW breeze on the water. Ashore for lobster at Dead Eye Dick's at 1900. *Very* calm at sundown.
> Then, fun and games in Great Salt Pond when a screaming squall hit at

0200. *Brett* riding well, and holding (on a 22-pound Danforth) until a two-boat raft dragged down on our starboard bow. Waves *off* the beach! Wind (reported later) 60 knots. Fended the raft off twice, second time from port bow. Turned on motor to swing wide of them and realized *we* were now dragging. "M" crawled forward to check anchor rode. Came aft and calmly reported:

"There's an anchor on our bow."

"There's a *what?!*"

"There's a plow anchor hooked on our bow."

"Jesus. . . !"

Turned off engine; worried about wrapping our anchor line in the prop. Dragging in pitch darkness N across ferry channel. Impossible to face wind and spray. Then realized we were holding—the Danforth had dug in again.

A big plow was indeed on our bow, hooked over our rode, the shank under *Brett*'s stem at the chock and the chain and line running aft under our hull. We were trailing the two-boat raft that had attacked us twice before, the three of us just upwind of a dozen anchored boats. Raft on *very short scope*. Cast them off when the wind moderated at 0230. Back to bed at 0430.

That was a Force 11 summer squall—brief but devastating in its fury, and all the more dangerous because it hit a sleeping fleet in a crowded harbor. A number of boats were damaged that night, and

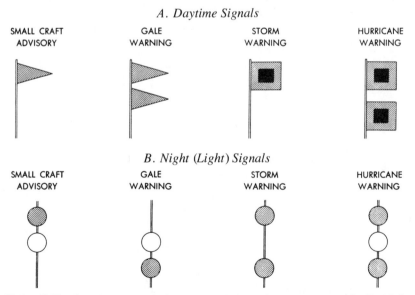

National Weather Service coastal warning displays. A. Daytime signals. B. Night (light) signals. The shaded area represents the color red on flags and lights.

BEAUFORT WIND SCALE
WITH CORRESPONDING SEA STATE CODES

Beaufort number or force	Wind speed				World Meteorological Organization (1964)	Effects observed far from land	Effects observed near coast	Effects observed on land	Sea State	Code
	knots	mph	meters per second	km per hour					Term and height of waves, in meters	
0	under 1	under 1	0.0–0.2	under 1	Calm	Sea like mirror.	Calm.	Calm; smoke rises vertically.	Calm, glassy, 0	0
1	1–3	1–3	0.3–1.5	1–5	Light air	Ripples with appearance of scales; no foam crests.	Fishing smack just has steerage way.	Smoke drift indicates wind direction; vanes do not move.	Calm, rippled, 0–0.1	1
2	4–6	4–7	1.6–3.3	6–11	Light breeze	Small wavelets; crests of glassy appearance, not breaking.	Wind fills the sails of smacks which then travel at about 1–2 miles per hour.	Wind felt on face; leaves rustle; vanes begin to move.	Smooth, wavelets, 0.1–0.5	2
3	7–10	8–12	3.4–5.4	12–19	Gentle breeze	Large wavelets; crests begin to break; scattered whitecaps.	Smacks begin to careen and travel about 3–4 miles per hour.	Leaves, small twigs in constant motion; light flags extended.	Slight, 0.5–1.25	3
4	11–16	13–18	5.5–7.9	20–28	Moderate breeze	Small waves, becoming longer; numerous whitecaps.	Good working breeze, smacks carry all canvas with good list.	Dust, leaves, and loose paper raised up; small branches move.	Moderate, 1.25–2.5	4
5	17–21	19–24	8.0–10.7	29–38	Fresh breeze	Moderate waves, taking longer form; many whitecaps; some spray.	Smacks shorten sail.	Small trees in leaf begin to sway.	Rough, 2.5–4	5
6	22–27	25–31	10.8–13.8	39–49	Strong breeze	Larger waves forming; whitecaps everywhere; more spray.	Smacks have doubled reef in mainsail; care required when fishing.	Larger branches of trees in motion; whistling heard in wires.	Very rough, 4–6	6
7	28–33	32–38	13.9–17.1	50–61	Near gale	Sea heaps up; white foam from breaking waves begins to be blown in streaks.	Smacks remain in harbor and those at sea lie-to.	Whole trees in motion; resistance felt in walking against wind.		
8	34–40	39–46	17.2–20.7	62–74	Gale	Moderately high waves of greater length; edges of crests begin to break into spindrift; foam is blown in well-marked streaks.	All smacks make for harbor, if near.	Twigs and small branches broken off trees; progress generally impeded.		
9	41–47	47–54	20.8–24.4	75–88	Strong gale	High waves; sea begins to roll; dense streaks of foam; spray may reduce visibility.		Slight structural damage occurs; slate blown from roofs.		
10	48–55	55–63	24.5–28.4	89–102	Storm	Very high waves with overhanging crests; sea takes white appearance as foam is blown in very dense streaks; rolling is heavy and visibility reduced.		Seldom experienced on land; trees broken or uprooted; considerable structural damage occurs.	High, 6–9	7
11	56–63	64–72	28.5–32.6	103–117	Violent storm	Exceptionally high waves; sea covered with white foam patches; visibility still more reduced.		Very rarely experienced on land; usually accompanied by widespread damage.	Very high, 9–14	8
12	64 and over	73 and over	32.7 and over	118 and over	Hurricane	Air filled with foam; sea completely white with driving spray; visibility greatly reduced.			Phenomenal, over 14	9

Note: Since January 1, 1955, weather map symbols have been based upon wind speed in knots, at five-knot intervals, rather than upon Beaufort number.

The complete Beaufort Wind Scale.

many dinghies were lost. More boats dragged early the next morning when the wind came up again, but it never seems as bad in bright sunshine. Need we add that none of the above was written *during* the squall?

Force 11 is a wind of 56–63 knots (64–72 M.P.H.) on the Beaufort Wind Scale, just under hurricane force. The chart shows the Beaufort scale from 0 to 12, with the state of the sea at each level.

10

Reading the Clouds

The sky above us is rarely totally empty. The sun is usually up there someplace, or if it has dropped below the horizon it has been replaced by the moon or stars. And there is usually a cloud or two, if no more than a few cotton-ball clouds above the distant shore or a smudge just above the horizon.

Bowditch tells us that "Clouds are visible assemblages of numerous tiny droplets of water, or ice crystals, formed by condensation of water vapor in the air, with the bases of the assemblages above the surface of the earth. . . . Fog is a similar assemblage in contact with the surface of the earth."

That's one way of putting it. It's more important to know that the shape, size, thickness, and nature of clouds depend on the weather conditions that form them. Clouds are indicators of various processes occurring in the atmosphere. The ability to "read the clouds" and recognize different types, and a knowledge of the conditions under which they have formed are useful in predicting future weather.

Although the variety of clouds is virtually endless, they may be classified according to general type. Clouds are grouped generally into three "families" according to some common characteristic. *High clouds* are those having a mean lower level above 20,000 feet. They are composed principally of ice crystals. *Middle clouds* have a mean level between 6500 and 20,000 feet. They are composed largely of water droplets, although the higher ones have a tendency toward ice particles. *Low clouds* have a mean lower level of less than 6500 feet. These clouds are composed entirely of water droplets.

Within these three families are ten principal cloud types. The names of these are composed of various combinations and forms of the following basic words, all from Latin:

cirrus, meaning "curl, lock, or tuft of hair."
cumulus, meaning "heap, a pile, an accumulation."
stratus, meaning "spread out, flatten, cover with a layer."
alto, meaning "high, upper air."
nimbus, meaning "rainy cloud."

Individual cloud types have variations or combinations of these. The ten principal cloud types are:

HIGH CLOUDS

Cirrus (Ci) are detached high clouds of delicate and fibrous appearance, without shading, generally white in color, and often of a silky appearance. Their fibrous and feathery appearance is due to the fact that they are composed entirely of ice crystals. Cirrus appear in varied forms such as isolated tufts; long, thin lines across the sky; branching, featherlike plumes; and curved wisps which may end in tufts. These clouds may be arranged in parallel bands which cross the sky in great circles and appear to converge toward a point on the horizon. This may indicate, in a general way, the direction of a low-pressure area. Cirrus may be brilliantly colored at sunrise and sunset. Because of their height, they become illuminated before other clouds in the morning and remain lighted after others at sunset. Cirrus are generally associated with fair weather, but if they are followed by lower and thicker clouds, they are often the forerunner of rain or snow.

Cirrus.

Cirrocumulus (Cc) are high clouds composed of small white flakes or scales, or of very small globular masses, usually without shadows and arranged in groups or lines, or more often in ripples resembling those of sand on the seashore. One form of cirrocumulus is popularly known as "mackerel sky" because the pattern resembles the scales on the back of a mackerel. Like cirrus, cirrocumulus are composed of ice crystals and are generally associated with fair weather, but may precede a storm if they thicken and lower. They may turn gray and appear hard before thickening.

Cirrocumulus.

Cirrostratus (Cs) are thin, whitish, high clouds sometimes covering the sky completely and giving it a milky appearance, and at other times presenting, more or less distinctly, a formation like a tangled web. The thin veil is not sufficiently dense to blur the outline of sun or moon. However, the ice crystals of which the cloud is composed refract the light passing through in such a way that halos may form with the sun or moon at the center. The illustration shows cirrus thickening and changing into cirrostratus. In this form it is popularly known as "mares' tails." If it continues to thicken and lower, the ice crystals melting to

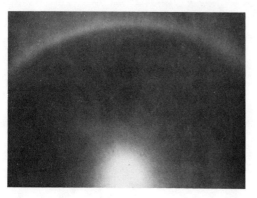

Cirrostratus.

form water droplets, the cloud formation is known as altostratus. When this occurs, rain may normally be expected within 24 hours. The more brushlike the cirrus when the sky appears, as in this illustration, the stronger the wind at the level of the cloud.

MIDDLE CLOUDS

Altocumulus (Ac) are middle clouds consisting of a layer of large, ball-like masses that tend to merge together. The balls or patches may vary in thickness and color from dazzling white to dark gray, but they are more or less regularly arranged. They may appear as distinct patches, as shown, and are similar to cirrocumulus. They can be distinguished by the fact that individual patches are generally larger, and show distinct shadows in some places. They are sometimes mistaken for stratocumulus. If this form thickens and lowers, it may produce thundery weather and showers, but it does not bring prolonged bad

Altocumulus in patches.

Altocumulus in bands.

Turreted altocumulus.

weather. Sometimes the patches merge to form a series of big rolls that resemble ocean waves, but with streaks of blue sky. Because of perspective, the rolls appear to run together near the horizon. These regular parallel bands differ from cirrocumulus in that they occur in larger masses with shadows. These clouds move in the direction of the short dimension of the rolls, as do ocean waves. Sometimes altocumulus appear briefly in the form shown here, usually before a thunderstorm. They are generally arranged in a line with a flat horizontal base, giving the impression of turrets on a castle. The turreted tops may look like miniature cumulus and possess considerable depth and great length. These clouds usually indicate a change to chaotic, thundery skies.

Altostratus.

Altostratus (As) are middle clouds having the appearance of a grayish or bluish, fibrous veil or sheet. The sun or moon, when seen through these clouds, appears as if it were shining through ground glass, with a corona around it. Halos are not formed. If these clouds thicken and lower, or if low and ragged "scud" or rain clouds (nimbostratus) form below them, continuous rain or snow may be expected within a few hours.

Low Clouds

Stratocumulus (Sc) are low clouds composed of soft, gray, roll-shaped masses. They may be shaped in long, parallel rolls similar to altocumulus, moving forward with the wind. The motion is in the direction of their short dimension, like ocean waves. These clouds, which vary greatly in altitude, are the final product of the characteristic daily change that takes place in cumulus clouds. They are usually followed by clear skies during the night.

Stratus (St) is a low cloud in a uniform layer resembling fog. Often the base is not more than 1000 feet high. A veil of thin stratus gives the sky a hazy appearance. Stratus is often quite thick, permitting so little sunlight to penetrate that it appears dark to an observer below it. From above it looks white. Light mist may descend from stratus. Strong wind sometimes breaks stratus into shreds called "fractostratus."

Stratocumulus.

Stratus.

Nimbostratus (Ns) is a low, dark, shapeless cloud layer, usually nearly uniform, but sometimes with ragged, wet-looking bases. Nimbostratus is the typical rain cloud. The precipitation which falls from this cloud is steady or intermittent, but not showery.

Cumulus (Cu) are dense clouds with vertical development (clouds formed by rising air that is cooled as it reaches greater heights). They have a horizontal base and dome-shaped upper surface, with protuberances extending above the dome. Cumulus appear in small patches, and never cover the entire sky. When the vertical development is not great, the clouds appear in patches resembling tufts of cotton or wool, being popularly called "woolpack" clouds. The horizontal bases of such clouds may not be noticeable. These are called "fair weather" cumulus because they always accompany good weather. However, they may merge with altocumulus, or may grow to cumulonimbus before a thunderstorm. Since cumulus are formed by updrafts, they are accompanied by turbulence, causing "bumpiness" in the air. The extent of turbulence is proportional to the vertical extent of the clouds. Cumulus are marked by strong contrasts of light and dark.

Cumulus.

Cumulonimbus (Cb) is a massive cloud with great vertical development, rising in mountainous towers to great heights. The upper part consists of ice crystals, and often spreads out in the shape of an anvil which may be seen at such distances that the base may be below the horizon. Cumulonimbus often produces showers of rain, snow, or hail, frequently accompanied by thunder. Because of this, the cloud is often popularly called a "thundercloud" or "thunderhead." The base is horizontal, but as showers occur it lowers and becomes ragged.

Cumulonimbus.

Several excellent cloud identification books are available to the small-boat skipper. Shop your local bookseller or marine store for the latest and the best.

III

The Pilot's Locker

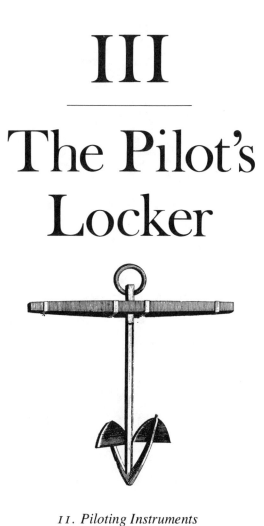

11

Piloting Instruments

Let's talk some more about the one totally "essential" thing aboard your boat—your marine magnetic compass.

On a "most important" scale of 1 to 10, your primary steering compass is an undisputed "10." On the same scale, new skippers might rate a "6" or "7," only slightly below the ship's cook but well above potted geraniums and pillows with crocheted anchors.

Magnetic Magic

The magnetic compass has been around a very long time. Early in the history of navigation seamen noted that the Pole Star remained close to one point in the northern sky. This served as his compass. When it was not visible, he used other stars, the sun and moon, winds, clouds, and waves. The development of the magnetic compass, perhaps a thousand years ago, offered a better method of steering a reasonably accurate course. The origin of the magnetic compass is not known. In 203 B.C., when Hannibal set sail from Italy, his pilot was said to be one "Pelorus." The compass may have been in use then, but no one is sure. To many, it was *magic*—but it *worked,* so no one cared. There is little to substantiate the story that the Chinese invented it, and the legend that Marco Polo introduced it into Italy in the thirteenth century is almost certainly false. It is sometimes stated that the Arabs brought it to Europe, but this too is unlikely. Probably it was known first in the West. The Norsemen of the eleventh century were familiar with it, and about 1200 a compass used by mariners when the Pole Star was hidden was described by a French poet, Guyot de Provins.

A needle thrust through a straw and floated in water in a container comprised the earliest compass known. In 1248 a writer named Hugo de Bercy spoke of a new compass construction, the needle "now" being supported on two floats. Petrus Peregrinus de Maricourt, in his *Epistola de Magnete* of 1269, wrote of a pivoted floating compass with a lubber's line, and said that it was equipped with sights for taking bearings.

The reliability of the magnetic compass today is a comparatively recent achievement. It was not until the 1870s that Sir William Thomson (Lord Kelvin) was able to successfully combine all of the requirements for a good dry-card compass and mount it in a well-designed binnacle. The dry-card compass was the standard compass in the Royal Navy until 1906 when the Board of Admiralty adopted the liquid compass as the standard compass.

The *compass card,* according to tradition, originated about the beginning of the fourteenth century, when Flavio Gioja of Amalfi attached a sliver of lodestone or a magnetized needle to a card. But the rose on the compass card is probably older than the needle. It is the wind rose of the ancients. Primitive man naturally named directions by the winds. The prophet Jeremiah speaks of the winds from the four quarters of heaven (Jer. 49:36) and Homer named the four winds— Boreas, Eurus, Notus, and Lephyrus. Aristotle is said to have suggested a circle of twelve winds, and Eratosthenes, who measured the world correctly, reduced the number to eight about 200 B.C.. The "Tower of the Winds" at Athens, built about 100 B.C., had eight sides. The Latin rose of twelve points was common on most compasses used in the Middle Ages.

Variation was understood 200 years ago, and navigators made allowance for it, but the earliest recognition of its existence is not known. Columbus, and even the eleventh-century Chinese, have been given credit for its discovery, but little proof can be offered for either claim.

The continuing change in variation was determined by a series of magnetic observations made at Limehouse, England. In 1580 William Borough fixed the variation in that area at approximately 11° 25' east. Thirty-two years later Edmund Gunter, professor of astronomy at Gresham College, determined it to be 6° 13' east. At first it was believed that Borough had made an error, but in 1633 a further decrease was found, and the changing of the earth's magnetic field was established.

A South Atlantic expedition was led by Edmond Halley at the close of the seventeenth century to gather data and to map, for the first time, lines of variation. In 1724 George Graham published his observations in proof of the diurnal change in variation. Canton determined that the change was considerably less in winter than in summer, and about 1785 the strength of the magnetic force was shown by Paul de Lamanon to vary in different places.

The existence of *deviation* was known to John Smith in 1627 when he wrote of the "bittacle" as being a "square box nailed together with wooden pinnes, because iron nails would attract the Compasse." But no one knew how to correct a compass for deviation until Capt. Matthew Flinders, while on a voyage to Australia in H.M.S. *Investigator* in 1801–1802, discovered a method. Flinders did not understand deviation completely, but the vertical bar he erected to correct for it was part of the solution, and the *Flinders bar* used today is a memorial to its discoverer. Between 1839 and 1855 Sir George Airy, then astronomer royal, studied the matter further and developed combinations of permanent magnets and soft iron masses for adjusting the compass. The introduction, by Lord Kelvin, of short needles as compass magnets made adjustment more precise.

COMPASS ERROR

Your charts take variation into account; it is your responsibility to allow for compass deviation. It is also your responsibility to see that your compass is as accurate *as possible,* recognizing that *no compass is 100 percent perfect.*

Bowditch states it this way: "To adequately serve its purpose, a navigational compass needs to have certain characteristics . . . accuracy, reliability, and convenience. The most important characteristic is accuracy."

To this, the author would add: *And it better be tough!*

Although your compass deserves your tender loving care, it possibly won't get it. Compasses aboard small vessels are often neglected shamefully. They are soaked in seawater, bumped, vibrated, baked in the sun, and chilled in frigid weather. Only when they rebel (usually by weeping fluid) do many skippers give them the care and attention they deserve. Whether your compass is a Ritchie, a Danforth, a Sestrel, or another reliable make, call a *professional* if your compass acts up; don't attack it with your handy screwdriver. Professional compass adjusters and marine instrument shops can be found in all major ports and most yachting centers. If none is available, contact the manufacturer of your compass for anything other than minor adjustments. The author once spent a most pleasant afternoon in the offices of Henry Browne & Son Limited in Barking, England, discussing the growing bubble in his faithful Sestrel. He came away armed with gaskets, screws, and cans of fluid—and a final word of caution: "Don't forget, place your compass in your fridge for two hours before you fill it. . . ." Not *this* skipper! He took the lot to New York Nautical; their modest charge to clean and repair the Sestrel was money well spent.

Compass Variation

Keep in mind that a magnetic compass does not point directly to true north—the needle or card is attracted toward the magnetic pole. The angle between "true" and "magnetic" north—variation—is a measurable quantity and is clearly marked on your charts. Variation changes with your location on the globe.

Compass Deviation

Deviation, on the other hand, is the difference between magnetic north and where your compass is *actually* pointing. Deviation is caused by the influence of fixed magnetic masses in the vicinity of the compass—probably built into your boat.

A compass in a vessel is normally subjected to magnetic influence other than that of the earth. These may be metal, or electrical circuits. Some metal in the vicinity of the compass may have acquired permanent magnetism. Since the direction of this magnetic field is generally not the same as that of the earth's field, their relative position will change as you change course—and the deviation or error will vary with your heading. Your compass should be sited as far as possible away from any form of magnetic influence—at least three feet from electrical equipment, the engine, radios, and radar. And don't forget that portable radios, tool boxes, marlin spikes, and knives may cause error too.

Fixed deviation can be determined by "swinging the compass"—that is, turning your vessel to various headings through 360° while sighting with a transit along two known bearings. You *can* learn to do this, and you *could* make the necessary adjustments, but the author

U.S.S. _____ NO. _____
(BB, CL, DD, etc.)

[X] PILOT HOUSE [ ] SECONDARY CONNING STATION [ ] OTHER _____

BINNACLE TYPE: [X] NAVY ST'D [ ] OTHER _____

COMPASS 7-1/2 MAKE C.G. Conn SERIAL NO. 8560

TYPE CC COILS "K" DATE 9 September 1975

READ INSTRUCTIONS ON BACK BEFORE STARTING ADJUSTMENT

SHIPS HEAD MAGNETIC	DEVIATIONS DG OFF	DEVIATIONS DG ON	SHIPS HEAD MAGNETIC	DEVIATIONS DG OFF	DEVIATIONS DG ON
0	0.5E	0.5E	180	0.5W	0.0
15	1.0E	1.0E	195	1.0W	0.5W
30	1.5E	1.5E	210	1.0W	1.0W
45	2.0E	1.5E	225	1.5W	1.5W
60	2.0E	2.0E	240	2.0W	2.0W
75	2.5E	2.5E	255	2.0W	2.5W
90	2.5E	3.0E	270	1.5W	2.0W
105	2.0E	2.5E	285	1.0W	1.5W
120	1.5E	2.0E	300	1.0W	1.0W
135	1.5E	1.5E	315	0.5W	0.5W
150	1.0E	1.0E	330	0.5W	0.5W
165	0.0	0.5E	345	0.0	0.0

DEVIATIONS DETERMINED BY: [ ] SUN'S AZIMUTH [X] GYRO [ ] SHORE BEARINGS

B 6 MAGNETS RED [ ] FORE [X] AFT AT 12" FROM COMPASS CARD

C 4 MAGNETS RED [ ] PORT [X] STBD AT 6" FROM COMPASS CARD

D 2-7" [X] SPHERES [ ] CYLS AT 12" [X] ATHWART-SHIP [ ] SLEWED — ___° [ ] CLOCKWISE [ ] CTR. CLOCKWISE

HEELING MAGNET: [ ] RED UP [X] BLUE UP 6" FROM COMPASS CARD FLINDERS BAR: [X] FORE [ ] AFT 12"

[X] LAT 18°00'N [X] LONG 120°00'E
[ ] H 0.385 [ ] Z 0.151

SIGNED (Adjuster or Navigator) _____ APPROVED (Commanding) _____

VERTICAL INDUCTION DATA
(Fill out completely before adjusting)

RECORD DEVIATION ON AT LEAST TWO ADJACENT CARDINAL HEADINGS

BEFORE STATING ADJUSTMENT: N 8 W, E 0, S 4 E, W 9 E.

RECORD BELOW INFORMATION FROM LAST NAVSHIPS 3120/4 DEVIATION TABLE:

DATE 5 December 1974 [ ] LAT 32 53N [ ] LONG 117 18W
[ ] H .260 [ ] Z .420

12" FLINDERS BAR [X] FORWARD [ ] AFT DEVIATIONS N 2.5W E 7E S 6.5E W 5W

RECORD HERE DATA ON RECENT OVERHAULS, GUNFIRE, STRUCTURAL CHANGES, FLASHING, DEPERMING, WITH DATES AND EFFECT ON MAGNETIC COMPASSES.

Shipyard overhaul:
    3 Oct - 2 Dec 1974
Depermed at Norfolk, Va.:
    3 Dec 1974

PERFORMANCE DATA

COMPASS AT SEA:	[ ] UNSTEADY	[X] STEADY	
COMPASS ACTION:	[ ] SLOW	[X] SATISFACTORY	
NORMAL DEVIATIONS:	[X] CHANGE	[ ] REMAIN RELIABLE	
DEGAUSSED DEVIATIONS:	[X] VARY	[ ] DO NOT VARY	

REMARKS

INSTRUCTIONS

1. This form shall be filled out by the Navigator for each magnetic compass as set forth in Chapter 9240 of NAVAL SHIPS TECHNICAL MANUAL.

2. When a swing for deviations is made, the deviations should be recorded both with degaussing coils off and with degaussing coils energized at the proper currents for heading and magnetic zone.

3. Each time this form is filled out after a swing for deviations, a copy shall be submitted to: Naval Ship Engineering Center Hyattsville, Maryland 20782. A letter of transmittal is not required.

4. When choice of box is given, check applicable box.

5. Before adjusting, fill in section on "Vertical Induction Data" above.

NAVSEA 3120/4 (REV. 6-72) (REVERSE) C-24858

A U.S. Navy deviation table.

prefers to repeat his earlier advice: Your compass should be corrected by a qualified compass adjuster. It is dangerous to cruise with a compass of unknown deviation; it is foolish to tinker with the safety of your vessel.

Even when deviation has been reduced to a minimum, some residual deviation will remain. This deviation should be recorded in some form of *deviation table*. The illustration shows both sides of the form used by the United States Navy. This table is entered with the magnetic heading, and the deviation on that heading is determined from the tabulation. If the deviation is not more than about 2° on any heading, satisfactory results may be obtained by entering the values at intervals of 45° only.

Your boat's deviation table—*as provided by your professional compass adjuster*—may be relatively simple. One method has one column for magnetic heading, a second column for deviation, and a third for compass heading. Still another solution, most popular among yachts-men, is to center a compass rose inside a larger one so that an open space is between them, and a radial line would connect points of the same graduation on both roses. Each magnetic heading for which deviation has been determined is located on the outer rose, and a straight line is drawn from this point to the corresponding compass heading on the inner rose.

A variation of this method is to draw two parallel lines a short dis-tance apart, and graduate each from 1 to 360 so that a perpendicular between the two lines connects points of the same graduation. Straight lines are drawn from magnetic directions on one line to the correspond-ing compass directions on the other. If the graduated lines are horizon-tal and the upper one represents magnetic directions, the slope of the lines you draw indicates the direction of the deviation. That is, for westerly deviation the upper part of the connecting line is left (west) of the bottom part, and for easterly deviation it is right.

Again, it is important to remember that deviation varies with *head-ing*. Therefore a deviation table is *never* entered with a bearing. If the deviation table converts directly from one type of heading to another, deviation is found by taking the difference between the two values. On the compass rose or straight-line type, the deviation can be written alongside the connecting line and the intermediate values determined by estimate. If you have trouble determining whether to add or subtract deviation when bearings are involved, you need only note which head-ing, magnetic or compass, is larger. The same relationship holds between the two values of bearing.

Your deviation table should be protected from damage due to han-dling or weather, and placed in a position where it will always be available when needed. One method commonly used is to mount it on a board, cover it with shellac or varnish, and attach it to the binnacle. Another method is to post it under glass near the compass. It is good practice for the pilot to keep a second copy available at a convenient place, possibly mounted above your chart table or in your yacht log.

To recap:

1. There are at least two solutions to the problem of compass error: the error can be permitted to remain and the various directions com-pensated for through the use of a deviation chart, or compass error can be removed by a qualified compass adjuster. In practice, a combination of both of these methods is used.

2. Variation depends on location of the vessel, and the navigator

has no control over it. Variation does not affect the operation of the compass itself.

3. Deviation is undesirable because it is troublesome to apply. As the vessel rolls and pitches, or as it changes direction, the magnetic field changes, producing a corresponding change in the deviation of an unadjusted compass.

4. Deviation can be eliminated, as nearly as practicable, by introducing at the compass a magnetic field that is equal in magnitude and opposite in polarity to that of the vessel. This process is called *compass adjustment,* or sometimes *compass compensation.* In general, the introduced field is of the same kind of magnetism as well as of the same intensity as those of the field causing deviation. That is, permanent magnets are used to neutralize permanent magnetism, and soft iron to neutralize induced magnetism, so that the adjustment remains effective with changes of heading and magnetic latitude. A relatively small mass of iron near the compass introduces a field equal to that of a much larger mass at a distance.

5. When a compass is properly adjusted, its remaining or residual deviation is small and practically constant at various magnetic latitudes, the directive force is as strong as is obtainable on all headings, and the compass returns quickly from deflections and is comparatively steady as the vessel rolls and pitches.

6. A compass is reliable when its operation is not often interrupted; when its indications are relatively free from unknown or unsuspected disturbances; when it is little affected by extremes of temperature, moisture, vibration, or shock; and when it is not so sensitive that large errors are introduced by ordinary changes in conditions or equipment near the compass.

7. The value of a compass is dependent somewhat on the convenience with which it can be used. Accuracy too may be involved. Thus a compass should not be installed at a location that does not permit an unobstructed view in most directions. The compass graduations and index should be clean, adequately lighted if it is to be used at night, and it must be clearly marked.

8. And finally, you *must* have one compass, you should have two—and three is even *better!*

OTHER PILOTING INSTRUMENTS

The instruments in the concluding paragraphs of this chapter are neither gadgetry nor panaceas; in actual use they probably fall someplace in between. Most of the instruments below are electrically powered, and because they are, they are prone to failure. To paraphrase a familiar axiom:

Water corrodes; salt water corrodes absolutely.

It is well and good if you wish to equip your small ship with electrical piloting aids, but each should be just that—an *aid,* not a *crutch.* If you can't pilot your vessel safely from here to there—and home again—with nothing more than the basic piloting "tools," perhaps you *should* plant geraniums in your cockpit and stay tied to a marina or yacht club dock.

Although this book will not deal with radar, one of the more sophisticated of piloting instruments, the following illustrates our premise that *total* dependence on electronics is questionable, if not downright dangerous. The author has the highest regard for radar—we both came of age in the early 1940s. Admittedly, radar has improved more than the author over the past four decades, but somehow—luck, perhaps—this skipper has managed to pilot two boats safely for many of those years without radar. The following isn't conclusive, but it does make a point:

Fragments from the log of *Lady Brett:*

August 6, Sunday—Fog. Still foggy at 1015. Some boats leaving [Cutty Hunk in New England's Elizabeth Islands]. Still foggy at 1050, but departed anyway. Motored with main through peasoup fog to Quicks Hole, then through on C 180°. Neither shore visible.

Visibility was getting better in Buzzards Bay, but still foggy in Vineyard Sound. Turned up Sound at 1202—main and #1. Visibility nil, with light breeze out of SW. St'b'd tack. Found each buoy and turned at Bell 16 off Falmouth [Cape Cod]. Circled buoy to lower sails and work out a course to Falmouth breakwater. Visibility perhaps 10 yards. Nothing visible except Bell 16 and a magnificent big sloop, *Volcano,* also circling the buoy.

At this point *Volcano* turned away, heading in the general direction of the invisible breakwater. *Lady Brett* fell in behind her, almost nudging her stern.

"Where are you going?" Foredeck called aft.

"She's got radar!"

"Are you on *your* course?"

"Well—almost."

Foredeck shrugged and peered ahead through the fog.

At this point, the big sloop ahead did an abrupt U-turn—only yards off a sandy beach. She had missed the harbor entrance by a good 50 yards.

A short time later both boats found the breakwater and motored slowly into Falmouth Harbor, where they tied up to a floating dock at MacDougal's. We were there for an oil change and a dinner ashore.

And *Volcano?*

You guessed it. She was there because her radar wasn't working.

MEASURING DISTANCE TRAVELED

One of the simplest mechanical distance-measuring devices is the *taffrail log,* consisting of (1) a rotor that turns like a screw propeller when it is towed through the water; (2) a braided log line that tows the rotor and transmits its rotation to an indicator on the vessel; and (3) a dial and pointer mechanism that registers the distance traveled through the water.

The taffrail log is usually streamed from the ship's quarter or a small vessel's stern. The log line should be sufficiently long, and attached in such position, that the rotor is clear of the disturbed water of the wake of the vessel; otherwise error is introduced. Errors may also be introduced by a head or following sea; by mechanical wear or damage, such as a bent fin; or by fouling of the rotor, as by seaweed or refuse.

An accurately calibrated taffrail log in good working order provides information of sufficient reliability for most purposes of navigation. Its readings should be checked at various speeds by towing it over a known distance in an area free from currents. Usually, the average of several runs, preferably in opposite directions, is more accurate than a single one. If an error is found, it should be expressed as a percentage and applied to later readings. The calibration should be checked from time to time.

A wide variety of electrical logs and knotmeters are available for small yachts. If you elect to go this route, compare them all before you buy; some *are* gadgets—and none is a panacea.

MEASURING SPEED

Speed can be determined indirectly by means of distance and time, or it can be measured directly. All instruments now in common use for measuring speed determine rate of motion *through the water*. Instruments for measuring speed, like those for measuring distance, are called logs.

Before the development of modern logs, speed was determined in a number of ways. Perhaps the most common primitive device is the *chip log,* although a *ground log* (a weight, with line attached, which was thrown overboard and rested on the bottom in shallow water) and a *Dutchman's log* have also been used. These devices have been used by modern pilots (see Chapter 13).

Problems of Measuring Speed

Bowditch states it this way:

Speed measured relative to water is not a stable well-defined quantity because of the motion of the water itself. Most speed logs now used to measure speed through the water measure speed relative to water within the hydro-dynamic influence of the vessel's hull and in the immediate vicinity of the motion sensor. . . . In addition, the motions of a vessel, such as yaw and pitch, introduce variations in the speed over ground. These speed variations can generate appreciable errors in the speed measurement. Many of the uncertainties and errors in the measurement of a vessel's speed are functions of the ocean environment and of the characteristics of the vessel carrying the speed sensor.

The key words above are "the motion of water itself." Water *moves*. Even if your vessel is moored to a buoy, water flows past her hull, and that movement will not be uniform. A variety of excellent, highly accurate knotmeters are available, most with digital readouts. Some even combine boat speed, distance traveled, and water depth in one neat, easy-to-read electronic package. Like radar, knotmeters and logs and depth sounders are aids, not panaceas. And keep in mind that knotmeters and logs measure speed and distance *through* the water, not speed and distance *over the bottom*.

Radio Direction Finders

Some small-boat skippers swear by their portable radio direction finders; most swear at them. Big-ship radio direction finders seem to work well, but the author has seen few portables that consistently pick up anything other than rock or country music.

The principle of the RDF is relatively simple. A bearing obtained by radio, like one determined in any other manner, provides the means for establishing a line of position. By heading in the direction from which the signal is coming, one can proceed toward, or *home* on, the transmitter. In thick weather you should avoid heading directly toward the source of the radiobeacon, unless you feel secure that the station is a considerable distance away. In 1934 the Nantucket Lightship was rammed and sunk by a ship homing on its radiobeacon. You can't estimate the distance from a radiobeacon by either the strength of the signals received or the time at which the signals were first heard. You should give this fact careful consideration in approaching radiobeacons. You should also keep in mind that most lightships and large buoys are anchored to a very long scope of chain, and as a result the radius of their swinging circle is considerable. The charted position is the location of the anchor. Under certain wind and current conditions they are subject to sudden, unexpected sheers, and may be hazardous to a small vessel attempting to pass close aboard.

There's no reason you shouldn't equip your boat with a portable RDF—if you have a fat wallet and a passion for country music.

Depth Measurement

First there was the lead line; now there is the echo depth sounder. A lead line is perfectly adequate for routine soundings, especially when anchoring, but an electronic depth sounder—like a VHF radiotelephone—is a very useful instrument to have aboard. A knowledge of the depth beneath your keel is critical, and you should have one or the other—a lead or a depth sounder.

Lead Line

The *lead line* is probably the oldest of all navigation aids. It is still a highly useful device, particularly in periods of reduced visibility. It is most useful in shoal water near the shore.

Many marine equipment catalogs and most yacht chandlers carry leads, with lines marked in feet and fathoms. A big-ship hand lead weighs from 7 to 14 pounds and has a line marked to about 25 fathoms. The markings commonly used on lead lines are as in Table 3.

Table 3. **Markings on Lead Lines**

Distance from Lead in Fathoms	Marking
2	two strips of leather
3	three strips of leather
5	white rag (usually cotton)
7	red rag (usually wool)
10	leather with hole
13	same as 3 fathoms
15	same as 5 fathoms
17	same as 7 fathoms

Fathoms marked on the lead line are called *marks*. The intermediate whole fathoms are called *deeps*. In reporting depths it is customary to use these terms, as "by the mark five," "deep six," etc. The only fractions of a fathom usually reported are halves and quarters, the customary expressions being "and a half, eight," "less a quarter, four," etc. A practice sometimes followed is to place distinctive markings on the hand lead line at each foot near the critical depths of the vessel, or in the case of smaller vessels, along the total length of the line, which may measure no more than 20 or 30 feet.

Echo Sounders

Most soundings are made by means of an *echo sounder*. In this instrument, a pulse of electrical energy is converted periodically to sound energy and transmitted downward by a transducer. When the energy strikes the bottom (or any other object having acoustic properties different from those of water), a portion is reflected back to the transducer as an echo. This energy is reconverted to electrical energy for presentation. Because the speed of sound in water is nearly constant, the amount of time that elapses between the transmission of a pulse and the reception of its echo is a measure of the distance traveled, or in this case, the depth.

BAROMETERS

The sea of air surrounding the earth exerts a pressure of about 14.7 pounds per square inch on the surface of the earth. This *atmospheric pressure*, sometimes called *barometric pressure*, varies from place to place, and at the same place it varies with time.

Atmospheric pressure is one of the basic elements of a meteorological observation. When the pressure at each station is plotted on a synoptic chart, lines of equal atmospheric pressure, called *isobars*, are drawn to indicate the areas of high and low pressure and their centers. These are useful in making weather predictions, because certain types of weather are characteristic of each type of area, and the wind patterns over large areas are deduced from the isobars. Atmospheric pressure is measured with a *barometer*.

The *aneroid barometer*, most commonly found aboard smaller boats, measures atmospheric pressure by means of the force exerted by the weight of air on a partly evacuated, thin-metal element called a *sylphon cell* (aneroid capsule). A small spring is used, either internally or externally, to partly counteract the tendency of the atmospheric pressure to crush the cell. Atmospheric pressure is indicated directly by a scale and a pointer connected to the cell by a combination of levers. The linkage provides considerable magnification of the slight motion of the cell, to permit readings to higher precision than could be obtained without it. An aneroid barometer should be mounted permanently, usually on a prominent bulkhead. A good marine barometer is a beautiful and decorative instrument, useful but not essential to the safe piloting of your boat.

BINOCULARS

That description—"useful but not essential"—might also apply to another nonelectronic piloting "tool," binoculars. Most good marine binoculars are sturdy, reasonably lightweight, and waterproof. Better glasses also provide good night vision. No, binoculars aren't totally essential, but they're mighty useful to have aboard when you're trying to pick out a distant buoy or determine the safest approach to an unfamiliar and tricky harbor.

12

The New-Skipper's Bookshelf

The following selection of books, publications, and sources is not intended to be totally comprehensive; few bibliographies are. Nor does the author pretend that you can't pilot your little ship safely and happily unless you have each of these volumes on your bookshelf.

Some—those in the first category—are important, if not essential, to the art of piloting; others would be useful to read or own, and a few others are merely fun. Except for the three main groupings—"Must Have," "Should Have," and "Good to Have"—the selections here are listed in no particular order.

Must Have

Log Books

Buy one—*and use it!* Over the past dozen years or so the author has purchased six or more yacht log books. Some were well designed and potentially useful; others were shoddy and cluttered. One, a beautiful book, would have been more appropriate on the bridge of *Queen Elizabeth 2* than aboard an auxiliary sailboat.

We have used none of them. Instead we have purchased—and filled—three well-bound accounting ledgers. Each measures 8½ inches by 10 inches, and each has plenty of room for random jottings, and only a few columns for the date, motor hours, or whatever. Most marine stores offer a variety of yacht logs; you'll find a ledger at your local stationer. Ask for a "Columnar."

Nautical Chart Catalog (Nos. 1 to 4)

The Nautical Chart Catalog for your area will probably be available (free) at your favorite marine store, chandler, or local authorized chart dealer, or you can write to: Distribution Division (OA / C44), National Ocean Survey, Riverdale, MD 20737. Request your chart catalog by number: (1) Atlantic and Gulf Coasts, (2) Pacific Coast, including Hawaii, (3) Alaska, and (4) Great Lakes and Adjacent Waterways.

Coast Pilots, Waterway Guides, and Boating Almanacs

A *United States Coast Pilot* (Volumes 1 to 9), available from NOA, is a valuable book to have aboard, but you may prefer one of the commercial guides or almanacs, such as the annual *Waterway Guide* or *Boating Almanac* series. Each is packed with essential information; the choice is yours. The nine *Coast Pilots* cover in detail regulations, landmarks, anchorages, dangers, and navigational aids; the commercial guides concentrate mainly on marine facilities, usually keyed to an inset chart. The following examples illustrate the differences between the *Coast Pilot 2* (Cape Cod to Sandy Hook), *Waterway Guide*'s

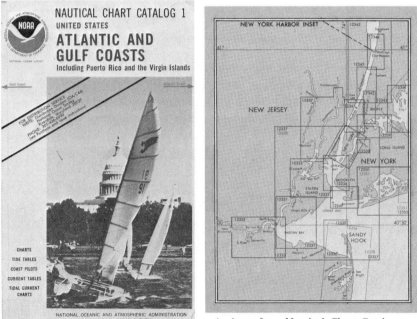

Cover of Nautical Chart Catalog 1.

An inset from Nautical Chart Catalog 1 *showing New York Harbor.*

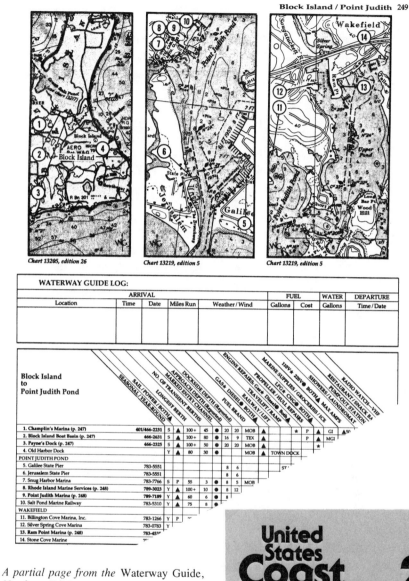

Chart 13205, edition 26   **Chart 13219, edition 5**   **Chart 13219, edition 5**

WATERWAY GUIDE LOG:

Location	ARRIVAL					FUEL		WATER	DEPARTURE
	Time	Date	Miles Run	Weather / Wind		Gallons	Cost	Gallons	Time / Date

Block Island to Point Judith Pond

		SEASONAL / YEAR-ROUND	SAIL / POWER / BOTH	NO. OF TRANSIENT BERTHS	LONGEST BERTH	APPROACH DEPTH / MARKED ENTRY CHANNEL	DOCKSIDE DEPTH (Reported)	GAS* DIESEL BOTH	FUEL BRAND	ENGINE REPAIRS / RAILWAY / LIFT	PROPELLER / HULL REPAIRS / TRAVELIFT / LIFT	MARINE SUPPLIES / LPG / CNG	110V / 220V / BOTH	SHOWERS / MAX AMPS	GROCERIES / ICE	PUMP-OUT STATION	RESTAURANT / SNACK BAR / RADIO WATCH—VHF / LAUNDROMAT
1. Champlin's Marina (p. 247)	401/466-2231	S	▲	100+	45	●	20	20	MOB	▲			★	P	▲	GI	▲50
2. Block Island Boat Basin (p. 247)	466-2631	S	▲	100+	80	●	16	9	TEX	▲				P	▲	MGI	
3. Payne's Dock (p. 247)	466-2325	S	▲	100+	50	●	20	20	MOB	▲						★	
4. Old Harbor Dock		Y	▲	80	30	●			MOB	▲	TOWN DOCK						
POINT JUDITH POND																	
5. Galilee State Pier	783-5551						8	6			ST'						
6. Jerusalem State Pier	783-5551						8	6									
7. Snug Harbor Marina	783-7766	S	P	55	3	●	8	5	MOB								
8. Rhode Island Marine Services (p. 248)	789-3023	Y	▲	100+	10	●	8	12									
9. Point Judith Marina (p. 248)	789-7189	Y	▲	60	6	●	8										
10. Salt Pond Marine Railway	783-5310	Y	▲	75	8	●											
WAKEFIELD																	
11. Billington Cove Marina, Inc.	783-1266	Y	P	~													
12. Silver Spring Cove Marina	783-0783	Y															
13. Ram Point Marina (p. 248)	783-453?																
14. Stone Cove Marine	7?																

A partial page from the Waterway Guide, *Northern Edition.*

Title page from United States Coast Pilot *2, covering the Atlantic Coast from Cape Cod to Sandy Hook.*

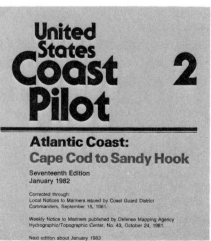

United States Coast Pilot 2

Atlantic Coast: Cape Cod to Sandy Hook

Seventeenth Edition
January 1982

Corrected through:
Local Notices to Mariners issued by Coast Guard District Commanders, September 15, 1981.

Weekly Notice to Mariners published by Defense Mapping Agency Hydrographic/Topographic Center, No. 43, October 24, 1981.

Next edition about January 1983

Northern Edition, and *Boating Almanac,* Volume 2 (Long Island to Massachusetts) in their coverage of Rhode Island's Point Judith area.

Here is how the *Coast Pilot* presents Point Judith and the Harbor of Refuge:

Chart 13219.—Point Judith Light (41° 21.7'N., 71° 28.9'W.), 65 feet above the water, is shown from an octagonal tower, 51 feet high, with the lower half white, upper half brown. The station has a fog signal and a radiobeacon. About 100 yards north of the light is a Coast Guard station. Storm warning signals are displayed. (See chart.) A lighted whistle buoy is 2.6 miles southward of the light. (See chart 13218.) A prominent elevated water tank is about 1.8 miles northward of the light, and another globular water tank is about 3 miles northwestward of the light.

The area around Point Judith, including the approaches to Point Judith Harbor of Refuge, is irregular with rocky bottom and indications of boulders. Caution is advised to avoid the shoal spots, even with a smooth sea, and to exercise extra care where the depths are not more than 6 feet greater than the draft.

Point Judith Harbor of Refuge, on the west side of Point Judith, is formed by a main V-shaped breakwater and two shorearm breakwaters extending to the shore. The harbor is easy access for most vessels except with a heavy southerly sea. It is little used by tows. The only soft bottom in the harbor is found in the southern part of the deeper water enclosed by the main breakwater. On the north side the shoaling is gradual; the 18-foot curve is about 0.3 to 0.5 mile offshore.

Near the central part of the harbor are two shoals; the northernmost one has depths of 14 to 18 feet, and the southernmost one has depths of 14 to 16 feet and is marked by a buoy.

The area within the V-shaped breakwater affords protected anchorage for small craft. The breakwater should be given a berth of 200 yards to avoid broken and hard bottom; a rocky shoal area about 100 yards wide, paralleling the west side of the main breakwater northward from the angle should be avoided. A good berth for a vessel is on a line between Point Judith Harbor of Refuge East Entrance Light 3 and Point Judith Harbor of Refuge West Entrance Light 2, midway between them in 22 to 30 feet. This position falls on the edge of the east-west thoroughfare used by pleasure craft and fishing boats.

The southern entrance to the Harbor of Refuge, known locally as the East Gap, is 400 yards wide; in July 1981, it had a reported controlling depth of about 24 feet, with deeper water in the western half of the channel.

The western entrance to the Harbor of Refuge, known locally as the West Gap, is 500 yards wide; in July 1981, it had a reported controlling depth of about 18 feet, with lesser depths on the north side of the entrance.

Tides and Currents.—The mean range of tide in the Harbor of Refuge is 3.1 feet. The tidal currents have a velocity of about 0.7 knot at the south entrance. The currents off the west entrance are rotary, with a velocity at strength of 0.5 knot. (See Tidal Current Tables for predictions.)

Considerably stronger currents have been reported to develop especially when the tide is ebbing.

Point Judith Pond is a saltwater tidal pond entered between two rock jetties at The Breachway in the northwestern part of Point Judith Harbor of Refuge. The east jetty is marked near its seaward end by a daybeacon. The pond extends 3.3 miles northerly to the town of Wakefield. It is used extensively by small fishing vessels and pleasure craft, and numerous fish wharves are inside the entrance. The north end of Point Judith Pond affords good anchorage for boats of 4 feet draft or less during a heavy blow.

The village of Galilee on the east side of the entrance and Jerusalem on the west side at Succotash Point have State piers and numerous small piers chiefly used by fishermen. A State fisheries laboratory is just above the State pier at Jerusalem. A State pier superintendent controls the State piers at Galilee and Jerusalem; his office is at the head of the Galilee State Pier.

A channel with three dredged sections marked by buoys extends from Point Judith Harbor of Refuge along the west side of the pond to the State Pier at Jerusalem, and thence northerly to the turning basin at Wakefield. A branch channel, on the east side, extends northeasterly from the entrance to the pond to the State Pier at Galilee, and into anchorage areas westward of Galilee and southward of Little Comfort Island.

In May–June 1978, the controlling depths were 7 feet (14 feet at midchannel) to the junction with the Galilee branch channel, thence 12 feet to the State Pier at Jerusalem, thence 2½ feet (3 feet at midchannel) in the dredged sections of the channel above Jerusalem to the turning basin at Wakefield with 6 feet in the basin except for shoaling to 5 feet along the west limit. The east branch channel had a controlling depth of 15 feet to the State Pier at Galilee, thence 12 feet to the anchorage basin southward of Little Comfort Island, thence in July 1981, 7 feet was reported in the anchorage except for shoaling to 2 feet along the east limit. In May–June 1978, the anchorage westward of Galilee had depths of 10 feet.

Tides and Currents.—The mean range of tide in the pond is 2.8 feet and occurs later than in the Harbor of Refuge by about 10 minutes just inside the entrance to 30 minutes at the north end. The tidal currents in the entrance have a velocity of 1.8 knots on the flood and 1.5 knots on the ebb, and cause slight rips and overfalls at changes of tide. Higher current velocities are reported to occur. (See Tidal Current Tables for predictions.)

Several boatyards and marinas are at Galilee, Jerusalem, Wakefield, and at Snug Harbor, on the west side of the pond about 0.8 mile above the entrance. Berths, electricity, gasoline, diesel fuel, water, ice, marine supplies, storage, launching ramps, and hull and engine repairs are available. The largest marine railway in the area, at the southern end of the waterfront at Snug Harbor, can handle craft up to 150 feet long or 400 tons. In July 1981, a reported depth of 12 feet could be carried to the railway.

Storm warnings are displayed. (See chart.)

Daily ferry service is available to Block Island from Galilee. Daily bus service is operated to Providence.

The *Waterway Guide* sees the same area this way:

Point Judith / Harbor of Refuge

Rocky Point Judith, sticking out to sea from Rhode Island mainland, has wrecked many a ship in past years. There are still rocky shoals, but a Coast Guard station and 65-foot stone lighthouse help you into the big Harbor of Refuge.

Westward of the Point, the Rhode Island shore to Watch Hill is 17 miles of beach, with occasional rocky projections, and a few "inlets" navigable only by very small boats, mainly at high tide. For the boatman this section of coast between Watch Hill and Point Judith has little to offer except perhaps, on a calm day, anchorage in the roadstead and a dinghy trip ashore for a swim. East of Point Judith are the cruising grounds of Narragansett Bay.

Harbor of Refuge. Entry to the breakwater-enclosed Harbor of Refuge is through either of two passages, both easy in good weather. In foul weather use whichever one is leeward.

If your approach is the one from the northeast, maintain a watch for fish traps and lobster-trap buoys; keep at least two miles off the lighthouse. The east light of the V-shaped breakwater, now named Light 3, is a four-second flashing green with a square-shaped green daymark. The west light on this breakwater, now called Light 2, has a red reflector and triangle red daybeacon.

Anchor in the angle of the main breakwater but not too far to the south. A heavy layer of kelp covers most of the bottom of the harbor and provides poor holding ground; occasionally boats have dragged anchor following a northeast squall.

And the *Boating Almanac* takes the approach shown in the two illustrations.

Each of the above is excellent; each has its unique use, and each to a degree complements the others and the other cruising guides listed below. A small-boat skipper in the Northeast who has the cash and the space should consider buying all three. The same is true for *Coast*

A page from the Boating Almanac, *Vol. 2, covering Point Judith.*

A partial page from the Boating Almanac, *Vol. 2.*

Pilots, Waterway Guides, and *Boating Almanacs* for other cruising areas.

A Variety of Cruising Guides

Guides are available for cruising grounds from Hawaii to Maine, Alaska to the Bahamas—or, if you're *really* adventurous—Scotland's Inner Hebrides, Europe's Inland Waterways, or the Tyrrhenian Sea. You may find some of them at your local marine or book store, but Dolphin Book Club (see below) or The Armchair Sailor (also below) are probably your best bet for a full selection. Recent Dolphin mailings offered the following "local" guides to its members:

Richardson's Chartbook & Cruising Guide (1981): Lake Erie Edition, Lake Huron Edition, Lake Michigan Edition.

Well-Favored Passage: A Guide to Lake Huron's North Channel, by Marjorie C. Brazer (1982).

Cruising Nova Scotia: From Yarmouth to Canso, by Wayne Clarke, Judith Penner, and George Rogers (1979).

A Cruising Guide to the New England Coast, Including the Hudson River, Long Island Sound, and the Coast of New Brunswick, by Roger F. Duncan and John P. Ware (1979).

Exploring Coastal New England: Gloucester to Kennebunkport, by Barbara Clayton and Kathleen Whitley (1979).

Cape Cod—Where to Go, What to Do, How to Do It, by Julius M. Wilensky (2nd edition, 1976). Spiral-bound softcover.

A Cruising Guide to the Chesapeake, by William T. Stone and Fessenden S. Blanchard (1973).

The Intracoastal Waterway: A Cockpit Cruising Handbook, by Jan and Bill Moeller.

Cruising Guide to the Florida Keys by Capt. Frank Papy (new revised 3rd edition, 1979). Spiral-bound softcover.

Waterway Guide (softcover). Northern Edition—Maine to New York Harbor. Mid-Atlantic Edition—New York to the Florida Line. Southern Edition—Florida and the Gulf Coasts of Alabama Mississippi, Louisiana, and Texas.

California Coastal Passages, by Brian Fagan. Softcover.

Cruising Guide to the Channel Islands (of California), by Brian Fagan and Graham Pomeroy (1979). Softcover.

Cruising the Pacific Coast: Acapulco to Skagway, by Carolyn and Jack West (3rd edition, 1974).

Sea Guide, Vol. 1, *Southern California,* by Leland R. Lewis, charts and illustrations by Peter E. Ebeling (3rd edition, 1973).

Cruising Guide for the Hawaiian Islands, edited by Arlo W. Fast and George Seberg (1980).

Pacific Boating Almanacs (1982). Softcover. Southern California, Arizona, Baja Claifornia. Northern California and Nevada. Pacific Northwest.

A Cruising Guide to the Southern Coast, by Robert S. Roscoe and Fessenden S. Blanchard (3rd edition, 1974).

Cruising the San Juan Islands by Bruce Calhoun (1973).

Cruising the Northwest: A Practical Guide for the Pacific Coast Boater, by Donald Holm (1977).

Yachtsman's Guide to the Bermuda Islands, by Michael Voegeli (1981). Spiral-bound softcover.

Cruising Guide to the Abacos and the Northern Bahamas, by Julius M. Wilensky (2nd edition 1981; with tide tables). Spiral-bound softcover.

A Cruising Guide to the Caribbean and the Bahamas, by Jerrems C. Hart and William T. Stone (1976).

Bahama Islands: A Boatman's Guide to the Land and the Water, by J. Linton Rigg, revised by Harry Kline (1973).

Bahama Diver's Guide, by Shlomo Cohen (1977).

Yachtsman's Guide to the Bahamas, by Harry Kline (1981). Spiral-bound softcover.

Street's Cruising Guide to the Eastern Caribbean: Vol. 1, *Getting There;* Vol. II, *Puerto Rico to Dominica;* Vol. III, *Martinique to Trinidad;* Vol. IV, *Venezuela,* by Donald M. Street, Jr. (1981–1982). Spiral-bound softcover.

Yachtsman's Guide to the Greater Antilles, by Harry Kline (1981). Spiral-bound softcover.

Stevens' Cruising Guide to the Windward Islands (1979). Spiral-bound softcover.

Yachtsman's Guide to the Windward Islands by Julius M. Wilensky (1978). Spiral-bound with water-resistant softcover.

Chart-Kits® by Better Boating Association (Marine atlases, 17″ by 22″). The Bahamas—105 aerial photographs, all charts (1979). The Virgin Islands.

Cayman Islands Handbook and Businessman's Guide, edited by Jim Graves (1979). Softcover.

Tide and Tidal Publications

Tide Tables, Tidal Current Tables, Tidal Current Charts, and Tidal Current Diagrams are available from National Ocean Survey's Distribution Division (see above).

Coast Guard Light Lists

These lists furnish more information about aids to navigation than can be shown on your charts. They are *not* to be used instead of charts or *Coast Pilots*. Five volumes are available:

Light List, Vol. I—Atlantic Coast, St. Croix River, Maine, to Little River, South Carolina.

Light List, Vol. II—Atlantic and Gulf Coasts, Little River, South Carolina, to Rio Grande, Texas.

Light List, Vol. III—Pacific Coast and Pacific Islands.

Light List, Vol. IV—Great Lakes.

Light List, Vol. V—Mississippi River System.

The various *Light Lists* and prices are listed in your chart catalog. They are available from the Superintendent of Documents, U.S. Government Printing Office, Washington, DC 20402.

SHOULD HAVE

Again, you don't need *all* of the books from the following selection—but each is excellent in its own right, and none would be out of place on a new-skipper's bookshelf. Most nautical book publishers, distributors, or clubs are owned, run, or influenced by sailors (Roger Taylor at International Marine, Eric Swenson at W. W. Norton, Spencer Smith at Dolphin, to name but a few), but one of the very best, John de Graff, never went near the water if he could avoid it. And one of de Graff's best titles, *Heavy Weather Sailing,* is the first selection on this "Should Have" list.

Heavy Weather Sailing, K. Adlard Coles (de Graff).

By most definitions, Adlard Coles's classic *Heavy Weather Sailing* wouldn't be considered essential reading for a new skipper-pilot. But this book defies definition. If *Heavy Weather Sailing* doesn't make you run for the hills, you are a dedicated sailor, hopelessly in love with the sea. Published by John de Graff (Clinton Corners, N.Y.), a third revised edition of *Heavy Weather Sailing* was issued in 1981. It can be ordered through most better bookstores or marine catalogs, or from Dolphin Book Club, International Marine, or The Armchair Sailor. Buy, beg, or borrow a copy of this book—but, above all, *read it.*

Reed's Nautical Almanac and Coast Pilot—East Coast Edition (W. W. Norton).

An American edition of a world-famous nautical almanac. This annual contains tidal charts and more than 150 pages of visual navigational aids. *Commonsense Coastal Navigation,* Hewitt Schlereth (W. W. Norton).

One of the most successful teachers of navigation, Schlereth's "commonsense" book is for both the beginner and the old hand. (Even Old Salt could learn from Schlereth.)

Coastal Navigation for Yachtsmen, Ken Duxbury (Van Nostrand Reinhold).

Duxbury, a British yachtsman, is also the author of *Seastate and Tides.* Each is available from the publisher or Dolphin Book Club.

Piloting, Frederick Graves.

Ed Graves has structured his book on piloting to provide "an easy source of information, tables, and examples for both the raw beginner and the experienced navigator. It serves as a ready reference as well as a textbook."

Chapman: Piloting, Seamanship, and Small Boat Handling, 55th edition (Hearst).

Thousands of new skippers buy *Chapman*s each year, whether they read it or not. Widely known as the "bible" of pleasure boating, *Chapman* is packed with information on every aspect of coastal or lakes boating.

Coastwise Navigation, Frances W. Wright (Cornell Maritime Press).

Basic, but good—and published by an excellent nautical publisher. Illustrated with charts and diagrams.

Coastal Navigator's Notebook, Tony Gibbs (International Marine).

Gibbs, former editor of *Yachting,* compiled this handy notebook for the skipper-navigator "who enjoys or would like to enjoy the process of piloting his vessel."

Coastal Navigation, Step by Step, Warren Norville.

Norville's book draws together all the elements of piloting and dead reckoning—for fishermen, tugboatmen, and yachtsmen. Well written, well illustrated.

Navigation for Yachtsmen, Mary Blewitt (David McKay).

An Americanized edition of Blewitt's compact, tightly structured volume on those aspects of coastal and offshore navigation that do not involve celestial. *Navigation for Yachtsmen* is based on the British author's experiences in small vessels.

Yacht Cruising, Patrick Ellam (W. W. Norton).

Much of value for the coastal cruiser from a veteran of countless ocean voyages, including piloting, Intracoastal Waterways, dead reckoning, current and leeway, bound coastwise, and checking the compass.

GOOD TO HAVE

You really don't *need* any of the following publications, but they would be "good to have" or "fun to have," and each is likely to enhance your enjoyment of cruising and piloting.

The Elements of Seamanship, Roger C. Taylor (International Marine).

In a captivating writing style, Roger Taylor covers the world of boats and the various aspects of seamanship from "Keeping from Hitting Anything" to "Keeping Your Reputation." Taylor's glossary—"Keeping a Civil Tongue at Sea"—includes seagoing expressions that have withstood the test of time.

Best of Sail Navigation, Editors of *Sail* magazine (Sail Books).

More than fifty articles from a decade of *Sail* magazines—piloting, equipment, and charts.

This Is Rough Weather Cruising, Erroll Bruce (Sail Books).

Handling winds of Force 5 or more, by a sailor-author who ought to know. Beautifully illustrated with color photographs and drawings.

The Proper Yacht, 2nd edition, Arthur Beiser.

This second edition of Beiser's classic is almost—*almost,* but not quite—as good as the first, which was published by Macmillan in 1966. We have owned and cherished the first edition of *The Proper Yacht* since 1966; we wouldn't lend it to anyone.

Great Voyages in Small Boats: Solo Circumnavigations (published by John de Graff).

Here they are—the best of the best: *Sailing Alone around the World* by Joshua Slocum, *Alone through the Roaring Twenties* by Vito Dumas, and *Trekka round the World* by John Guzzwell. De Graff, in one volume, has given the new skipper the start of a great nautical library.

Great Voyages in Small Boats: Solo Transatlantic (published by John de Graff).

Not content with the success of *Solo Circumnavigations,* de Graff has now added a second volume: *My Ship Is So Small* by Ann Davidson, *The Ship That Would Not Travel Due West* by David Lewis, and *Alone at Sea* by Hannes Lindemann.

The Saga of Cimba, Richard Maury (de Graff, 1973).

First published in 1939, this is a gentle account of an incredible adventure—the battle of a 26-foot schooner against Atlantic winter gales.

Celestial Navigation for Yachtsmen, Mary Blewitt (de Graff).

Mary Blewitt's "little book" has been called "idiot-proof"—and it is. As an introduction to celestial navigation (using the *Air Almanac* and H.O. 249), it can't be surpassed. It is difficult to image a better introduction to the mysteries of celestial navigation—in only 94 pages!

Sun Sight Sailing, S. L. Seaton (David McKay).

Seaton uses only 100 pages to explain his "foolproof, step-by-step method of finding your position at sea." Like Blewitt, above, Seaton's little book is wonderfully basic, an excellent first book for the beginner.

The Riddle of the Sands, Erskine Childers.

Available in a variety of editions (some out of print and difficult to find), Childers's classic sea mystery is the only novel on this list. We agree with The Armchair Sailor, which lists a paperback edition: "We do not hesitate to recommend it."

Voyaging under Power, Robert P. Beebe (Seven Seas Press).

Carleton Mitchell, in his introduction to Beebe's fine book, says that "voyaging under power is not merely a time of life, but a way of life."

Mitchell, who was also a fine author of nautical books, was a self-described "escapee from the tyranny of sail."

Celestial Navigation: Captain Joe Thompson's Cookbook Method, J. E. Thompson (David McKay).

Captain Thompson takes the "cookbook" approach to getting a line of position from a celestial observation: step one, step two, step three . . . and a pinch of that. Especially valuable to the skipper who uses celestial only occasionally.

Cruises with Kathleen, Donald Hamilton (David McKay).

You probably know Donald Hamilton as the creator of the Matt Helm thrillers, but Hamilton is also an intrepid small-boat skipper. The author has strong opinions on all aspects of cruising—and he's not shy about expressing them.

The Circumnavigator's Handbook, Steve and Linda Dashew (W. W. Norton).

Much of value for the coastal skipper from the experiences of 36 circumnavigators.

The Self-Sufficient Sailor, Larry and Lin Pardey (W. W. Norton).

The Pardeys, Larry and Lin, aren't like us ordinary folks, and perhaps for that reason their books are a good cut above the ordinary. Look for the *Seraffyn* books; the most recent, and perhaps the best, is *Seraffyn's Oriental Adventure.*

Cruising under Sail, 3rd edition, Eric Hiscock (Oxford).

The Hiscocks, like the Pardeys, are very special people who *do* what the rest of us dream about. Any Hiscock is worth reading, but this one, which incorporates *Voyaging under Sail,* was written for small-boat skipper-pilots.

Yachtsman's Winterbook, edited by Spencer Smith (David McKay).

This is the antidote to those long, dark winter evenings when your boat's under cover and trussed up like a Thanksgiving turkey: more than fifty articles from nautical periodicals from around the world. An ideal collection for your cruising library, published in oversize paperback.

The Sailing Book, edited by Michael Bartlett and Joanne A. Fishman (Arbor House).

A surprisingly good entry from a publisher who doesn't know a dinghy from a dhow, *The Sailing Book* has been put together by two editors who obviously know and love their subject—the sea, and those who sail and write about the sea.

Princess, Joe Richards (David McKay).

A rare book in more ways than one, *Princess* is again out of print. Here is the story of one man's love for a boat, told in a style that is unique. Illustrated by the author.

Finish with Engines, Mike Peyton (Nautical Publishing Co. Ltd.).

British cartoonist Peyton admits he is losing his battle to warn us away from the water—but he keeps trying, and *Finish with Engines* is his most recent hilarious effort. The others are *Come Sailing, Come Sailing Again,* and *Huricane Zoe and Other Sailing.*

Sources: Books, Publications, and Charts

We apologize that the following list of names and addresses is not complete; many fine publishers, stores, clubs, and distributors have not been included. This is a personal list, those sources that have been especially helpful to the author; you will undoubtedly add some of your own.

National Ocean Survey, Distribution Division, C44, National Ocean Survey, Riverdale, MD 20840.

Hydrographic Chart Distribution Office, Department of Environment, 1675 Russel Road, P.O. Box 8080, Ottawa, Ontario, KIG 3H6, Canada.

U.S. Army Corps of Engineers, Chicago District, 219 South Dearborn Street, Chicago, IL 60604; Omaha District, U.S. Post Office, 215 North 17th Street, Omaha, NE 68102; Ohio River Division, P.O. Box 1159, Cincinnati, OH 45201; Mobile District, P.O. Box 2288, Mobile, AL 36628.

Superintendent of Documents, U.S. Government Printing Office, Washington, DC 20402.

U.S. Coast Guard Headquarters, Commandant, USCG (or Marine Inspection Office), 400 7th Street SW, Washington, DC 20590.

National Weather Service, % Distribution Division, NOS, Riverdale MD 20840 (or Superintendent of Documents, U.S. Government Printing Office, Washington, DC 20402).

Dolphin Book Club, 485 Lexington Avenue, New York, NY 10017. (Ask for their current new-member offer, or see Dolphin's ads in *Sail, Yachting, Cruising World,* et al.)

International Marine Publishing Company, 21 Elm Street, Camden, ME 04843. (Seasonal and monthly catalogs.)

The Armchair Sailor Bookstore, Lee's Wharf, Newport, RI 02840. (Books, charts, and navigation instruments. A $3 charge for this catalog, but worth every penny.)

The Sea Heritage Society, 254–26 75th Avenue, Glen Oaks, NY 11004.

W. W. Norton & Company, Inc., 500 Fifth Avenue, New York, NY 10110.

Julian Burnett, Books, P.O. Box 229, Atlanta, GA 30301. (Out-of-print nautical books, $2 for catalog.)

Sail Books, 34 Commercial Wharf, Boston, MA 02110.

Mystic Seaport Museum, Inc., Mystic, CT 06355.

Boat Owners Association of the United States, 880 South Pickett St., Alexandria, VA 22304. (Services include a Boating Book Buyers Guide.)

13

Some Definitions, Tables, and a Few Salty Terms

abeam—bearing approximately 090° relative (''abeam to starboard'') or 270° relative (''abeam to port'').

advanced line of position—a line of position which has been moved forward to allow for the run since the line was established.

aground—touching, resting, or lodged on the bottom—an embarrassing and dangerous situation.

aid to navigation—a device external to a craft, designed to assist in determination of position of the craft, or of a safe course, or to warn of dangers.

alternating fixed and flashing light—a fixed light varied at regular intervals by one or more flashes of greater brilliance, with color variations in either the fixed light or flashes, or both.

alternating fixed and group flashing light—a fixed light varied at regular intervals by a group of two or more flashes of greater brilliance, with color variations in either the fixed light or flashes, or both.

alternating flashing light—a light showing one or more flashes with color variations at regular intervals, the duration of light being less than that of darkness.

alternating group flashing light—a light showing groups of flashes with color variations at regular intervals, the duration of light being less than that of darkness.

alternating group occulting light—a light having groups of total eclipses at regular intervals and having color variations, the duration of light being equal to or greater than that of darkness.

alternating light—a light having periodic color variations, particularly one with constant luminous intensity.

alternating occulting light—a light having one or more total eclipses at regular intervals and having color variations, the duration of light being equal to or greater than that of darkness.

anchorage—an area where a vessel anchors or may anchor, either because of suitability or designation. *See* Harbor of Refuge.

anemometer—an instrument for measuring the speed of the wind. Some instruments also indicate the direction from which it is blowing.

aneroid barometer—an instrument that determines atmospheric pressure by the effect of such pressure on a thin-metal cylinder from which the air has been partly exhausted.

anticyclone—an approximately circular portion of the atmosphere, having relatively high atmospheric pressure and winds which blow clockwise around the center in the northern hemisphere.

apparent wind—wind relative to a moving point, such as a vessel.

astern—bearing approximately 180° relative.

awash—situated so that the top is intermittently washed by by waves or tidal action. If it's your small ship, it's time to break out the life jackets.

back—of the wind, to change direction counterclockwise in the northern hemisphere and clockwise in the southern hemisphere.

barometer—an instrument for measuring atmospheric pressure.

barometric pressure—atmospheric pressure as indicated by a barometer.

beacon—1. a fixed aid to navigation; 2. an unlighted aid to navigation; 3. anything serving as a signal or conspicuous indication, either for guidance or warning.

bearing (B, Brg.)—the horizontal direction of one terrestrial point from another, expressed as angular distance from a reference direction, usually from 000° at the reference direction, clockwise through 360°. When measured through 90° or 180° from *either* north or south, it is called *bearing angle* (*B*), which bears the same relationship to east or west as a craft proceeds from one point to another.

bearing line—a line extending in the direction of a bearing.

Beaufort Scale—a numerical scale for indicating wind speed, named after Admiral Sir Francis Beaufort, who devised it in 1806. *See* force.

binnacle—the stand in which a compass is mounted, *not* the compass itself.

bobbing a light—quickly lowering the height of eye several feet and then raising it again when a light is first sighted, to determine whether the observer is at the geographical range of the light.

bow and beam bearings—successive relative bearings (right or left) or 45° and 90° of a fixed object.

"Bowditch"—*American Practical Navigator,* an epitome of navigation, maintained continuously since it was first published in 1802. The intent of the original author, Nathaniel Bowditch, was "to provide a compendium of navigational material understandable to the mariner." *The New-Skipper's Bowditch* has the same objective for new skippers.

Bowditch, Nathaniel—Nathaniel Bowditch (1773–1838) was born at Salem, Massachusetts, fourth of the seven children of Habakkuk and Mary Bowditch. Like most of Salem's residents, Nathaniel Bowditch spent his life close to the sea. His father reportedly lost two ships at sea and two of his brothers died at sea. Bowditch, who was an astronomical and mathematical genius, made a total of five ocean voyages over a period of nine years, the last as master of the three-masted ship *Putnam.* Since 1802, more than 700,000 copies of "Bowditch" have been printed in seventy editions.

Nathaniel Bowditch.

boxing the compass—the naming of the various graduations of the compass card in order is called boxing the compass, an important attainment by the student mariner of earlier generations. The point system of indicating relative bearings survived long after degrees became almost universally used for compass and true directions. Except for the cardinal and intercardinal points, and occasionally the two-point graduations, all of which are used to indicate directions generally (as "northwest winds," meaning winds from a general northwesterly direction), the point system has become largely historical.

broad on the beam—bearing 090° relative ("broad on the starboard beam") or 270° relative ("broad on the port beam").

broad on the bow—bearing 045° relative ("broad on the starboard bow") or 315° relative ("broad on the port bow").

broad on the quarter—bearing 135° relative ("broad on the starboard quarter") or 225° relative ("broad on the port quarter").

buoyage—a system of buoys.

can buoy—a buoy the above-water part of which is in the shape of a cylinder.

cardinal point—north, east, south, or west.

Celsius temperature—temperature based on a scale in which, under standard atmospheric pressure, water freezes at 0° and boils at 100°; called "centigrade temperature" before 1948.

chip log—a method of measuring boat speed. Attach a long line to a heavy, floating object. Tie a knot in the line 12 or 15 fathoms from the object, and another 10 fathoms (or any convenient distance) from the first. Stream the device over the side and let the line run out freely, noting the elapsed time between the passage of the two knots through your hand. Speed in knots is determined by the following formula:

$$S = \frac{60 \text{ seconds per minute} \times 60 \text{ minutes per hour} \times \text{feet between marks}}{6000 \text{ feet per mile} \times \text{seconds of elapsed time}}$$

This is equal to:

$$S = \frac{3600 \times \text{feet between marks}}{6000 \times \text{seconds of elapsed time}} = \frac{0.6 \times \text{feet between marks}}{\text{seconds of elapsed time}}$$

Since the feet between marks is constant, a convenient number can be selected. Thus if the length is 16⅔ feet, the formula becomes

$$S = \frac{10}{\text{seconds of elapsed time}}$$

chronometer—a timepiece with a nearly constant rate.

circle of position—a circular line of position.

coastal current—an ocean current flowing roughly parallel to a coast, outside the surf zone.

coasting—proceeding approximately parallel to a coastline and near enough to be in pilot waters most of the time.

Coast Pilot—a descriptive book for the use of mariners, containing detailed information on the coastal waters, harbor facilities, etc., of an area, particularly along the coasts of the United States.

command—"the ability to control," or "the authority and right to command." A new skipper earns that "right" by learning more, caring more, and trying harder than anyone else aboard (plus remembering: "Port is left—starboard is right").

compass card—that part of a compass on which the direction graduations are placed. The compass card is composed of light, nonmagnetic material. In most modern compasses the card is graduated into 360°, increasing clockwise from north through east, south, and west. Some compass cards are graduated in "points," usually in addition to the degree graduations. There are thirty-two *points of the compass*, 11¼° apart. The four cardinal points are north, east, south, and west. Midway between these are four *intercardinal points* at northeast, southeast, southwest, and northwest. The eight points between cardinal and intercardinal points are named for the two directions between which they lie, the cardinal name being given first, as north-northeast, east-northeast, east-southeast, etc. The remaining sixteen points are named for the nearest cardinal or intercardinal point "by" the next cardinal point in the direction of measurement, as north by east, northeast by north, etc.

compass heading—heading relative to compass north.

compass north—the direction north as indicated by a magnetic compass.

compass points—the thirty-two divisions of a compass, at intervals of 11¼°. *See* compass card.

compass rose—a circle graduated in degrees, clockwise from 0° at the reference direction to 360°, or in compass points, or in both degrees and points.

conversions—refer to the conversion table.

Conversions

Meters into yards:	Add one-tenth.
Yards into meters:	Deduct one-tenth.
Kilometers into miles:	Multiply by 5 and divide by 8.
Miles into kilometers:	Multiply by 8 and divide by 5.
Liters into pints:	Multiply by 7 and divide by 4.
Pints into liters:	Multiply by 4 and divide by 7.
Liters into gallons:	Multiply by 2 and divide by 9.
Gallons into liters:	Multiply by 9 and divide by 2.
Kilograms into pounds:	Divide by 9 and multiply by 20.
Pounds into kilograms:	Divide by 20 and multiply by 9.
Fahrenheit into Celsius:	Subtract 32, multiply by 5, and divide by 9.
Celsius into Fahrenheit:	Multiply by 9, divide by 5, and add 32.

course (C, Cn)—the horizontal direction in which a vessel is steered or intended to be steered, expressed as angular distance from north, usually from 000° at north, clockwise through 360°. Strictly, the term applies to direction *through the water,* not the direction intended to be made good over the ground. The course is often designated as *true, magnetic, compass,* or *grid* as the reference direction is true, magnetic, compass, or grid north, respectively. *Course made good* (CMG) is the single resultant direction from the point of departure to point of arrival at any given time. Sometimes the expression *course of advance* (COA) is used to indicate the direction intended to be made good over the ground, and *course over ground* (COG) the direction of the path actually followed, usually a somewhat irregular line. *Course line* is a line extending in the direction of a course. The symbol *C* is always used for *course angle,* and is usually used for *course* where there is little or no possibility of confusion.

course line—1. a line extending in the direction of a given course; 2. a line of position approximately parallel to the course. *See* course.

course made good—the direction of a point of departure to point of arrival. *See* course.

cross bearings—two or more bearings used as intersecting lines of position for fixing the position of a vessel.

danger angle—the maximum or minimum angle between two points (separated either horizontally or vertically), as observed from a vessel, indicating the limit of safe approach to an off-lying danger.

danger bearing—the maximum or minimum bearing of a point for safe passage past an off-lying danger.

danger line—a line drawn on a chart to indicate the limits of safe navigation for a vessel of specific draft.

danger sounding—a minimum sounding chosen for a vessel of specific draft in a given area to indicate the limit of safe navigation.

daybeacon—an unlighted beacon.

daymark—a distinctive structure serving as an aid to navigation during daylight, whether or not the structure has a light.

dead ahead—bearing 000° relative.

dead astern—bearing 180° relative.

dead reckoning—the determination of your position by advancing a known position for courses and distances. A position so determined is called a *dead reckoning position*. It is generally accepted that the *course steered* and the *speed through the water* should be used, but the expression is also used to refer to the determination of position by use of the course and speed expected to be made good over the ground, thus making an estimated allowance for disturbing elements such as current and wind. A position so determined is better called an *estimated position*. The expression "dead reckoning" may have originated from use of the Dutchman's log, a buoyant object thrown overboard to determine the speed of the vessel relative to the object, which was assumed to be *dead* in the water. Apparently, the expression *deduced reckoning* was used when allowance was made for current and wind. It was often shortened to *ded reckoning* and the similarity of this expression to *dead reckoning* was undoubtedly the source of the confusion that still exists.

deck log—a written record of the movements of a vessel with regard to courses, speeds, positions, and other navigational information, and important events aboard the vessel.

Defense Mapping Agency Hydrographic Center—In 1830 the U.S. Navy established a Depot of Charts and Instruments in Washington, D.C., primarily to serve as a storehouse where such charts and sailing directions as were available, together with navigational instruments, could be assembled for issue to navy ships. Lt. L. M. Goldsborough and one assistant, Midshipman R. B. Hitchcok, constituted the entire staff. The first chart published by the Depot was produced from data obtained in a survey made by Lt. Charles Wilkes, who had succeeded Goldsborough in 1834. From 1842 until 1861 Lt. Matthew Fontaine Maury served as officer-in-charge. Under his command the Depot rose to international prominence. Maury decided upon an ambitious plan to increase the mariner's knowledge of existing winds, weather, and currents. He began by making a detailed record of pertinent matter included in old log books stored at the Depot. He then inaugurated a hydrographic reporting program among shipmasters, and the thousands of answers received, along with the log book data, were first utilized to publish the *Wind and Current Chart of the North Atlantic* of 1847. In 1854 the Depot was redesignated the U.S. Naval Observatory and Hydrographical Office, and in 1866 Congress separated the two, broadly increasing the functions of the latter. One of the first acts of the new Office was to purchase the copyright of *The New American Practical Navigator*. Several volumes of sailing directions had already been published. The first *Notice to Mariners* appeared in 1869. Daily broadcast of navigational warnings was inaugurated in 1907, and in 1912, following the sinking of the *Titanic*, Hydrographic Office action led to the establishment of the International Ice Patrol. In 1962 the U.S. Navy Hydrographic Office was redesignated the U.S. Naval Oceanographic Office. In 1972 certain hydrographic functions of the latter office were transferred to the Defense Mapping Agency Hydrographic Center.

direction of current—the direction *toward* which a current is flowing.

direction of wind—the direction *from* which a wind is blowing.

distance on the earth (D, Dist.)—the separation of two points, expressed as the length of a line joining them. On the surface of the earth it is usually stated in miles. Navigators customarily use the *nautical mile* (mi., M) of 1852 meters exactly. This is the value suggested by the International Hydrographic Bureau in 1929 and since adopted by most maritime nations. It is often called the International Nautical Mile to distinguish it from slightly different values used by some countries. On July 1, 1959, the United States adopted the exact relationship of 1 yard = 0.9144 meter. The length of the International Nautical Mile is consequently equal to 6076.11549 feet (approximately). For most navigational purposes the nautical mile is considered the length of 1 minute of latitude, or of any great circle of the earth, regardless of location. On the Clarke spheroid of 1866, used for mapping North America, the length of 1 minute of latitude varies from about 6046 feet at the equator to approximately 6108 feet at the poles. The length of 1 minute of a great circle of a sphere having an area equal to that of the earth, as represented by this spheroid, is 6080.2 U.S. feet. This was the standard value of the nautical mile in the United States prior to adoption of the international value. A *geographical mile* is the length of 1 minute of the equator, or about 6087 feet.

drift—1. the speed of a current; 2. the distance a vessel is moved by current and wind; 3. downwind or downcurrent motion due to wind or current.

Dutchman's log—a variation of the chip log. A floating object is thrown overboard at the bow, and the elapsed time required for it to pass the known length of your vessel is noted. Use the formula under "chip log" to determine speed.

easy conversions—*See* conversions.

ebb current—tidal current moving away from land or down a tidal stream.

estimating the wind at sea—observers on board ships at sea usually determine the speed of the wind by estimating its Beaufort force. Through experience, mariners have developed various methods of estimating this force. The effect of the wind on the observer himself, the ship's rigging, flags, etc., is used; estimates based on these indications give the relative wind which must be corrected for the motion of the ship before an estimate of the true wind speed can be obtained. The most common method involves the appearance of the sea surface. The state of the sea disturbance, i.e., the dimensions of the waves, the presence of white caps, foam, or spray, depends principally on three factors: (1) *the wind speed*—the higher the speed of the wind, the greater is the sea disturbance; (2) *the duration of the wind*—at any point on the sea, the disturbance will increase the longer the wind blows at a given speed, until a maximum state of disturbance is reached; (3) *the fetch*—this is the length of the stretch of water over which the wind acts on the sea surface from the same direction. For a given wind speed and duration, the longer the fetch, the greater is the sea disturbance. If the fetch is short, say, a few miles, the disturbance will be relatively small no matter how great the wind speed is or how long it has been blowing. *See* force.

estimated position—the most probable position of a craft, determined from incomplete data or data of questionable accuracy.

Fahrenheit temperature—temperature based on a scale in which, under standard atmospheric pressure, water freezes at 32° and boils at 212°.

fathom—a unit of length equal to 6 feet. The fathom as a unit of length or depth is of obscure origin, but primitive man considered it a measure of the outstretched arms, and the modern seaman still estimates the length of a line in this manner. That the unit was used in early times is indicated by reference to it in the detailed account given of the Apostle Paul's voyage to Rome, as recorded in Chapter 27 of the Acts of the Apostles. Posidonius reported a sounding of more than 1000 fathoms in the second century B.C. How old the unit was at that time is unknown.

fix—a relatively accurate position determined without reference to any former position.

fixed and flashing light—a fixed light varied at regular intervals by one or more flashes of greater brilliance.

fixed and group flashing light—a fixed light varied at regular intervals by a group of two or more flashes of greater brilliance.

fixed light—a light having constant luminous intensity.

flashing light—a light showing one or more flashes at regular intervals, the duration of light being less than that of darkness.

flood current—tidal current moving toward land or up a tidal stream.

force (wind, Beaufort Scale)—refer to the Beaufort Scale table.

Beaufort Scale

Force Number	Description	Wind Speed (knots)	Wind Speed (M.P.H.)
Force 0	calm	under 1	under 1
Force 1	light air	1–3	1–3
Force 2	light breeze	4–6	4–7
Force 3	gentle breeze	7–10	8–12
Force 4	moderate breeze	11–16	13–18
Force 5	fresh breeze	17–21	19–24
Force 6	strong breeze	22–27	25–31
Force 7	moderate gale	28–33	32–38
Force 8	fresh gale	34–40	39–46
Force 9	strong gale	41–47	47–54
Force 10	whole gale	48–55	55–63
Force 11	storm	56–63	64–72
Force 12	hurricane	64–71	73–82

Force 13 to 17: Winds up to 118 knots (136 M.P.H.), "air filled with foam, sea completely white with driving spray, visibility greatly reduced"

general chart—a nautical chart intended for offshore coastwise navigation.

grounding—when the bottom of your boat touches the floor of the sea (and you've got a problem).

group flashing light—a light showing groups of flashes at regular intervals, the duration of light being less than that of darkness.

group occulting light—a light having groups of eclipses at regular intervals, the duration of light being equal to or greater than that of darkness.

harbor chart—a nautical chart intended for navigation and anchorage in harbors and smaller waterways.

harbor of refuge—a man-made protective harbor (but *any* harbor is a "harbor of refuge" when it's blowing like stink outside).

heading (Hdg., SH)—the direction in which a vessel is pointed, expressed as angular distance from north, usually from 000° at north, clockwise through 360°. Heading should not be confused with course. Heading is a constantly changing value as a vessel oscillates or yaws back and forth across the course due to the effects of sea, wind, and steering error.

helmspersons—when they are good, they are very, very good; and when they are bad, they are terrible. If the crew member at the helm of your vessel is bad or indifferent, look to *your* laurels; sloppy steering is a nautical menace.

high tide—the maximum height reached by a rising tide.

high water—high tide.

inshore—in or near the shore.

International Nautical Mile—the standard nautical mile, of 1852 meters.

interrupted quick-flashing light—a light showing quick flashes for several seconds, followed by a period of darkness.

isobar—a line connecting points having the same atmospheric pressure reduced to a common datum.

junction buoy—a buoy marking the junction of two channels or two parts of a channel, when proceeding from seaward.

kilometer—1000 meters (about 0.54 nautical mile).

knot—a unit of speed equal to one nautical mile per hour.

landfall—the first sighting of land when approached from seaward.

landmark—a conspicuous object on land, serving as an indicator for guidance or warning.

lateral marks—Generally used for well-defined channels, they indicate the port and starboard hand sides of the route to be followed, and are used in conjunction with a conventional direction of buoyage. This direction is defined in one of two ways: (1) local direction of buoyage—the direction taken by the mariner when approaching a harbor, river estuary, or other waterway from seaward; (2) general direction of buoyage—in other areas, a direction determined by the buoyage authorities, following a clockwise direction around continental landmasses, given in sailing directions, and if necessary, indicated on charts by a symbol. By night a port-hand buoy is identifiable by its red light, and a starboard-hand buoy by its green light.

latitude (L, lat.)—the angular distance from the equator, measured northward or southward along a meridian from 0° at the equator to 90° at the poles. It is designated *North* (N) or *South* (S) to indicate the direction of measurement.

lee shore—a nasty place to be when the wind is up.

leeway—the leeward motion of a vessel, due to wind, expressed as distance, speed, or an angle.

leg—one part of a track, consisting of a single course line.

lengths—refer to the table of length equivalents.

Length Equivalents

1 inch	= 25.4 millimeters
	= 2.54 centimeters
1 foot (U.S.)	= 12 inches
	= 1 British foot
	= ⅓ yard
	= 0.3048 meter
	= ⅙ fathom
1 foot (U.S. Survey)	= 0.30480061 meter
1 yard	= 36 inches
	= 3 feet
	= 0.9144 meter
1 fathom	= 6 feet
	= 2 yards
	= 1.8288 meters
1 cable	= 720 feet
	= 240 yards
	= 219.4560 meters
1 cable (British)	= 0.1 nautical mile
1 statute mile	= 5,280 feet
	= 1,760 yards
	= 1,609.344 meters
	= 1.609344 kilometers
	= 0.86897624 nautical mile
1 nautical mile	= 6,076.11548556 feet
	= 2,025.37182852 yards
	= 1,852 meters

	= 1.852 kilimeters
	= 1.150779448 statute miles
1 meter	= 100 centimeters
	= 39.370079 inches
	= 3.28083990 feet
	= 1.09361330 yards
	= 0.54680665 fathom
	= 0.00062137 statute mile
	= 0.00053996 nautical mile
1 kilometer	= 3,280.83990 feet
	= 1,093.61330 yards
	= 1,000 meters
	= 0.62137119 statute mile

light list—a publication tabulating navigational lights and related information.

light sector—a sector in which a navigational light is visible or has a distinctive color.

line of position—a line on some point of which a vessel may be presumed to be located, as a result of observation or measurement.

log—1. an instrument for measuring the speed or distance, or both, traveled by a vessel; 2. deck log, or yacht log.

longitude (long.)—the arc of a parallel or the angle at the pole between the prime meridian and the meridian of a point on the earth, measured eastward or westward from the prime meridian through 180°. It is designated *East* (E) or *West* (W) to indicate the direction of measurement.

low tide—the minimum height reached by a falling tide.

low water—low tide.

lubber's line—a reference line on any direction-indicating instrument marking the reading which coincides with the heading.

magnetic bearing—bearing relative to magnetic north.

magnetic compass table—deviation table.

magnetic course—course relative to magnetic north.

magnetic heading—heading relative to magnetic north.

magnetic north—the direction north as indicated by the earth's magnetic lines of force.

maximum ebb—the greatest speed of an ebb current.

maximum flood—the greatest speed of a flood current.

"Mayday, mayday, mayday"—Like S O S, "Mayday" is a call for help. With luck and good pilotage, you will probably cruise for years and *never* make that call. *But see* radio distress procedures—just in case.

mean sea level—the average height of the surface of the sea for all stages of the tide, usually determined from hourly readings.

mean tide level—half-tide level.

mercator projection—the only cylindrical projection widely used for navigation is the *Mercator* or *equatorial cylindrical orthomorphic,* named for its inventor Gerhard Kremer (Mercator), a Flemish geographer. It is not perspective and the parallels cannot be located by geometrical projection, the spacing being derived mathematically. The use of a cylinder to explain the relationship of the terrestrial latitude and longitude lines to those on the cylinder often results in misleading illustrations. The distinguishing feature of the Mercator projection among cylindrical projections is that both the meridians and parallels are expanded in the same ratio with increased latitude. Expansion is the same in all directions and angles are correctly shown, the projection being conformal. Rhumb lines appear as straight lines, the directions of which can be measured directly on the chart. Distances can also be measured directly, to practical accuracy, but not by a single distance scale over the entire chart, unless the spread of latitude is small. The latitude scale is customarily used for measuring distances, the expansion scale being the same as that of distances at the same latitude. Great circles, except meridians and the equator, appear as curved lines concave to the equator. Small areas appear in their correct shape but of increased size unless they are near the equator. Plotting of positions by latitude and longitude is done by means of rectangular coordinates, as on any cylindrical projection.

meridian—a meridian is a great circle through the geographical poles of the earth. Hence, all meridians meet at the poles, and their planes intersect each other in a line, the polar axis. The term ''meridian'' is usually applied to the upper branch only, that half from the pole to pole which passes through a given point. The other half is called the ''lower branch.''

most probable position—that position of a craft judged to be most accurate when the exact position is not known.

mutiny, desertions, and other minor aggravations—mutiny, desertions, and general discontent occur when the skipper *doesn't* learn more, care more, or try harder—or when the skipper forgets that the purpose of the whole thing is ''fun.''

National Ocean Survey—founded in 1807 when Congress passed a resolution authorizing a survey of the coast, harbors, outlying islands, and fishing banks of the United States. On the recommendation of the American Philosophical Society, President Jefferson appointed Ferdinand Hassler, a Swiss immigrant who had founded the Geodetic Survey of his native land, the first director of the Survey of the Coast. The survey was renamed Coast Survey in 1836. The approaches to New York were the first sections of the coast charted. In 1878 the survey was renamed Coast and Geodetic Survey, and in 1970 the survey became the National Ocean Survey. NOS today provides the mariner with the charts and *Coast Pilots* of all waters of the United States and its possessions, and tide and tidal current tables for much of the world.

navigation—the process of directing the movements of a craft, expeditiously and safely, from one point to another. The word *navigate* is from the Latin *navigatus,* the past participle of the verb *navigere,* which is derived from the words *navis,* meaning "ship," and *agere,* meaning "to move" or "to direct." Navigation of water craft is called *marine navigation* to distinguish it from navigation of aircraft. Navigation of a vessel on the surface is sometimes called surface navigation to distinguish it from underwater navigation of a submerged vessel.

navigator's chart—a *map* is a conventional representation, usually on a plane surface, of all or part of the physical features of the earth's surface or any part of it. A *chart* is such a representation intended primarily for navigation. A new skipper is demoted the first time he or she calls a "chart" a "map." A *nautical* or *marine chart* is one intended primarily for marine navigation. It generally shows depths of water (by soundings and sometimes also by depth curves), aids to navigation, dangers, and the outline of adjacent land and such land features as are useful to the navigator. A map projection or chart projection is a method of representing all or part of the surface of a sphere or spheroid on a plane surface. The process is one of transferring points on the surface of the sphere or spheroid onto a surface that can be flattened to form a plane, such as a cylinder or cone. If points on the surface of the sphere or spheroid are projected from a single point (including infinity), the projection is said to be perspective or geometric. Most map projections are not perspective.

neap tides—the tides occurring near the times of first and last quarter of the moon, when the range of tide tends to decrease.

new skipper—*"new,"* as in "having existed but a short time," and *"skipper,"* as in "the master of a fishing, small trading, or pleasure boat." *See* command.

nightmark—an object of distinctive characteristics serving as an aid to navigation during darkness.

nun buoy—a buoy the above-water part of which is in the shape of a cone or a truncated cone.

occluded front—the weather front formed when a cold front overtakes a warm front.

occulting light—a light totally eclipsed at intervals, the duration of light being equal to or greater than that of darkness.

offshore—away from the shore.

off soundings—in an area where the depth of water cannot be measured by an ordinary sounding lead, generally considered to be beyond the 100-fathom line.

old salt—*"old,"* as in "from an earlier time," and "salt," as in "cured or seasoned with salt." Put the two words together and there's no telling what you'll get.

on soundings—in an area where the depth of water can be measured by ordinary sounding lead, generally considered to be within the 100-fathom line.

on the beam—bearing approximately 090° relative ("on the starboard beam") or 270° relative ("on the port beam").

on the bow—bearing approximately 045° relative ("on the starboard bow") or 315° relative ("on the port bow").

on the quarter—bearing approximately 135° relative ("on the starboard quarter") or 225° relative ("on the port quarter").

pilot chart—a chart giving information on ocean currents, weather, and other items of interest to a navigator.

piloting—piloting or pilotage is navigation involving frequent or continuous determination of position or a line of position relative to geographic points, and usually requiring need for close attention to the vessel's draft with respect to the depth of water. It is practiced in the vicinity of land and other hard places, and requires good judgment and almost constant attention and alertness on the part of the pilot. Celestial navigation is navigation using information obtained from celestial bodies.

plot—a drawing consisting of lines and points graphically representing certain conditions, as the progress of a craft.

plotting chart—a chart designed primarily for plotting dead reckoning and lines of position from celestial observations or radio aids, etc.

plotting sheet—a blank chart showing only the graticule and one or more compass roses, so that the plotting sheet can be used for any longitude.

position—a point defined by stated or implied coordinates, particularly one on the surface of the earth.

prime meridian—the meridian used as the origin for measurement of longitude. The prime meridian used almost universally is that through the original position of the British Royal Observatory at Greenwich, near London, England.

quick-flashing light—a light showing short flashes at the rate of not less than 60 per minute.

radio distress procedures—distress calls are made on channel 16 (156.80 MHz) for VHF radiotelephony. For less serious situations than warrant the distress procedure, the urgency signal is "Pan" (*pahn,* spoken three times). Distress calls indicate that a vessel is threatened by grave and imminent danger and requests immediate assistance. They have absolute priority over all other transmissions. All stations that hear a distress call must immediately cease any transmission capable of interfering with the distress traffic and shall continue to listen on the frequency used for the emission of the distress call. This call shall not be addressed to a particular station, and

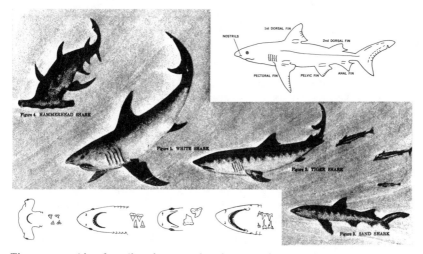

The reverse side of a pilot chart can be almost as fascinating as the face. These critters—"Dangerous Sea Life"—can be found on the back side of the July Pilot Chart of the North Atlantic.

acknowledgement of receipt shall not be given before the distress message is sent. Follow this procedure: (1) Send the distress call, consisting of the distress signal "Mayday" (spoken three times) and the words "This is" (spoken once) the call sign or name of the vessel in distress (spoken three times). (2) The distress message follows immediately and consists of: the distress signal "Mayday," then (a) the call sign and name of the vessel in distress; (b) particulars of its position—true bearing and distance from a known geographical position; (c) the nature of the distress; (d) the kind of assistance desired; (e) the number of persons aboard and the condition of any injured; (f) present seaworthiness of vessl; (g) description of the vessel (length; type; cabin; masts; power; color of hull, superstructure, tri; etc.); (h) any other information that might facilitate the rescue, such as display of a surface-to-air identification signal or a radar reflector; and (i) your listening frequency and schedule; finally, "This is" (call sign and name of vessel in distress). "Over." Complete radio prcedures are given in *Coast Pilots,* under "General Information."

radio operating procedures (General)—(1) Keep your transmissions brief. (2) Identify your vessel—name and call sign. (3) Listen before transmitting. (4) Give priority to distress or safety communications. (5) Speak normally—don't shout or whisper. (6) Signify you are finished by saying "Over." (7) Signify that no response is necessary by saying "Out." (8) Signify that you are a decent, thoughtful skipper by keeping your kids off the air and away from your radiotelephone.

radiobeacon—a radio transmitter emitting a characteristic signal to permit a craft with suitable equipment to determine its position relative to the beacon.

radionavigation—navigation using radio waves for determination of position or of a line of position. Radar navigation and satellite navigation are parts of the radionavigation division. Radar navigation involves the use of radio waves, usually in the centimeter band, to determine the distance and direction of an object reflecting the waves to the sender. Satellite navigation involves the use of artificial earth satellites for determination of position. The term *electronic navigation* is used to refer to navigation involving the use of electronics in any way. Thus the term includes the use of the gyrocompass for steering and the echo sounder when piloting.

range—1. two or more objects in line; 2. the extreme distance at which an object or light can be seen or a radio signal can be used.

range lights—two or more lights in the same horizontal direction, particularly those lights so placed as navigational aids to mark any line of importance to vessels, as a channel.

red sector—a sector of the circle of visibility of a navigational light in which a red light is exhibited.

relative bearing—a bearing relative to the heading, or to the vessel itself. It is usually measured from 000° at the heading, clockwise through 360°. However, it is sometimes conveniently measured right or left from 0° at the ship's head through 180°. Older methods, such as indicating the number of degrees or points from some part of the vessel (10° forward of the starboard beam, two points on the port quarter, etc.) are seldom used today to indicate precise directions, except for bearings ahead or astern, or broad on the bow, beam, or quarter. To convert a relative bearing to a bearing from north, express the relative bearing in terms of the 0°–360° system and add the heading (true bearing = relative bearing + true heading). Thus if another vessel bears 127° relative from your ship whose heading is 150°, the bearing from north is 127° + 150° = 277°. If the total exceeds 360°, subtract this amount. To convert a bearing from north to a relative bearing, subtract the heading (relative bearing = true bearing − true heading). Thus a lightship which bears 241° from north bears 241° − 137° = 104° relative from your vessel whose heading is 137°. If the heading is larger than the true bearing, add 360° to the true bearing before subtracting.

rhumb lines and great circles—the principal advantage of a rhumb line is that it maintains constant true direction. A ship following the rhumb line between two places does not change true course. A rhumb line makes the same angle with all meridians it crosses and appears as a straight line on a Mercator chart. It is adequate for most purposes of navigation. Bearing lines (except long ones, like those obtained by radio) and course lines are both plotted on a Mercator chart as rhumb lines, except in high latitudes. The equator and the meridians are great circles, but may be considered special cases of the rhumb line.

rotary current—a tidal current which changes direction progressively through 360° during a tidal-day cycle, without coming to slack water.

running fix—a position determined by crossing lines of position with an appreciable time difference between them and advanced or retired to a common time.

sailing chart—a small-scale nautical chart for offshore navigation.

sailing directions—a descriptive book for the use of mariners, containing detailed information on the coastal waters, harbor facilities, etc., of an area, particularly along coasts other than those of the United States. The publication of modern sailing directions by the Defense Mapping Agency Hydrographic Center is one of the achievements properly attributed to Matthew Fontaine Maury. During the two decades he headed the Depot of Charts and Instruments (renamed U.S. Naval Observatory and Hydrographical Office in 1854), Maury gathered data that led to the publication of eight volumes of sailing directions.

salty—salty, as in "smacking of the sea or nautical life."

seamark—a conspicuous object in the water, serving as an indicator for guidance or warning of a craft.

sectored light—a light having sectors of different colors or the same color in specific sectors separated by dark sectors.

Seven-Eights Rule—a rule of thumb which states that the approximate distance to an object broad on the beam equals ⅞ of the distance traveled while the relative bearing (right or left) changes from 30° to 60° or from 120° to 150°.

Seven-Tenths Rule—a rule of thumb which states that the approximate distance to an object broad on the beam equals $7/10$ of the distance traveled while the relative bearing (right or left) changes from 22.5° to 45° or from 137° to 157.5°.

Seven-Thirds Rule—a rule of thumb which states that the approximate distance to an object on the beam equals $7/3$ of the distance traveled while the relative bearing (right or left) changes from 22.5° to 26.5°, 67.5° to 90°, 90° to 112.5°, or 153.5° to 157.5°.

shallow water—waves running into shallow water increase in steepness and in their tendency to break. With an onshore wind there will be more white caps over the shallow waters than over the deeper water farther offshore. It is only over relatively deep water that the sea criterion can be used with confidence.

short-long flashing light—a light showing a short flash of about 0.4 second, and a long flash of four times that duration, this combination recurring about six to eight times per minute.

slack water—the condition when the speed of a tidal current is zero— a happy condition if you are approaching a drawbridge or a dock.

speed (S)—rate of motion, or distance per unit of time. A *knot* (kn.), the unit of speed commonly used in navigation, is a rate of one nautical mile per hour. The expression *knots per hour* refers to acceleration, not speed. The expression *speed of advance* (SOA) is used to indicate the speed intended to be made along the track, and *speed over ground* (SOG) the speed along the path actually followed. *Speed made good* (SMG) is the speed along the course made good.

speed comparisons—refer to speed comparisons table.

Speed Comparisons

1 statute mile per hour	= 88 feet per minute
	= 29.33333333 yards per minute
	= 1.609344 kilometers per hour
	= 0.86897624 knot
	= 0.44704 meter per second
1 knot	= 101.26859143 feet per minute
	= 33.75619714 yards per minute
	= 1.852 kilometers per hour
	= 1.68780986 feet per second
	= 1.15077945 statute miles per hour
	= 0.51444444 meter per second
1 kilometer per hour	= 0.62137119 statute mile per hour
	= 0.53995680 knot
1 meter per second	= 196.85039340 feet per minute
	= 65.6167978 yards per minute
	= 3.6 kilometers per hour
	= 3.28083990 feet per second
	= 2.23693632 statute miles per hour
	= 1.94384449 knots

spring tides—the tides occurring near the times of full moon and new moon, when the range of tide tends to increase.

sound buoy—a buoy equipped with a characteristic sound signal.

sounding—measured or charted depth of water, or the measurement of such depth.

spar buoy—a buoy made of a tapered log or of metal similarly shaped.

stand—the condition at high tide or low tide when there is no change in the height of the water.

station buoy—a buoy used to mark the approximate station of an important buoy or a lightship.

statute mile—a unit of distance equal to 5280 feet in the United States, a land mile. The land or statute mile (mil., St M) is commonly used for navigation on rivers, notably the Great Lakes of North America. The nautical mile is about 38/33 or approximately 1.15 statute miles.

steering compass—a compass by which a craft is steered.

swell—the name given to waves, generally of considerable length, which were raised in some distant area by winds blowing there, and which have moved into your vicinity; or to waves raised nearby and which continue to advance after the wind in your area has abated or changed direction. The direction of swell waves is usually different from the direction of the wind and the sea waves. Swell waves should not be considered when estimating wind speed and direction. Only those waves raised by the wind blowing at the time are of any significance. The wind-driven waves show a greater tendency to break when superimposed on the crests of swell—more white caps may be formed than if the swell were absent. Under these conditions it is easy to overestimate the wind speed.

taffrail log—a log consisting essentially of a rotor towed through the water by a line attached to a distance-registering device secured at the taffrail.

tidal current tables—tables listing predictions of the times and speeds of tidal currents at various places, and other pertinent information.

tide rips—small waves formed by the meeting of opposing tidal currents or by a tidal current crossing an irregular bottom.

tide tables—tables listing predications of the times and heights of tides.

tides and currents—a wind blowing against a tide or strong current causes a greater sea disturbance than normal, which may result in an overestimate of the wind speed. On the other hand, a wind blowing in the same direction as a tide or strong current causes less sea disturbance than normal, and may result in an underestimate of the wind speed.

track—the horizontal component of the path followed or expected to be followed by a vessel or a storm center. The terms *intended track* and *trackline* are also used to indicate the path of intended travel. The path actually followed is usually a somewhat irregular line. The track consists of one or a series of course lines from the point of departure to the destination, along which it is intended the vessel will proceed. A great circle that a vessel intends to follow is called a *great circle track*.

true bearing—bearing relative to true north.

true course—course relative to true north.

true heading—heading relative to true north.

true north—the direction of the north geographical pole.

true wind—wind relative to a fixed point on the earth.

turning buoy—a buoy marking a turn, as in a channel.

veer—of the wind, (1) to change direction clockwise in the northern hemisphere and counterclockwise in the southern hemisphere, or (2) to shift aft.

warm front—that line of discontinuity, at the earth's surface or at a horizontal plane aloft, where the forward edge of an advancing warm air mass is replacing a colder air mass.

wind shifts—following a rapid change in the direction of the wind, as occurs at the passage of a cold front, the new wind will to a great extent flatten out the waves that were present before the wind shift. This is so because the direction of the wind after the shift may differ by 90° or more from the direction of the waves, which does not change. Hence the wind may oppose the progress of the waves and dampen them out quickly. At the same time the new wind begins to generate its own waves on top of this dissipating swell, and it is not long before the cross pattern of waves gives the sea a ''choppy'' or confused appearance. During the first few hours following the wind shift the appearance of the sea surface may not provide a reliable indication of the wind speed. The wind is normally stronger than the sea would indicate, as old waves are being flattened out and new waves are just beginning to be developed.

wind and the sea—the action of the wind in creating ocean currents and waves. There is a relationship between the speed of the wind and the state of the sea in the immediate vicinity of the wind. This is useful in predicting the sea conditions to be anticipated when future wind speed forecasts are available. It can also be used to estimate the speed of the wind when an anemometer is not available. Wind speeds are usually grouped in accordance with the Beaufort Scale. *See* estimating the wind at sea.

wind direction—the direction *from* which wind blows.

wind rose—a diagram showing the relative frequency and sometimes the average speed of the winds blowing from different directions in a specified region.

zone time—the local mean time of a reference or zone meridian whose time is kept throughout a designated zone.

14

Looking Aft

There comes a time in any cruise, voyage, personal relationship, career, or manual when it is wise to look back to see where you *were* and where you *are*—and *where you want to be*. Whether your view is from your bunk, your piloting station, or a comfortable cockpit cushion, the time has come to look aft—to review and contemplate where you started and what you've learned along the way. This, then, is a review of our brief passage through *The New-Skipper's Bowditch*.

THE PILOT AS NAVIGATOR

In the preceding thirteen chapters, dead reckoning, piloting, equipment, weather, and the sea were discussed separately. In this concluding chapter the interrelationship of these various elements of pilotage—and coastal navigation—are discussed. However, the *most important* element of piloting and navigation cannot be acquired from this book—or from any other book or instructor. The *science* of navigation can be taught, but the *art* of navigation must be acquired. Navigation is a blending of the two—a *scientific art*. The truly successful navigator is one who supplements his knowledge with judgment, utilizing every opportunity to improve his judgment through experience. Even with knowledge and judgment, the navigator cannot expect to be fully reliable unless he is alert, constantly evaluating the situation as it develops, avoiding dangerous situations before they arise, or recognizing them if they do occur—always keeping "ahead of the vessel." The elements of successful navigation, then, are *knowledge, judgment,* and *alertness.* To the skipper who possesses or nurtures these qualities, navigation can be a pleasure. The skipper-pilot who tries to navigate without them is at best a doubtful asset. At worst he may be a menace to his vessel and his shipmates.

It is not wise to attempt to reduce navigation to a series of mechanical steps to be followed by rote. Nor is it wise to allow your responsibilities as "navigator" to become an all-consuming task, forgetting the pleasures of cruising and the well-being and morale of your crew. The Bligh syndrome has no place aboard a *pleasure* craft, but Captain Bligh is certain to slip aboard if *you* get uptight. Don't forget what *his* crew did to him.

The methods and techniques of coastal navigation that should be used are those that are applicable to your type of vessel, the equipment available, your training and experience as pilot or navigator, and the local situation. The navigation of a small craft proceeding up the Choptank River, for instance, might be quite different from that of an ocean liner entering New York Harbor, yet each navigator shares the same responsibility—the sure, safe passage of his vessel. It is important that a navgator make an "estimate of the situation" and use the methods and techniques that are best suited to the conditions at hand. The discussion that follows is generally applicable to any vessel under average conditions.

Advance Preparation

The initial planning for a long or tricky passage includes: (1) a brief review of the appropriate books, tables, or guides (e.g., *Coast Pilot, Boating Almanac,* or *Waterway Guide; Eldridge Tide & Pilot Book;* tidal current charts and diagrams; and perhaps one or another of the various cruising guides), (2) laying out each of the nautical charts you expect to use, in the sequence you expect to use them, and (3) a check of the weather, either visually or by radio. Although at this point you have not picked up a pencil, you will have begun to "feel" the day's run—when you should start, what to expect, and when you may expect to arrive.

As your planning progresses, you will start to form an "overview" of the passage, and you will develop an *intended* track that is based on (1) the weather, (2) navigational hazards ahead, (3) your capabilities and equipment, (4) the well-being of your crew and your vessel, and (5) a snug, safe, comfortable destination (or alternative if the weather goes to pot). The detailed planning of the approach and entry at the destination is usually deferred until some time during the transit but before making landfall.

At this point, a word of caution is appropriate. *Less is usually better.* Rather than maximize distance traveled, try to maximize pleasure. Anchoring or docking in an unfamiliar harbor, with a tired and cranky crew, neglects some of the *real* pleasures of cruising—a relaxed "happy hour" and dinner, a quiet evening in the cockpit, preferably after a swim or a shower, and finally, the satisfaction of watching as the late arrivals feel their way into *your* harbor amid angry orders and counter-orders, while you are smug in the knowledge that *you planned it better.*

However, *before* you get underway from *here* to go *there,* you may want to adopt some or all of the following as you study your publications and charts: (1) determine and circle which soundings are in feet and which are in fathoms, (2) read the various notes on your charts, (3) mark on your charts or note in your yacht log or pilot's notebook critical turning points, lights, buoys, or landmarks, and (4) work out and mark any "danger angles" you must skirt during the day's passage ahead. If a danger sounding is useful, it should be marked on your chart.

The extent of your preliminary study should depend on your previous knowledge of the area. But however familiar you may be with local conditions, don't overlook the importance of refreshing your memory regarding all *critical* information. The prudent navigator leaves nothing to chance and *assumes nothing* that he doesn't know to be fact.

Getting Underway—Here

In a harbor, your largest scale chart should be used for greatest accuracy and detail. Your dead reckoning should be started as soon as you steady on your first course. If the desired track has not been plotted in advance, the dead reckoning is run ahead a short distance. In either event, the predicted time of arrival at the next turning bearing or of passing the next aid to navigation should be noted on your chart or at least tucked away in your head. If there is *any* chance of fog or a sudden summer squall, plot a magnetic compass course *back into the harbor* before you weigh anchor or take in your lines. Fog may set in rapidly and without warning, obscuring landmarks before a round of bearings can be observed. Lights should be timed and identified by their characteristics. At a distance, the color and shape of buoys may not be apparent. Sometimes a sailboat may be mistaken for a buoy.

Buoys may be out of position. Bearings and ranges on fixed objects are better than on floating aids which may not remain at fixed points. Soundings should be taken continuously in the vicinity of shoal water. It is good practice to check the compass at convenient opportunites, as when on a range or passing between two headlands.

By skillful navigation you can save many miles, but "saving miles" should never be at the expense of safety. Always keep in mind the possibility of equipment failure, unexpected fog, traffic, or the possibility of strong and variable currents.

A detailed *running* record should be kept in a pilot's notebook, your log, or on your charts. Entries should show bearings and ranges, important soundings, changes of course and speed, the times of passing important aids to navigation, and other pertinent information. The record should leave nothing in doubt, indicating whether bearings are true or by magnetic compass, whether soundings are in feet, fathoms, or meters. This record is useful in preparing a permanent yacht log, providing guidance for future runs over the same area, establishing your position if fog sets in, and in providing a pleasant and/or exciting "diary" of your days on the water. Your charts should also present a neat and intelligible record of the passage. Course lines and lines of position should be drawn boldly and neatly, and should be no longer than needed. Standard labels should be used wherever they contribute to an understanding of the plot. They should be so placed and worded that no doubt is left as to their applicability and meaning. If possible, lines and labels should not be drawn through chart symbols. Outside the harbor, if your course is parallel to the coast you may prefer to hug the shore to utilize aids to navigation and other landmarks, but always keep in mind that a set toward the beach, particularly off the entrance to an estuary, can surprise you, and many yachts have grounded in sparkling-clear weather because a course was set too close to off-lying dangers.

Landfall—There

Bowditch states it this way: "After a voyage at sea, the first contact with the land is of considerable importance." This is no less true if *your* "voyage" is the crossing of a major sound or a 50-mile passage offshore between two harbors.

Before entering port you should have a mental picture of what to expect under the anticipated conditions of lighting and visibility. The characteristics of aids to navigation by day (or night) should be known, for you *should* have broken out and studied your harbor chart and tide table *before* you arrived. Useful ranges, natural or artificial, should be noted. Danger bearings and danger circles should be drawn and labeled, if this has not already been done. A danger sounding should be selected and drawn on the chart, if needed. Any shoal areas, wrecks, or areas of unusually swift current should be noted. If the entrance is especially difficult, courses to be steered and the distance on each should be determined and recorded, or drawn and labeled on the chart. The identification of turning points should be indicated. Course changes should occur at preselected points having definite identification.

Once you are safely inside, and if you are anchoring, your "spot" should be selected carefully, taking into account local regulations, the consideration of others, and safety, including holding qualities of the bottom. If there is any doubt as to the depth of the water, take soundings. If space is limited, the approach to the anchorage should be planned and executed carefully. As soon as the anchor is let go, the position should be determined accurately. Bearings of a number of prominent landmarks and lights should be measured and recorded, as a guide for determining later whether or not your little ship is dragging its anchor. A *swing circle,* with a radius equal to the scope plus your vessel's length, should be observed, especially if there is no current and the breeze is light. Weigh anchor and move if you aren't *totally* satisfied; it's far better to move when you're wide awake and it's light than in darkness when the wind pipes up during the night.

THE PLEASURE OF IT ALL

In principle the navigation of your small vessel is the same as that of a large ship, but because your boat has a relatively shallow draft, greater maneuverability, and less equipment, there are some important differences. Most small craft spend much of their time within sight of land, where navigation is largely a matter of piloting. They often skirt the beach close enough to be able to reach safety in case of storm or fog, and since most of them are used primarily for pleasure, there is a natural tendency for navigation to be more casual than in larger craft.

The equipment carried and the type of navigation employed depend primarily on the use of the craft and the preference of the user. If a rowboat, canoe, or small sailboat is to be used only close to the shore in good weather, "seaman's eye" might be sufficient for all navigational purposes. But if there is any possibility that the craft might be out in a fog, or proceed to greater distances from shore, fog-signaling apparatus, a compass, and some means of taking soundings must be carried.

A wide variety of equipment is available for yachts, and from this, suitable items can be selected. A minimum list should include a compass, charts, plotting equipment (many types are available), means for determining speed or distance, log book, tide and tidal current tables, light list, coast pilot or sailing directions, hand lead, binoculars, flashlight, and fog-signal apparatus. A barometer is also useful.

Several items of electronic equipment, some of which are relatively inexpensive, are available for use in small craft to aid in navigation and increase safety. From the standpoint of safety the principal item of radio equipment is a marine radiotelephone, which in addition to providing normal communication to other boats and the shore, permits the boat carrying it to call for help in distress, or to assist in the location of another distressed vessel. Portable broadcast receivers permit reception of weather information on even the smallest boats. For larger craft, where ample power is available, radar and Loran (long-range radio navigation system) may be good investments. In addition every small craft should carry a corner radar reflector. In an emergency a metal bucket might be of some value as a reflector.

If your craft is to proceed out of sight of land for more than short intervals, celestial navigation equipment should be carried. This includes a sextant, an accurate timepiece, an almanac, sight reduction tables, and perhaps a star finder. If there is any doubt as to advisability of including some item of equipment, the safer decision is to include it.

The practice of navigation in small craft varies even more widely than the equipment carried. The variation extends from complete navigation similar to that of a large ocean steamer to no navigation other than by eye. The completeness of the navigation should fit the circumstances. There is an understandable tendency among small-craft navigators of limited experience to underestimate the need for thorough and complete navigation. In general, it is good practice for the navigator of a small craft to establish the routine of always following definite courses from buoy to buoy or landmark to landmark, so that the sudden onset of low visibility will not find him unable to proceed to safety without delay. He should change course at established points, maintain knowledge of his position at all times, and have reliable information on the deviation of his compass. There is a place in small-craft navigation for a complete, accurate, neat plot. Where this is impractical because of heavy weather or limited plotting space, a careful log and dead reckoning should be substituted.

The accounts given in yachting magazines, and the large number of calls for assistance received by the Coast Guard, indicate an inadequacy in the navigation of many small craft. Part of this is due to a lack of appreciation of the need for careful navigation. Much of it is due to lack of knowledge on the part of the small-craft skipper. The decision to omit some part of navigation should stem from knowledge, not ignorance. If you, the new skipper, are adequately informed, navigation will be an important part of *your* yachting pleasure.

Index